PUBLIC OR PRIVATE EDUCATION?

LESSONS FROM HISTORY

EDITOR
RICHARD ALDRICH

Institute of Education
University of London

WOBURN PRESS
LONDON • PORTLAND, OR

First published in 2004 in Great Britain by
WOBURN PRESS
Crown House, 47 Chase Side, Southgate
London N14 5BP

and in the United States of America by
WOBURN PRESS
c/o ISBS, 920 N.E. 58th Avenue, Suite 300
Portland, Oregon 97213-3786

Website: www.woburnpress.com

British Library Cataloguing in Publication Data
Public or private education?: lessons from history. –
(Woburn education series)
1. Education – Great Britain – History 2. Privatisation in
education.
I. Aldrich, Richard
370.9′41

ISBN 0-7130-0230-1 (cloth)
ISBN 0-7130-4061-0 (paper)
ISSN 1462-2076

Library of Congress Cataloging-in-Publication Data
Public or private education?: lessons from history/editor, Richard Aldrich.
p. cm. – (Woburn education series, ISSN 1462-20760)
Includes bibliographical references and index.
ISBN 0-7130-0230-1 (cloth)
1. Private schools – History. 2. Privatization in education – History.
3. Education – Social aspects – Cross-cultural studies. I. Aldrich, Richard.
II. Series.

LC47.P83 2004
371.02–dc22   2003060737

Typeset by Cambridge Photosetting Services, Cambridge and in 10.5/12.5 Times
Printed in Great Britain by MPG Books Ltd, Bodmin, Cornwall

CONTENTS

LIST OF CONTRIBUTORS

Richard Aldrich is Emeritus Professor of History of Education at the Institute of Education, University of London and a former President of the International Standing Conference for the History of Education and of the UK History of Education Society. His most recent book is *The Institute of Education 1902–2002: A Centenary History* (2002).

Michèle Cohen teaches at Richmond, the American International University in London, and is a visiting fellow at the Institute of Education, University of London. Her publications include *Fashioning Masculinity: National Identity and Language in the Eighteenth Century* (1996) and *English Masculinities 1660–1800* (1999), co-edited with Tim Hitchcock.

Dennis Dean taught at the University of North London and at the Institute of Education, University of London. His publications include *Education and Policy in England in the Twentieth Century* (1991), co-authored with Peter Gordon and Richard Aldrich, and articles in major educational and historical journals.

Lesley A. Hall is an archivist at the Wellcome Library for the History and Understanding of Medicine, London, and the author of several books and numerous articles on sexual attitudes and behaviour in Britain in the nineteenth and twentieth centuries.

Peter Leuner is Director of Syracuse University's London Centre. His career in international education has included teaching, founding new organisations, developing dual-accredited degrees, managing organisational change and curricular innovation, as well as researching and writing about the field.

Helen Penn is Professor of Early Childhood at the University of East London and a visiting fellow at the Institute of Education, University of London. She has published widely on the topic of policies in early education and childcare and is a contributor to the *New Dictionary of National Biography*.

Gary McCulloch is Brian Simon Professor of Education at the Institute of Education, University of London. His recent publications include *Failing the Ordinary Child?* (1998), *Historical Research in Educational Settings* (2000) with William Richardson, and *The Politics of Professionalism* (2000) with Gill Helsby and Peter Knight.

William J. Reese is Professor of Educational Policy Studies, History, and European Studies at the University of Wisconsin-Madison. He is a former editor of the *History of Education Quarterly* and has been Vice-President, Division F, History and Historiography, of the American Educational Research Association.

Geoffrey Sherington is Dean of the Faculty of Education at the University of Sydney, Australia, where he holds a personal chair in history of education. He has written extensively on the history of secondary schools in Australia as well as related studies on the history of youth.

Susan Williams is a research fellow at the Institute of Education, University of London. Her studies of social and cultural history include *Ladies of Influence* (2000), *The Children of London* (2001) with Pat Ivin and Caroline Morse, and *The People's King* (2003).

Mike Woolf is President of the Foundation for International Education and has held a number of other roles in international education. He has worked in broadcasting, as an academic, and has written widely on issues relating to literature and education.

ACKNOWLEDGEMENTS

I am very pleased to express my thanks to Mr Frank Cass, to Professor Peter Gordon, editor of the Woburn Education Series, and to my book editor, Ms Lisa Hyde. The ten contributors have responded most generously to my editorial requests. My colleagues at the Institute of Education have been unfailingly supportive. As ever, Averil Aldrich has played a major role in the preparation of the manuscript.

Richard Aldrich
School of Educational Foundations and Policy Studies
Institute of Education
University of London
September 2003

INTRODUCTION

Richard Aldrich

BACKGROUND AND PURPOSES

The industrial revolution of the late eighteenth and early nineteenth century had a major impact upon Britain. Industrialisation and urbanisation, coupled with the rise of the bureaucratic state, led to much clearer distinctions between private and public in terms of employment, the roles of females and males, general social organisation, politics and the provision of welfare and education. Two centuries later many of those distinctions are being eroded. Home-working, both for men and women, is on the increase, fuelled by the revolution in communications generated by computers and the internet. Girls and women are no longer predominantly associated with the private sphere, but have full access to, if not always full participation in, public life. The capacity of individuals to employ others for personal as opposed to productive services proliferates once more – as shown by the rise of the personal trainer and lifestyle counsellor.

The privatisation of the British political, economic and social agenda of modern times is often dated from the election of 1979, which brought Margaret Thatcher and the Conservative Party to power. Public utilities were sold to private companies, local authority tenants were given the right to purchase their council houses and the powers of trade unions and professions were curtailed. In the years 1979–97 Conservative educational policies aimed at bringing market principles to bear in education included: the publication of school examination results, increased parental choice of schools and greater parental representation on school governing bodies, devolution of budgets to schools and open enrolment, and the right of schools to opt out of local education authority control. Little turning back occurred under Labour governments from 1997. In 2001 Gordon Brown, Chancellor of the Exchequer in a

Labour government and member of a party historically associated with increases in public ownership, commented that 'For about a century the remedy to social problems was seen as the State acquiring more power to act on behalf of the people. Now the way forward is to move power closer to the people.'[1]

To a considerable degree British domestic history in the twentieth century was characterised by the rise, and subsequent decline, of the Welfare State. This book, however, places the issues of private and public in a longer time frame of 200, rather than 100, years. Thus it is possible not only to chart the rise, and subsequent challenges to public education, but also to identify and analyse some of those areas of education and of knowledge that have experienced different historical trajectories. One of the main benefits of this longer perspective is that the concepts of education and of knowledge employed in this volume are more varied than those in general use.

The growth of 'public' education in Britain is often dated from the £20,000 grant of 1833 and the establishment of a Committee of the Privy Council on Education in 1839, followed shortly by the appointment of two central government inspectors. Schooling was made compulsory between 1870 and 1880, and free from 1891. The leaving age was raised to 14 in 1918, 15 in 1947 and 16 in 1972, and was followed by substantial growth in participation rates in formal education at post-compulsory levels. Following the economic downturn of 1973, however, in his Ruskin College speech of 1976 the Labour Prime Minister, James Callaghan, expressed concern that all was not well with state schools. Results were not commensurate with the levels of public expenditure. Callaghan favoured a basic curriculum with basic standards, the better preparation of pupils for the world of work, and greater participation by parents in the running of schools. Growth in the percentage of GDP (Gross Domestic Product) devoted to education was halted and subsequently reduced. By the beginning of the twenty-first century, a massive increase in student numbers meant that the public financing of higher education was in chaos, with nearly a third of British universities trading at a loss in 2002. Major debates ensued about the respective roles of Treasury grants, top up fees, endowments and a graduate tax.

There is a vast literature on private and public education and it is impossible to provide a thorough review at this point. Some studies are written for the express purpose of identifying and promoting private dimensions. Thus in 1999 James Tooley noted that while in the UK some 7 per cent of pupils attended private schools:

> In countries such as Colombia, 28 per cent of total enrolment in kindergarten and primary education is in the private sector, increasing to 40 per cent at secondary school level; in Argentina and Côte d'Ivoire 30 per cent and 57 per cent respectively of secondary school enrolment is in the private sector; Indonesia has 23 per cent private primary and

secondary school students, and currently a massive 94 per cent of private higher education students.[2]

Tooley also regularly adduces historical perspectives, drawn from the work of E.G. West, to argue that in England and Wales voluntary and private means had supplied 'almost universal schooling and literacy before the 1870 Act allowed the state to "jump into the saddle" of the horse that was already galloping'.[3]

Private schools, however, may fulfil different functions in different societies and at different periods in history. In some countries private schools have principally been expressions of religious and other cultural identities. In England during the last 130 years they have mainly served to confirm or provide the social status of the children of the upper and upper middle classes. The recent advent of league tables of performance has demonstrated the success of the pupils of such schools in public examinations and in gaining access to prestigious universities.

On the other hand while Tooley argues that private schooling should displace much that is provided by the state, other authors such as Ted Tapper are concerned 'to examine the possibility of creating a more unified educational system'.[4] One example of such an attempt was the assisted places scheme, introduced under the 1980 Education (No. 2) Act. By 1996 there were some 30,000 pupils with assisted places in independent schools, with assistance based on a sliding scale according to parental income.[5] In their substantial review of the scheme, published in 1989, Tony Edwards, John Fitz and Geoff Whitty noted that 'the Scheme seems to have been yet another example of an educational reform targeted towards the working class but mainly benefiting children from middle-class backgrounds'.[6] Given that the scheme was available to only 1 per cent of pupils entering secondary schools for the first time, Edwards, Fitz and Whitty concluded that it had not 'fundamentally changed the traditional pattern of education in England and Wales'. Nevertheless, in their judgement its existence reinforced the idea that state schools could not 'match the quality of private provision' and had inhibited 'the development of credible alternatives'.[7]

It has been argued that in urban areas in England (and possibly more widely) 'the market system of education and the concomitant processes of decomprehensivisation mean that resources are flowing from those children with greatest need to those with least need ... children are rewarded largely in proportion to the skill and interest of their parents'.[8] Nevertheless, attempts in many parts of the world to restructure state schooling by devolving more powers to schools and parents, increasing the roles of private sector providers and introducing market forces, have been to some extent a reflection of major dissatisfaction, on the part of both governments and parents, with public education systems. In a recent study, Geoff Whitty, Sally Power and David Halpin have argued that the causes of such dissatisfaction are to be found in the fact that the mass schooling systems of the second half of the twentieth century were based upon traditional class and (particularly in the USA) racial divisions.[9] Thus they believe that current moves towards devolution and choice are simply shifting the blame further down the line and can only provide a temporary solution.[10] This does not mean, however, that ultimately there will be a return to the *status quo*. Whitty *et al*'s vision of educational reform is based upon 'a genuinely revitalised civil society' and the reconstruction of 'a truly public education system'.[11]

At least two broad positions can be identified in the current public/private debate on education in the UK, and may briefly be described here. The first is that the maintained education system was inefficient and being run in the interests of the producers – educational administrators and teachers – while the interests of the consumers – pupils, parents, employers and governments – were being neglected. The introduction of privatisation, competition and market forces is the best means of ensuring value for money, meeting the diverse needs and expectations of different religious and cultural groups, and securing a general raising of standards. Since (as is clearly demonstrated in the case of higher education) the state cannot fund from taxation the level of educational provision that students or it itself demands, private provision or assistance in some form or another is inevitable. The second position is that an education system that is public and directed by professionals does put the true interests of pupils and students first. Under-funding is the main problem faced by state schools, as demonstrated by the fact that pupils in private schools are typically taught in smaller classes and enjoy a much greater range of facilities. Private firms supplying educational services are fundamentally interested in making a profit, while in a market situation informed parents will obtain an even greater share of places in the best schools for their children. In contrast to the private sector, public institutions in higher education continue to make provision for the independent pursuit of truth.

Public or Private Education? Lessons from History is seeking to inform rather than to take sides in this debate. It acknowledges that education is both a public and a private good. It does not offer immediate solutions to general questions about the relative worth of public or private, or equity or choice, in education. This book, its editor and the several contributors recognise that education has exhibited, and will continue to exhibit, both public and private dimensions. We do, however, share two purposes. The first is to provide a series of historical insights into the relationships between the public and private dimensions of education and of knowledge. The second is to suggest that the examination of relationships that have occurred at other points in time has the potential to enhance and reconfigure the nature of the current public/

private debate. Concentration upon a narrow range of issues in the present may lead to the neglect of many of the concerns of the past, and of the future. For example, as several of the contributors to this volume demonstrate, issues of public and private in education are not just about the control and finance of formal systems but also relate to other educational locations, types and ownership of knowledge and ways of learning. It is for this reason that the term 'knowledge' frequently appears in this book. Much current discussion uses the word 'education' to mean simply, or essentially, the formal teaching and learning that takes place in schools and colleges. Of course all children in the UK are required to attend school between the ages of 5 and 16,[12] while post-16 participation rates in formal education have markedly increased in recent years. Compulsory school attendance in the UK, however, dates only from the last 30 years of the nineteenth century. Prior to that date it was recognised that knowledge was acquired in a variety of ways and that social, moral and vocational education took place principally in the home, the church and the workplace. If 'children are rewarded largely in proportion to the skill and interest of their parents', as Gewirtz *et al.* state, that may be because the family has been, is still, and may always be, a more powerful educational agency than some educational professionals are willing to admit. The concept of 'lifelong learning' is of relevance here. It suggests a recognition, or re-recognition, that education and knowledge are neither age specific nor necessarily dependent on professional teachers.

TERMINOLOGY AND ORGANISATION

The meanings of words change over time and may be interpreted in a variety of ways at any one point in time. One classic example is the use of the term 'public school' in England. In 1861 Charterhouse, Eton, Harrow, Rugby, Shrewsbury, Westminster and Winchester, together with two day schools, Merchant Taylors' and St Paul's, were recognised by the Clarendon Commissioners as the nine great public schools of England. Public schools, in this sense, were charitable foundations and thus the opposite of private schools, which might be run by individuals or groups of individuals essentially for profit. By 1900 the term 'public school' was being used more broadly, for example with reference to some 100 schools whose heads were members of the Headmasters' Conference. A century later such schools were more generally known as 'independent' or 'private' schools, terms applied to all schools financed from fees paid by parents and guardians, as opposed to 'maintained' or 'public' schools supported from rates and taxes.

Such changes and varieties in usage cannot be explored here in any depth, but some preliminary points may be made in respect of the key words employed in this volume. In current debate such terms as 'private', privatisation' and 'public' are frequently used with reference to producers or suppliers of education. In this book 'private' is also taken to mean pertaining to a person as an individual, or to a group of individuals as consumers of education; 'public' as affecting all people, as in a state or nation. In current debate and in general parlance the words 'private' and 'public' are frequently used as opposites. The employment of the phrase 'public or private education?' in the title of this book acknowledges such usage. It does not however, preclude the view that in an educational context, including the life history of an individual, these terms, concepts and experiences may also be complementary.

In this book the treatment of the private dimensions of education and knowledge is greater than in most contemporary or historical volumes. This does not imply a preference for 'private' over 'public'. Such treatment may be justified not only by the current majority position of public education but also because, as Sheldon Rothblatt pointed out in 1988, much of the historiography of English (and European) education:

> is pointed toward the development of centralised state systems of edu-cation, with governments as the principal suppliers of schools, colleges, and universities. ... Private or independent sectors of education are gen-erally viewed with suspicion or dislike as obstacles to political democracy and wider social opportunity ...[13]

On the other hand neither precedence in terms of worth nor historical sequence is implied by the order of 'public or private' in the title of this book. Indeed the very first chapter employs the term 'private/public'.

The inclusion of the term 'knowledge' at several points in this book has already been justified on the grounds that 'education' is frequently employed, not least in contemporary public/private debates, to mean only the formal educational system. Another reason for its inclusion is the perception that changes are occurring in the private and public dimensions and ownership of knowledge. Indeed, it has been argued that 'knowledge, as we have known it in the academy, is coming to an end'.[14] The assault upon knowledge in the academy is based not only upon a growing scepticism from outside about the credibility of some 'experts' and the establishment by many enterprises of their own systems of education and training, but also upon postmodernist arguments from within that there is no such thing as truth or objective reality and 'that all knowledge claims are partial, local and specific'.[15] Nevertheless, in the real world, including that element which exists within the academy itself, knowledge still thrives. Indeed, if it did not there would be no point in higher education or indeed in any other type of education. As Jonas Soltis has argued, 'knowledge seeking and using is both an individual and collective affair of trying to make sense of and operate effectively in the world'.[16] Knowledge may be defined as the fact or condition of knowing (which may be extended to include values and skills); education as the action or process of acquiring or dispensing of knowledge. Education frequently implies teaching and learning, but the terms 'self-educated' and 'self-taught' suggest that the teacher's role is neither essential to the process of education nor to the acquisition of knowledge. As noted above, the fact or condition of knowing, or of certain types of knowledge, may be less certain than before and this uncertainty has led to increasing use of the word 'information', which has a less grandiloquent ring. There can be no doubt, however, that, perhaps more than at any time in previous history, we live in a knowledge society and that knowledge is power. Finally it is worth noting that although the relationship between 'knowledge' and 'education' is complex, unlike 'private' and 'public', these words are rarely, if ever, seen as opposites.

The chapters in the middle section of this volume, for example those concerned with sex education and domestic education, indicate that distinctions between 'formal' and 'informal' education, and between 'private' and 'public', are frequently applied to the locations and processes of acquiring knowledge as much as to the nature of such knowledge. Thus formal education and public knowledge may be construed as that which takes place in institutions principally devoted to education – schools and colleges – while informal education and private knowledge are to be found elsewhere, for example in the family or the club. During the nineteenth and twentieth centuries, formal education in the UK increased in absolute and relative terms as a consequence of the rise of the schooled society. In the last 20 years, however, the revolution in communications, for example the internet which can be accessed from non-specialist sites, including the home, suggests that informal or self-education as reflected in the private acquisition of public, as well as of private, knowledge is on the increase.

The ten chapters of this book are organised into three parts. The first explores key themes and moments in British history in the eighteenth, nineteenth and twentieth centuries. The middle part also focuses upon the UK and comprises four chapters on areas of education and knowledge that have traditionally been located in the private rather than the public domain.[17] In the last part, two examinations of private and public are supplied from the USA and Australia, while the final chapter locates private and public issues of education and knowledge within contemporary and globalised contexts.

In the first chapter Michèle Cohen shows the centrality and importance of the eighteenth-century private/public debate on education and how this contributed to the articulation and shaping of gender difference. She argues that public schooling came to represent the natural site for the development of boys' masculinity, and private, domestic education the appropriate milieu for the fostering of girls' feminine identity. The gendered nature of the curriculum, ownership of knowledge and modes of knowing were intimately bound up with private and public, not only in terms of education but also of society at large. Some of their effects are still to be seen. While Cohen is concerned mainly with the education and knowledge acquired by those in the upper ranks of eighteenth-century society, Dennis Dean focuses upon the popular education and really useful knowledge of the mid-nineteenth century. He shows the strengths of this movement, the quality of its debates, and how from 1870 such private provision from below was swept away as schools and curricula for the working classes came almost entirely under the control of three 'public' bodies – central government, local government and the churches. Henceforth the educational insights and curricular concerns of the majority of the population were largely ignored. The re-designation of polytechnics as universities in the last decade of the twentieth century, coupled with ambitious targets at the start of the twenty-first for putting 50 per cent of the population through university, mean that the one-size-fits-all approach of twentieth-century primary and secondary schooling is now being extended even further. In the final chapter of this first section Gary McCulloch notes that the maintained system of education was frequently controlled and directed by those who had not attended such schools and would not consider sending their own children to them. He shows that the divide between private and public in secondary schooling has been one of the most distinctive features of twentieth-century English education and charts the many unsuccessful attempts that have been made to bring the two systems closer together. His chapter, when taken together with those of Reese and Sherington (Chapters 8 and 9), provides a basis for important comparative, as well as historical, perspectives upon secondary education.

The four areas of education and knowledge considered in the middle part of the book are early education and childcare, sex education, the domestic education of girls, and family history. In the first of these Helen Penn argues that during the twentieth century in the UK, early education and childcare were bedevilled by advances and retreats, muddle and reversal. Although this area of education and knowledge was traditionally characterised by a large voluntary and private sector, Penn concludes that the system should be publicly funded (if not publicly provided). She also makes the case for separate and coherent provision for these children of tender years, neither watered-down schooling nor a commercial baby park. Lesley Hall locates sex education not only in the context of public and private but also on the boundary between medical and educational concerns. She demonstrates the neglect of this vital area of knowledge. Her account, like that of Penn, is a 'sorry tale' of ambivalence, evasions and cautious expedients. The next two contributions have both familial and historiographical dimensions. Susan Williams argues that while much work has been undertaken on the entry of girls and women into the public world of education, the story of how female knowledge was handed down across the generations within the home has yet to be told or appreciated. She identifies three categories of this knowledge – basic instruction in the 3 Rs, domestic management and economy, morality and values – and argues that today 'there is barely any recognition of the educative role of the home'. Richard Aldrich distinguishes between the history of the family, which has become part of the public discipline of history, and family history, which has remained largely in private hands, and provides examples of potential links between these two domains. An example drawn from his own family history demonstrates the extent to which essential knowledge and values are acquired outside the formal educational system.

The final part of the book allows further comparisons and contrasts to be drawn. William Reese identifies a 'rediscovery of the public benefits of private education' in the recent history of American education. He traces the emergence of free public schooling in the USA after the Civil War, and shows how in the second half of the twentieth century that system came under increasing criticism. While many of the debates are very similar to those in the UK, and slightly more American children attend private schools (10 per cent as opposed to 7 per cent in the UK) the distinguishing feature of American private schools is their religious affiliation. Reese concludes that a recent Supreme Court decision in favour of a voucher plan in Cleveland, Ohio, may prepare the way for the substantial use of public funds to support pupils in private schools. Geoffrey Sherington's analysis of public commitment and private choice in Australian secondary education, with specific reference to New South Wales, focuses more on the interaction than the divide between public and private. He describes the influence of English grammar and public school traditions on Australian corporate schools for boys, and the culmination of the state's role in education with the growth of comprehensive secondary schooling from the 1960s under the 'Wyndham scheme'. At the start of a new century, Sherington envisages a possible re-definition of public education embracing multiple religious faiths and cultural diversities within separate institutions.

Finally, in their examination of international education Peter Leuner and Mike Woolf look to the future. They explore the concept of education as a commodity or service that can be traded internationally and argue that higher education is an expensive commodity where demand exceeds supply. They note that, particularly in some areas of the developing world, national governments cannot meet the demand for higher education, which results in a growth of internal private provision accompanied by public and private suppliers from abroad. Leuner and Woolf suggest that the boundaries between public and private education, as between nations and regions, will become more fluid, and that 'The university can no longer be the guardian of the Holy Grail of knowledge, protected by arcane regulations and complex, obscure practices.'

History is the study of human (and other) events with particular reference to the dimension of time – past, present and future. The first three chapters of this book demonstrate key historical moments and movements in the relationship between private and public education, events of considerable significance in their own time but which also have shaped and continue to shape our current situation. The four thematic studies shed light on types of education and knowledge that even today have remained largely outside the public sphere and, as yet, largely outside current public/private debates. The final part looks to possible future scenarios, by demonstrating similarities and differences in the private and public dimensions of education in two other English-speaking countries, and by raising fundamental questions about the demand for and supply of higher education within international and globalised contexts.

NOTES

1   Gordon Brown, 'Let the people look after themselves: The modern state must make more space for the voluntary sector', *The Times*, 11 January 2001.

2   J. Tooley, *The Global Education Industry: Lessons from Private Education in Developing Countries* (London: Institute of Economic Affairs, 1999), p. 11.

3   J. Tooley, *Reclaiming Education* (London: Cassell, 2000), p. 205. See also E.G. West, *Education and the Industrial Revolution* (London: Batsford, 1975).

4   T. Tapper, *Fee-Paying Schools and Educational Change in Britain: Between the State and the Marketplace* (London: Woburn Press, 1997), preface. See also G. Walden, *We Should Know Better: Solving the Education Crisis* (London: Fourth Estate, 1996).

5   Tapper, *Fee-Paying Schools*, p. 122.

6   T. Edwards, J. Fitz and G. Whitty, *The State and Private Education: An Evaluation of the Assisted Places Scheme* (London: Falmer, 1989), p. 218.

7   Ibid., pp. 219–20.

8   S. Gewirtz, S.J. Ball and R. Bowe, *Markets, Choice and Equity in Education* (Buckingham: Open University Press, 1995), p. 189.

9   G. Whitty, S. Power and D. Halpin, *Devolution and Choice in Education: The School, the State and the Market* (Buckingham: Open University Press, 1998), p. 132.

10 Ibid., p. 133.

11 Ibid., p. 141.

12 It is possible in the UK for parents to arrange for the education of their children by other means but the numbers who choose to do so are small. For a recent critique of the role of American schools in their economic and social contexts see R. Rothstein, *Out of Balance: Our Understanding of How Schools Affect Society and How Society Affects Schools* (Chicago: Spencer Foundation, 2002).

13 S. Rothblatt, 'Supply and Demand: "The Two Histories" of English Education', *History of Education Quarterly*, 28, 4 (1988), pp. 627–8.

14 A. Griffin, 'Knowledge under Attack: Consumption, Diversity and the Need for Values', in R. Barnett and A. Griffin (eds), *The End of Knowledge in Higher Education* (London: Cassell, 1997), p. 3.

15 Ibid., p. 5.
16 J.F. Soltis, *Education and the Concept of Knowledge* (New York: Teachers College, Columbia University, 1979), p. 15.
17 Although McCulloch specifically focuses upon England and other contributions do not distinguish between the educational experiences of the different countries that constitute the United Kingdom.

PART 1

1

GENDER AND THE PRIVATE/PUBLIC DEBATE ON EDUCATION IN THE LONG EIGHTEENTH CENTURY

Michèle Cohen

INTRODUCTION

The history of education is central to an understanding of the positioning of males and females as gendered beings since the Enlightenment. That history has generally foregrounded mainly 'the ideas and activities of men', though there have been some important contributions to the history of girls' education, especially in the past few years.[1] What is still lacking, however, is work that places gender at the heart of the analysis. This is the aim of this chapter. By examining an eighteenth century debate on education, the private/public debate, I hope to show how central gender has been to educational thought and prescription. My argument is that this debate contributed to the articulation of gender difference and the conceptualisation of gendered modes of knowing in the late eighteenth century.

'What shall I do with my son?' With these words, John Locke begins a discussion with an imaginary father about the respective merits of a private or public education. How should boys destined to be gentlemen be educated? Privately at home, or publicly at school?[2] Though for Locke, 'private' clearly refers to a domestic education and 'public' to education in a grammar or a 'great school',[3] the meanings of 'private' and 'public' in the eighteenth century were ambiguous enough for some commentators to feel the need to clarify their terms.[4] 'By private, I mean only *domestic* and *solitary* education', noted

Vicesimus Knox in a footnote at the start of a chapter on the debate in his *Liberal Education*.[5] 'Private' could also refer to a variety of small seminaries, though these could also be called 'public' to distinguish them from domestic education. 'Public' was always used with reference to grammar and great schools. As will be argued later, the terms private and public were more complex when applied to the education of girls.

THE DEBATE

Though the issue of a private or a public education was not new, Locke's articulation of the debate was a major point of reference for educationists throughout the eighteenth century. This may be because, as Yolton suggests, 'Locke systematised and made more readable what some of the earlier tracts attempted'.[6] Locke began his examination of the relative merits of private and public education for gentlemen's sons by conceding that 'both sides have their Inconveniences', but it is clear from the outset that for him the inconveniences of public education far outweighed its benefits.

Two key arguments in favour of public schools were that bringing together large numbers of boys encouraged confidence and fostered emulation. Locke dismissed these arguments, pointing out that the 'Boldness' and 'Spirit' gained at school were a 'mixture of Rudeness and an ill-turn'd Confidence' which were ultimately unbecoming to a gentleman. As for emulation, it might well be an incitement to hard work but, he noted not without irony, 'Observation and Industry' were not qualities boys tended to learn from one another. On the other hand, the 'Waggeries and Cheats' which schoolboys did teach each other were precisely not what a gentleman's son needed to learn.

A key disadvantage of domestic education was that it would foster 'Sheepishness and ignorance of the World'. But, Locke countered, it did preserve a boy's 'Innocence and Modesty', which it was 'preposterous to sacrifice to the attainment of Confidence and some little Skill of bustling for himself amongst others, by his conversation with ill-bred and vitious Boys'. At home, a boy was 'in his Father's sight, under a good Governor', and would be sure to acquire 'a genteel Carriage, more manly Thoughts ... with a greater Proficiency in Learning into the Bargain'. At school, masters had too many boys to look after, and could not be expected to 'instruct them Successfully in anything, but their Books'. For Locke, education was above all about virtue: 'Tis Vertue, then, direct Vertue, which is the hard and valuable part to be aimed at in Education.' Domestic education was 'much the best and safest way to this great and main End of Education'.[7]

The popularity of Locke's treatise may be one reason why the issue elicited such widespread interest.[8] From the early eighteenth century, most writers on education, whether private tutors or schoolmasters, included a chapter on the issue. Francis Brokesby reckoned that 'in private Education, the Person may be more closely followed, more carefully observed, more constantly attended, and more amply instructed', but he wondered whether these qualities would compensate for those 'defects which cleave to a private, but are discharged from a Publick education'. James Barclay, master of the Academy at Tottenham High Cross, argued that public education suited lively boys, and domestic education milder ones. It was their sons' 'tempers and dispositions' that parents should consider instead of deliberating about the 'good or bad consequences of private or publick education'. George Chapman, master of the Grammar School at Dumfries, considered that private education was 'defective ... towards rearing children for society', but that at public school, children's 'improvement is retarded and their morals endangered'.[9]

Comment was not confined to educationists. Essayists, novelists and poets also expressed their views on the subject, attesting to its prominence in the cultural life of the eighteenth century. Writing in the periodical paper, the *Spectator*, Budgell summarised the arguments of Locke's 'celebrated Treatise' before outlining both sides of the debate for readers' consideration. In *Pamela* (1739), Samuel Richardson's eponymous heroine has read Locke and exclaims: 'You can't imagine how these difficulties perplex me, as to my knowing how to judge which is best, a home or a school education.' Though she points out that the success of Locke's plan depends almost entirely on finding an ideal tutor, she follows his advice and opts for a home education. Her main worry is finding a way of inspiring the 'wished-for emulation' which 'would be so promotive' of learning. Mr Allworthy, in Fielding's *Tom Jones* (1749), also chooses a private education with a tutor for Tom Jones and Master Blifil. For 'having observed the imperfect institution of our public schools, and the many vices which boys were there liable to learn, [he] had resolved to educate his nephew ... in his own house'. On the other hand, it is because *Peregrine Pickle* (1751) is sent to a boarding school that this 'supposed dunce' becomes 'remarkable for the brightness of his parts', all because his 'spirit of emulation' was kindled. Rewarded for his efforts with 'honorary silver pennies', he gains popularity and many boys seek his company. Boswell tells us that Dr Johnson was so persuasive in his support of public schooling that he convinced Mr Murray, Solicitor General of Scotland, and Boswell himself, to send their sons to Eton and Westminster.[10] Johnson staunchly opposed domestic education, in part because he believed mothers' indulgence prevented their sons from achieving their potential, an attitude that recurs throughout the century.[11]

In the 1780s, a strong new voice emerged in favour of public schools, Vicesimus Knox, master of Tonbridge School.[12] Knox's importance rests on his attempt to regenerate public schools and restore their reputation, and on the popularity of his educational treatise, *Liberal Education* (1781).[13] However, it is Knox's position on the issue of private or public education that is considered here. I want to argue that his intervention irrevocably altered the meaning of the terms of the debate and opened up the possibility of thinking differently about it. Until Knox, private education's promise of virtue had been inviolable. Knox claimed rather that private education, far from automatically shielding youths from vice, actually predisposed them to it. Because youths educated at home are under constant surveillance, he reasoned, they are unprepared for future freedoms, and therefore more likely to turn to vice. 'I have known young men nearly ruined at university who attributed their wrong conduct to the immoderate restraints of a domestic education.'[14] Not only did this subvert the foundation of Locke's claim for the superiority of domestic education, but discursively shifting the site of vice from the school to the home made it possible to shift the site of virtue from the home to the school. A decade later, educationist Clara Reeve could comment: 'some have said, that a public education is most likely to produce eminent men – a private, virtuous ones; even this will bear a dispute, as the instances we see to the contrary refute all this kind of reasoning'.[15]

At the same time as he denounced domestic education, Knox secured the superiority of public schooling by linking the mechanism of learning and success to the very structure and organisation of the school, using a new vocabulary to articulate the conditions of possibility for this success: 'exertion' and the key notion that 'exertion strengthens the mind'. Knox explained that if a boy has 'parts',[16] he will become a better scholar at a school because many circumstances 'co-operate to force his own personal exertion, on which depends the increase of mental strength, and of course improvement, infinitely more than the instruction of any preceptor whatever'.[17]

Liberal Education was published at a time when the reputation of public schools, those 'nurseries of all vice and immorality', had reached an all-time low, and education had become 'one of the main areas of conflict in a changing society'.[18] An article in the *London Magazine* in 1779 described the 'gilded youth' of public schools as 'a herd of brutes in human shapes who glory in the violation of decency, of the common rules of society, and are the terror of the neighbourhood in which they reside'.[19] There was also continuing dissatisfaction with the public schools' narrow curriculum, and continuing disquiet with their methods of instruction, what I call the 3 Rs of eighteenth-century English pedagogy: rules, rote and the rod.

Though Knox has been credited with reforming public schools,[20] this was merely a step in a more ambitious programme. His aim was to reformulate the national character, by purging the nation of the 'levity' of France, an infection connected with 'luxury, effeminacy and everything ignoble'.[21] This called for a 'radical cure'. Knox's remedy was the study of the classics, inspiring youths to 'imbibe the spirit, the virtue, the elevation of sentiment and the rational love of liberty, which exalted the polished ancients'. Because the radical cure relied on laying a 'FIRM AND DURABLE FOUNDATION IN GRAMMAR', an objective attainable only by 'a strict, a long and laborious study of grammar at a puerile age', it is inextricably interwoven with Knox's arguments for public schooling, and his disparagement of domestic education.[22] Ostensibly, there was no reason why his cure could not be administered by tutors to home-educated boys with the same effect, but Knox claimed that the main reason that parents employed private tutors was to avoid the tough discipline of a great school. Tutors, he argued, did not have the authority to ground boys in Latin grammar and often failed to do so. Purging the nation of effeminacy required the resumption of a 'manly education'. Public schooling was essential to this project, while education at home, the site of indolence and idleness, was precisely inimical to it. Though Knox was not the first to complain about the infection of French 'levity', he was, I think, the first to forge a link between public schooling and the shaping of the national character, a link which was to become one of the defining features of Victorian public schools.

Following Knox, the discursive terrain on which the opposing arguments of the debate were increasingly disputed was masculinity. In other words, masculinity and effeminacy were mapped, respectively, onto 'public' and 'private'. Public schools were to represent the natural environment for boys who were going to be men. Thus the only circumstance when a public education would be 'improper', was for boys whose 'uncommon meekness', mental or physical weakness, infirmity or deformity, and 'imbecility of mind' required that, like tender plants, they be 'placed under glasses, in the shelter of a green house', unlike 'the oak' which flourishes best 'in open exposure'.[23] Not surprisingly, a 'model father' in a novel by Maria Edgeworth, who was still advocating a domestic education in the closing years of the eighteenth century, insists that his son be sent to school to be 'roughed about among boys, or he will never learn to be a man'.[24] Domestic education was suitable only for those who would never be men – weaklings, 'imbeciles' and, of course, girls.

GIRLS AND THE PRIVATE/PUBLIC DEBATE

Though girls' education was a subject of concern, advice, criticism and satire for most of the eighteenth century, there was no private/public debate about their education mirroring that for boys. 'With regard to women', Revd John Bennett noted in 1787, 'I do not know that this famous question about a public or a private education has ever been agitated.'[25] The lack of a debate points to one important difference in the attitudes to boys' and girls' education: while both private and public education for boys had their advocates and their critics, it is hard to find advocates of boarding schools for girls.[26] There had to be a good reason for a girl to be educated at school rather than at home, for 'whatever elegant or high-sounding schools may be sought out for a girl, a mother seems the only governess intended by nature'.[27] Throughout the century, and especially from the 1770s, boarding schools were generally considered the worse option. There are other differences, but the one most relevant to my discussion is size. The 'great schools' numbering over 50 children were boys' schools. Girls' boarding schools tended to group 15 to 20 girls, often less. This is one reason why it has been argued that they were private, 'essentially domestic rather than scholastic' and aiming primarily to replicate a home atmosphere.[28] This argument, however, conceals the complex and contradictory meanings associated with girls' education.

In an anonymous pamphlet published in 1779, *Thoughts on the Times, but Chiefly on the Profligacy of our Women*, the author, Francis Foster, made a comparison which had never, as far as I know, been articulated. He claimed that 'for the same reasons that public schools are proper for Boys, they are unfit for Girls'.[29] This is not one of the typical comments about girls' schools – which were usually ridiculed or censured for the levity or inappropriateness of girls' acquisitions there. What Foster did was to compare girls' schools with boys' schools, categorising both as public schooling. This discursive shift, which may seem like a slippage, in fact had major consequences. Including girls' boarding schools under the rubric of public education meant that girls' education had been brought into the private/public debate and was subject to the same criteria and scrutiny. Most crucially, it made it possible to compare boys' and girls' education and schooling. Thus, I take Bennett's remark that he did not think the famous question had ever been agitated with regards to girls, as evidence, on the contrary, that this is precisely what was taking place.

According to Foster, public schooling was suitable for boys but not for girls because the qualities a public school education allowed boys to develop were radically opposed to those that 'form the characteristick Beauties of the Sex'. In public schools, he noted, boys acquire the assurance necessary for them to 'bustle in the world' and girls, too, become 'self-assured, forward and impudent'. Yet, women ought to be 'all Timidity – bashful Reserve – Tenderness – and Delicacy'. Echoing Foster, Bennett went further. In *Strictures on Female Education* (1787) he listed three main advantages of public schools for boys: they fostered the confidence necessary for boys' future public roles; they encouraged emulation; and they produced lasting friendships which 'frequently lead the way to worldly honours and advancement'. He then demonstrated how these advantages were precisely not to be recommended for women. 'Confidence in them is "a horrid bore"'; women's greatest grace is 'the crimsoning *blush* and the retiring *timidity*'. Emulation they do not need, as they will not be called upon to compete in the public world. Nor, finally, do they need great friendships since their 'grand promotion' is a dignified marriage. Thus, he concluded, 'far ... from receiving any solid *advantages* from this method of exposure, I conceive that it often subjects girls to numerous inconveniencies, dangers and temptations' which they cannot resist.[30]

The critical consequence of the inclusion of girls' boarding schools in the private/public debate was that, as Foster's and Bennett's comments show, girls' education was perceived not just as being different but as diametrically opposed to that of boys. This opened up the possibility of constructing the character of each sex, not just as the product of, but as the condition for, a radically different form of education.[31] In the following section, I shall describe how these discourses took shape by comparing what educational and moral prescriptive literature said about confidence, friendships and emulation, Bennett's three criteria, in relation to girls' and boys' schools.

Confidence

Because they brought large numbers of boys together, public schools were believed to make them more confident, and, as Locke had put it, better able to 'bustle and shift amongst Boys of [their] own age'.[32] The opposite was true for girls. Not only was there no benefit to be gained in bringing girls together but, Revd Bennett lamented, the only consequences were corruption, infection and putrefaction.

> Thrown together in shoals, in one common reservoir, at a dangerous age, when nature bids an unusual fervour rise in their blood ... they insensibly convey an infection to each other by tales, sentiment, sympathy and friendship. ... Hence, from so many offensive breaths, all pent up together, proceeds a total putrefaction of the moral air ... a total forfeiture of that delicacy and softness, without which it is impossible for any woman to be lovely.[33]

Revd Chirol, another self-styled authority on girls' education, denounced boarding schools because girls developed minds of their own and even asserted their right to pronounce on the choice of a husband 'with a degree of pertness, arrogance and determination'.[34]

Friendships

The opportunity public schools gave boys to develop friendships was a recurring theme in educational and advice literature. While the private pupil 'languishe[d] in solitude', schoolboys were forming the kind of friendships 'which cannot be easily dissolved'.[35] Though there was always some dis-approval of interested friendships, cultivated for the sake of future gain or influence, schoolboys' relationships tended to be idealised as pure and trans-parent, marked by a kind of prelapsarian innocence. 'No friendship is more disinterested or more lasting, than that which is formed at an early age, before caution has taught hypocrisy and dissimulation.'[36]

The discourse on girls' friendships has a completely different tone. Girls' friendships were neither transparent nor pure, characterised rather by 'private correspondencies, assignations, and intrigue'.[37] This may explain why, in books of letters between mothers and their daughters at boarding school, a genre of moral literature that developed around the late 1760s, the daughter's choice of friends is a major topic of concern. The good girl was expected not to choose her friends quickly but rather to wait until she received approval from her mother, whom advice manuals also encouraged to remain her daughter's 'best friend'.[38] Some moralists positively discouraged girls' school friendships, arguing, like Chirol, that they were 'ephemeral connections in which the heart has no share, and which sometimes, even, prove extremely dangerous',[39] while others claimed that 'women are not so capable of firm and lasting friendship for each other as men'.[40] One possible explanation for the anxiety about girls' school friendships was the socially promiscuous nature of the pupils at boarding schools. By sending a daughter to an expensive school where she might associate with girls of higher rank while getting the same education, a middling family had much to gain: social cachet for the family, and improving the girl's chances on the marriage market. It was, however, feared that such girls would also acquire desires above their station and end up despising their own social milieu. Worse, this would make them vulnerable to the promises of – usually aristocratic – seducers, as *The Unfortunate Daughter* illustrates.[41] The advice Portia gives her daughter is to choose as a friend someone 'nearly equal to yourself in rank and station'.[42]

The promiscuous mixing of social classes was perceived differently for boys. Not only were great schools and many grammar schools endowed foundations where the mix of classes was integral to the structure of the school itself, but many advocates of public schooling actually extolled this mix as beneficial, especially to males of rank, because it would teach them that 'merit' alone, not rank, was the basis of distinction.[43] And if the practice of sending boys to prestigious schools for the useful connections they might form was strongly reproved, the attitude to this was, at the very least, equivocal. The formation of connections was an essential and avowed aspect of public school life, and one which went on strengthening throughout the nineteenth century.

Emulation

Emulation was probably the single most important argument for advocating public school education for boys in the eighteenth century, and though some educationists and moralists had reservations about it, most granted it quasi mystical powers for channelling boys' energies and motivating them to work.[44] In line with prevailing opinion, Knox had no doubts about its virtues. 'Emulation warms the passions on the side of all that is excellent, and more than counterbalances the weight of temptations to vice and idleness.' Without it, 'instruction will be always a tedious, and often fruitless labour'. Emulation could not be 'excited' without rivals, and, as the expression of this competition translated into a striving for excellence, was inseparable from the structure of schools. 'The boy … who stands at the head of his class, ranks, in the microcosm of the school, as a hero.'[45] Emulation amply compensated for the lack of individual attention in a school. As Dr John Moore, a strong supporter of public education, saw it:

> The active principle of emulation, when allowed full play, as in the chief
> schools in England, operates in various ways, and always with good
> effect. If a boy finds that he falls beneath his companions in literary
> merit, he will endeavour to excel them in intrepidity, or some other
> accomplishment. If he be brought to disgrace for neglecting his exercise,
> he will try to save himself from contempt by the firmness with which
> he bears his punishment.[46]

By contrast, the absence of emulation and the 'lack of compulsion' of domestic education meant not only that 'everything [was] languid and inefficient', but that youths were perverted and rendered effeminate. The home-educated youth, having no rivals to stimulate him, no standard but 'his own vanity', would eventually be a coxcomb.[47]

In relation to girls, emulation was unequivocally damaging. While emulation was thought to bring out the best in boys, its effects on girls were diametrically opposite. Girls of ability exert themselves beyond their capacity and impair their health. Girls of 'slender abilities' become even less interested in learning, and sink into listlessness, inactivity and despondence. The rivalry and competition exalted for boys were abhorred for girls. Girls were discouraged from entering into 'a personal contest for pre-eminence with the other party; [and] in contemplating superior merit, they are not to envy, but to admire; to copy, *not* to emulate'.[48] The problem, moralists argued, was that emulation in school had for its object the improvement of the understanding rather than of the heart. It was not exhortation to excel in 'humility, in patience, in charity, in piety, in holiness', but in skill, in languages, in other branches of knowledge, or more frequently, in merely ornamental accomplishments.[49] Would anyone maintain, asked Chirol, that improvement of the mind 'is to be purchased at the expence (sic) of morality' and improvement of the heart 'sacrificed to the cultivation of the understanding'? His solution was to reward virtue, not talents – in girls, of course. 'It is not the scholar of the greatest genius who ought to be proposed as an example to others, but she who is most laborious and persevering in her studies: for there is really some merit in application and efforts to improve, but none in mere display of talents which are the free gift of heaven.'[50] Writing to her mother from school, a virtuous daughter praises the governess who is taking 'great pains to check in us a spirit of competition and rivalry' and urges the girls to be 'more ambitious to excel ourselves, than to excel each other'. Good girls prefer to let others 'get all the start' and stand still themselves 'rather than to submit to the toil of competition or hazard the mortification of being outdone'.[51]

PUBLIC SCHOOLING AND THE DOMESTIC ENVIRONMENT

The representation of the domestic environment as dangerous to boys' masculinity had always been a problem for advocates of private education, and advocates of public schooling exploited this concern, pointing out, not without some justification, that domestic tuition's 'first principle' was to exclude 'compulsion and correction'.[52] Public schools alone, they claimed, exerted the discipline that would make men out of boys. 'I have perceived a certain hardihood and manliness of character in boys who have a public education, superior to what appears in those of the same age educated privately', noted a commentator.[53]

Girls' boarding schools were never envisaged to supersede the home, nor governesses to replace mothers. One reason was that the 'perfect intimacy between mothers and daughters' was said to be 'one of the most desirable objects in education'. But there was another reason, one which highlights a major difference in the way male and female education were perceived. A recurring objection to public schooling for girls was that it separated them from their families and threatened to weaken or even destroy 'the precious bonds of brotherly, sisterly and filial affection', while promoting mere 'friendship between strangers'.[54] This anxiety was unallayed in the nineteenth century, and even as strong a supporter of female education as George Eliot worried in a letter to Emily Davies, founder of Girton College, that women's participation in a collegiate system could weaken 'the bonds of family affection and family duties'.[55] Yet, no educational or moral manual throughout the whole period even hinted that distancing boys from their families might be problematic. Quite the opposite. It was distance from home that guaranteed the full expression of their masculine character. By the turn of the century, masculinity on the one hand and effeminacy and femininity on the other had been mapped respectively onto public and private. Public schooling had come to represent the 'natural' site for the development of boys' masculine identity, and private, domestic education the 'natural' site for the development of girls' feminine identity.

GENDER, EDUCATION AND KNOWLEDGE

When Mrs West declared in 1806 that 'each sex should be taught their proper "bias" for surely fribbles and viragos are equally contemptible and unnatural',[56] she was voicing her indignation at Mary Wollstonecraft's proposal that boys and girls should be educated together and study the same subjects.[57] The naturalisation of gendering that Mrs West was envisaging relies directly on the arguments deployed in the preceding decades over the private/public debate. Thus she asserts 'if public education seems most likely to form the active being that man ought to be, domestic instruction promises to introduce those habits which will prepare a woman for the retired part that she has to perform'.[58] How was education gendered to produce these 'natural' differences?

In the concluding section of this chapter, I want to look differently at the relation between gender, education and knowledge. The following discussion is exploratory, an attempt to rethink an old problem and hopefully to supply an outline for further research. What I am suggesting is that in the late eighteenth and early nineteenth centuries, gendered knowledge was shaped not, as is commonly argued, only by notions of the appropriate curriculum for each sex, but also by notions of what I call 'modes of knowing'. These were indirect but fundamental consequences of the private/public debate on education.

There can be little doubt, when looking at the language Knox used to describe the classical curriculum, that it was gender-coded: the 'exertion' and 'discipline' necessary to learn Latin grammar, and the rewards for having acquired it; the 'spirit', the 'virtue', the 'rational love of liberty' of the 'polished ancients'. As mentioned earlier, the arduousness of classical study was one reason why Knox claimed that public schooling would implement his 'radical cure' more successfully than domestic tutoring. Knox also imagined this discipline as a means of freeing the nation from the seduction and effeminacy consequent upon a Frenchified education. However, it was the revival of the classics as he conceived it that eventually served to create the divisions between male and female ways of modes of knowing that I am attempting to identify.[59]

Throughout the eighteenth century, most educationists thought, like Locke, that Latin was necessary to the education of boys destined to be gentlemen.

Dispute focused rather on whether Latin should be allowed to usurp the place of other subjects, especially English, and grammar and great schools were often criticised for their narrow curriculum and their exclusive focus on the classics. In the 1750s, there was even a 'powerful current of anti classical protest' by parents who wished their sons to be taught more useful subjects.[60] In reviving the study of the classics for commercial and professional classes as well as gentlemen, Knox was in effect going against 'the practical wisdom of the day'. Yet, Langford notes, it 'was to prove immensely attractive in the coming years'.[61] In his *Essay on Education*, William Barrow took up most of Knox's arguments and used his language of 'exertion' and 'discipline' to characterise the study of the classics in public schools. But he went further. He vaunted the absolute superiority of public schools over all other forms of education for teaching the classics rapidly and successfully. This, Barrow argued, is because the classics are 'almost the sole object of their attention'. It is not because Latin was arduous and demanded much concentration that this exclusive focus was justified. Rather, it was only if the classics were the subject of undivided attention, as they were in public schools, that 'a deep and critical' knowledge of the authors of antiquity was possible. If pupils were rushed from one subject to another, as they were in some academies which offered a whole range of subjects, their attention was divided 'amongst such a variety of pursuits [and] none can be more than superficially understood'.[62] In other words, by 1802, when Barrow's *Essay* was published, a crucial shift appears to have taken place with regard to the perception of the curriculum of public schools. Their narrow focus, so long an object of criticism, had been turned into a unique virtue. I have emphasised 'deep' and 'critical' because, along with 'thorough', these terms became key concepts describing a mode of knowing associated with public schools' unique ability to train the mind. Recalling his education at Eton in the 1820s, Gladstone could say with confidence:

> ... I claim for the old method of our public schools ... that it had merits and advantages for the loss of which no parade of universality, no increase of mere information, could possibly compensate. It taught with that rigid accuracy, which is the foundation of all really solid learning. It held thoroughness in a few things to be better than show in many. It enthroned in the seat of honour the most masculine studies.[63]

The modern curriculum that in the late eighteenth century was still in the process of being defined for female education, whether public or private, was not particularly feminine except for the accomplishments that formed a much contested part of it.[64] The core subjects that recur in the lists drawn up by various educationists and moralists include history, chronology, geography or the use of the globes, French, Italian, astronomy, natural and moral philosophy, and more rarely, arithmetic.[65] Girls were actively discouraged from learning Latin, though many did – from a father, as did Hannah More, from a brother, as did Harriet Martineau, by themselves, more unusually, as did Lady Mary Wortley Montagu,[66] or at school. As a pupil from 1797 to 1802 at the boarding school in Hans Place run by French émigrés, Mr and Mrs St Quentin, Mary Russell Mitford learned French, Italian, history, geography, astronomy, music, singing, drawing and dancing. She also learned Latin and read Virgil against her parents' expressed concern that it was unnecessary and occupied more of her time 'than could conveniently appropriate to it'. Mary 'carried her point'.[67]

It would be possible to argue that there was no essential gender difference in the subjects males and females could, in theory, study. Ruth Watts has shown that in the late eighteenth and early nineteenth centuries, many Unitarian families put into practice their belief that both sexes should receive the same education,[68] and Maria Edgeworth is believed to have advanced a notion of 'female education … in all essentials the same as men's'.[69] I want to suggest, however, that another kind of difference was emerging, a difference referring not to what, but rather to how, learning was acquired.

What is striking about the female curriculum is not necessarily its femininity, but its breadth. Although the historiography of education generally considers a broad curriculum to be an indication of progress, this may be at odds with the contemporary perceptions and practices alluded to by Barrow. According to these perceptions, although the range of subjects offered by girls' boarding schools or governesses constituted their main attraction and worth, the resulting knowledge could only be perceived as superficial. This reading would throw a different light on Miss Bingley's definition of the accomplished woman as one who 'must have a thorough knowledge of music, singing, drawing, dancing, and the modern languages to deserve the word'.[70] Ruth Watts, commenting on this passage in *Pride and Prejudice*, rightly doubts whether 'a thorough knowledge' of anything was ever given to women.[71] I would suggest in addition that Jane Austen was being ironic, an irony that would have been obvious to her contemporaries, not because those subjects might not lend themselves to thorough study but because the range of subjects would militate against the very possibility of any thoroughness. Thoroughness was, in any case, seen as unfeminine. 'Great eminence in almost anything is sometimes injurious to a young lady', noted Erasmus Darwin.[72] There was one exception. Women were advised to 'consider a thorough knowledge' of their native tongue.[73]

By the mid-nineteenth century, gender differences embedded in the variety of the curriculum had become embodied in the character of the sexes. Dorothea Beale, pioneer of girls' education and Principal of Cheltenham's Ladies' College, reports a comment made to her by the author Mrs Gaskell:

She did not think it desirable for a girl to learn to concentrate her attention on one subject at a time. The success of a man's life ... depended much on his power of doing this. Moreover, all the arrangements of society assume that he has business which must not be interrupted; he shuts himself up in his study, and whether he is doing little or much, it is a sin to disturb him. But a woman's usefulness depends on her power of diffusing herself, and making her influence felt at a number of points at once. She cannot withdraw herself to a study. Her place is in the drawing room, in the midst of others, within everyone's call, and at the ready disposal of a number of claimants, whose demands, though separately trifling, are collectively important. You would only make her unhappy by giving her the habit of fastening her intellectual powers on one thing at a time.[74]

What Gaskell was describing was a commonly held belief that men's capacity for absorption by a single subject and women's capacity for diffusion were 'natural' mental differences. J.S. Mill reflected that the problem was that women's mobility of mind was invoked to uphold their lack of fitness for what he called 'the higher class of serious business'.[75]

Superficiality was not just a feature of female knowledge, it could also be fused with the female learner. In *The Mill on the Floss*, when Maggie Tulliver wishes to learn Euclid like her brother Tom, he is indignant and declares that 'girls can't do Euclid'. Mr Stebbing, the tutor, reassures Tom. Girls, he says, 'can pick up a little of everything ... they've a great deal of superficial cleverness; but they couldn't go far into anything. They're quick and shallow.'[76] The superficial character of girls' intelligence explained their obvious brightness and ensured at the same time that, despite appearances, girls could never really match, let alone surpass, boys' mental superiority. The gender differences in modes of knowing embedded in the discursive bi-polarities 'deep/shallow', 'thorough/superficial', imply that the narrow but thorough knowledge of Latin imparted to boys strengthened their mind and became so intimate a part of its fabric that it gave them a 'peculiar aptitude', a sort of super-ordinate ability for grasping any new subject .[77] The broad and therefore superficial knowledge imparted to girls, on the other hand, precluded the possibility of their minds being strengthened, something the Assistant Commissioners of the Schools Inquiry Commission of 1868 noted again and again in their investigations of girls' schools.[78] Ironically, this meant that it was possible for girls to learn what was reserved for boys, on the assumption that they could never appropriate it.[79] As Ruskin would put it in 1882, 'a man ought to know any language or science he learns, thoroughly – while a woman ought to know the same language, or science, only so far as may enable her to sympathise in her husband's pleasures and those of his best friends'.[80]

CONCLUSION

My aim in this chapter has been to show how the private/public debate on education contributed to the articulation and shaping of gender difference. 'Public' became associated with masculinity, and 'private' with femininity and effeminacy. By the early nineteenth century, the debate no longer occupied the central place it had in eighteenth-century culture. In a sense, it had been resolved. Girls continued to be educated mostly privately, at home, and their brothers were increasingly educated publicly, at public or grammar schools. The debate can thus be said to have had a direct impact on the shape of upper- and middle-class education in the nineteenth century. Less direct, perhaps, is the impact the debate may have had on educational thought. I explored one aspect in particular: its relation to what I have called 'modes of knowing'.

I suggested that when the narrowness of the classical curriculum of boys' grammar and public schools, having been criticised for most of the eighteenth century, became valued, a different way of thinking about knowledge and modes of knowing also emerged. Why this shift took place when it did, and why it took place at all can only become clear with further research. What is certain, however, is that narrowness became emblematic of 'thoroughness'. The association of a single valued mode of knowing with a single type of educational institution, public schools, is likely to have had some impact on how other kinds of schooling and education for boys were perceived; it may also help explain why nineteenth-century parents were so keen for their sons to have a public school education if they could afford it. But it was on girls' education that the impact of the shift was most momentous. For once 'thoroughness' was associated with a mode of knowing available only in boys' public schools, the 'superficiality' that had long been the hallmark of girls' education and their curriculum acquired a new dimension of meaning. In other words, the term 'superficial' became a signifier for a lack of thoroughness. Because girls' curriculum was the very opposite of narrow, no matter what or how girls were taught, thoroughness would always elude them. It is significant that as late as the last years of the nineteenth century, a classics master at Rugby could proffer the opinion that classics could not be expected to be studied 'with the same thoroughness' in girls' schools as in boys'. Girls' schools, he explained:

> have grown with older traditions; music, drawing and modern languages have so long been the staple of girls' education that it is perhaps too late now to make any radical change. If the object of girls' education be, as many think, not so much to turn out finished scholars as to give an intelligent and sympathetic interest in life, this can be better achieved by grafting classics upon the existing curriculum, than by ousting other studies for the sake of these.[81]

By becoming fixed characteristics of gendered education, the discursive bi-polarities, 'thorough' and 'superficial', served to generate conceptions about what ideal education was and what it was not. For boys, the main object of education was training the mind. Learning the classics 'thoroughly' and almost exclusively was the best mode of knowing because it enabled all other potential knowledges; merely increasing instruction in a variety of subjects emphatically did not. Not only did 'too many subjects confuse the mind', argued one witness to the Clarendon Commission, but gaining an 'amount of knowledge' implied losing mental power.[82] The implications for a notion of girls' ideal education are less obvious, because defining what might constitute this ideal education remained fraught with tensions and contradictions, in part because of the anxiety about female intellectual specialisation. On the one hand, for reasons which are still not clear, women's minds were thought naturally 'more fitted for dividing their faculties among many things';[83] on the other, the 'multiplicity of subjects' they were taught was identified by the Schools Inquiry Commission as the single most important cause for the unsatisfactory state and 'want of thoroughness' of girls' education in England.[84]

A number of questions remain to be answered. It would be useful to discover the reasons for the enduring association of girls' education with a broad range of subjects.[85] It would also be important to know how other kinds of educational institutions for boys – the academies and private schools that flourished in the early nineteenth century – dealt with the modes of knowing associated exclusively with the key construct, 'thoroughness'. To what extent have notions of 'thoroughness' and 'superficiality' shaped education since the nineteenth century, in particular British insistence on early specialisation and suspicion of broad curricula? A more speculative and far-reaching question concerns the embodiment of gendered modes of knowing as a way of forging difference between the sexes. How far did male capacity to focus on a single narrow subject 'thoroughly' and female capacity for 'diffusion' extend beyond educational discourse, and interweave with other cultural perceptions of gender difference?[86] For example, in his analysis of the difference in mental powers of the two sexes, Charles Darwin identifies the genius which makes males pre-eminent over females as 'unflinching, undaunted perseverance', referring for his argument to J.S. Mill's remark that 'the things in which man excels are those which require most plodding, and long hammering at single thoughts'.[87]

The research I have outlined should also have consequences for the historiography of education. In particular, it highlights the need to situate the emergence of certain vocabularies in relation to their cultural and historical contexts. For example, I have argued elsewhere that the use of the term 'showy' to criticise girls' education in the late eighteenth century was related not to the knowledge itself so much as to its expression in the social spaces thought to corrupt girls' innocence.[88] It would be useful to trace more specifically the evolution of the term 'thorough' and its powerful hold on nineteenth-century educational imagination. This would enable us to rethink the sometimes uncritical acceptance that male education was essentially 'thorough' and female 'superficial', and instead regard 'thoroughness' and 'superficiality' as metaphorical oppositional categories representing gendered knowledge. This chapter has explored an important aspect of eighteenth-century vocabulary, the complex, shifting and increasingly gendered meanings of 'private' and 'public' in educational discourse, and has highlighted the resistance to the connotations of a public education for girls in the late eighteenth and early nineteenth centuries.[89] It is probably no coincidence that, nearly a century later, Maria Grey chose to call her educational foundation the Girls' *Public* Day School Company.[90]

NOTES

1 M. Hilton and P. Hirsch (eds), *Practical Visionaries: Women, Education and Social Progress 1790–1930* (London: Addison Wesley Longman, 2000), p. 1. See also J. Burstyn, *Victorian Education* (London: Croom Helm, 1980); C. Dyhouse, *Girls Growing up in Late Victorian and Edwardian England* (London: Routledge and Kegan Paul, 1981); D. Gorham, *The Victorian Girl and the Feminine Ideal* (London. Croom Helm, 1982); J. Purvis, *A History of Women's Education in England 1800–1914* (Buckingham: Open University Press, 1991).

2 John Locke, *Some Thoughts Concerning Education* [1693], J.W. and J.S. Yolton (eds), (Oxford: Clarendon Press, 1989), p. 128. All further references to Locke are from this edition.

3 In the eighteenth century, the terms 'great school' and 'public school' were used inter-changeably, although 'the demarcation between public and grammar schools . . . was uncertain', J. Lawson and H. Silver, *A Social History of Education in England* (London: Methuen and Co., 1973), p. 254. The term 'public school' was finally clarified and given legal definition by the Public Schools Act of 1864. 'The Clarendon Commission, by its investigation of only nine schools formally recognised those schools' claims to a superior, distinct, status', C. Shrosbree, *Public Schools and Private Education: The Clarendon Commission 1861–64 and the Public Schools Acts* (Manchester: Manchester University Press, 1988), p. 16.

4 See J.M. Sanderson, 'The Grammar School and the Education of the Poor, 1786–1840', *British Journal of Educational Studies*, 11 (1962–3), pp. 29–43.

5 10th edn, 2 vols, (London, 1789), vol. 1, pp. 34–5. This footnote was added only in the fourth edition of his text.

6 J.W. Yolton, *A Locke Dictionary* (Oxford: Blackwell, 1993), p. 263.

7 Locke, *Thoughts*, pp. 128–32.

8 It went through four editions in Locke's lifetime. He died in 1704.

9 [Francis Brokesby], *Of Education with Respect to Grammar Schools and the Universities* (London, 1701), A3. Brokesby was a Scholar and Fellow of Trinity College, Cambridge; James Barclay, *A Treatise on Education* (London, 1749), pp. 10–11; George Chapman, *A Treatise of Education* [1773], (London, 1784), pp. 55–6. See also J. Girrard, *Practical Lectures on Education* (1756); Sir John Fielding, *The Universal Mentor* (1763); Percival Stockdale, *An Examination of the Important Question,*

Whether Education, at a Great School, or by Private Tuition, is Preferable; with Remarks on Mr Knox's book entitled Liberal Education (London, 1782); George Croft, *A Plan of Education* (Wolverhampton, 1784), to name but a few.

10 *Spectator*, No. 313. Samuel Richardson, *Pamela* [1739], 2 vols (London: Everyman's Library, Dent, 1969), vol. 2, Letters XCII, p. 383, XCIV, p. 398. Henry Fielding, *The History of Tom Jones, A Foundling* [1749], 2 vols (London: Hutchinson and Co, 1904), vol. 1, Book III, ch. V, p. 99. Tobias Smollett, *The Adventures of Peregrine Pickle* [1751], 2 vols (London: Hutchinson and Co, 1904), vol. 1, ch. XII, p. 72. James Boswell, *Life of Johnson* [1791], (Oxford: Oxford University Press, 1980), p. 725. William Cowper, *The Letters of William Cowper Esq. to his Friends* (1827), and his poem *Tirocinium* (1785).

11 M. Cohen, 'Mothers of sons, mothers of daughters: the ambiguous figure of the mother in eighteenth-century educational discourse', paper read at the conference 'Parenthood in Early Modern England and Europe', Bedford Centre for the History of Women, January 2000.

12 So strong indeed that Knox himself added, in later editions of his text, that he might have expressed himself 'too strongly, in preferring public to private education': *Liberal Education* (1789), vol. 1, pp. 34–5.

13 It went through ten editions in the ten years after publication.

14 Vicesimus Knox, *Liberal Education* (Dublin, 1781), p. 24. All subsequent references are to this edition.

15 Clara Reeve, *Plans of Education* (London, 1792), p. 219.

16 Brightness, intelligence, capacity to learn. *Oxford English Dictionary*.

17 Knox, *Liberal Education*, p. 26.

18 Henry Fielding, *The History of Joseph Andrews* [1742], (London: Hutchinson and Co, 1904), Book III, ch. 5, p. 228. Lawson and Silver, *Social History*, p. 226.

19 *London Magazine* (1779), quoted in P. Langford, *A Polite and Commercial People: England 1727–1778* (Oxford: Clarendon Press, 1989), p. 88.

20 Langford, *Polite and Commercial*, pp. 88–9.

21 Knox, *Liberal Education*, p. 265.

22 Ibid., p. 36. By grammar, Knox meant Latin not English grammar, which was not studied at public school.

23 Ibid., p. 30.

24 Maria Edgeworth, 'Frank', in *Early Lessons* (1822), quoted by N. Vance, *The Sinews of the Spirit: The Ideal of Christian Manliness in Victorian Literature and Religious Thought* (Cambridge: Cambridge University Press, 1985), p. 11.

25 [John Bennett], *Strictures on Female Education* (London, 1787), p. 138.

26 One notable exception is Erasmus Darwin, *A Plan for the Conduct of Female Education in Boarding Schools* (Derby, 1797).

27 Bennett, *Strictures*, p. 138.

28 M. Bryant, *The London Experience of Secondary Education* (London: Athlone Press, 1984), pp. 145–8.

29 [Francis Foster], *Thoughts on the Times, but Chiefly on the Profligacy of our Women* (London, 1779), p. 16.

30 Ibid., p. 17. Bennett, *Strictures*, pp. 139–40.

31 See M. Cohen, *Fashioning Masculinity: National Identity and Language in the Eighteenth Century* (London: Routledge, 1996), ch. 6.

32 Locke, *Thoughts*, p. 128.

33 Bennett, *Strictures*, p. 141.

34 J.L. Chirol, *An Enquiry into the Best System of Female Education: Or Boarding School and Home Education Attentively Considered* (London, 1809), p. 118.

35 Knox, *Liberal Education*, pp. 28–9.

36 Croft, *Plan*, p. 10.
37 Bennett, *Strictures*, p. 141.
38 Portia, *The Polite Lady, or a Course of Female Education in a Series of Letters from a Mother to a Daughter* (London, 1769), p. 37.
39 Chirol, *Enquiry*, p. 118.
40 Revd Henry Kett, *Emily, a Moral Tale; Including Letters from a Father to his Daughter upon the Most Important Subjects*, 2 vols (London, 1809).
41 John Corry, *The Unfortunate Daughter* (London, 1803).
42 Portia, *Polite Lady*, pp. 60–1. The belief that boarding schools produced déclassé girls became commonplace and can be traced into the nineteenth century. It is the pivot of the story in Thomas Hardy, *The Woodlanders* (1886–7).
43 Croft, *Plan*, p. 12.
44 Locke, *Thoughts*; Thomas Gisborne, *An Enquiry into the Duties of the Female Sex* (London, 1796); David Williams, *A Treatise of Education* (London, 1774). Williams was a Dissenting minister and home tutor.
45 Knox, *Liberal Education*, p. 26.
46 John Moore, *A View of Society and Manners in France, Switzerland, and Germany*, 2 vols (Dublin, 4th edn, 1784), vol. 1, p. 204.
47 William Barrow, *An Essay on Education*, 2 vols (London, 1802), vol. 1, pp. 104–5.
48 Gisborne, *Enquiry*, pp. 36, 41; Chirol, *Enquiry*, p. 151.
49 Gisborne, *Enquiry*, p. 38.
50 Chirol, *Enquiry*, pp. 96, 153.
51 Mrs Taylor and Jane Taylor, *Correspondence Between a Mother and her Daughter at School* (London, 1817), pp. 12–13.
52 Cohen, 'Mothers of sons'. Barrow, *Essay*, vol. 1, p. 103.
53 Moore, *View*, vol. 1, p. 201.
54 Chirol, *Enquiry*, pp. 119.
55 Quoted in P. Nestor, *Female Friendships and Communities: Charlotte Brontë, George Eliot, Elizabeth Gaskell* (Oxford: Clarendon Press, 1985), p. 161.
56 Mrs West, *Letters to a Young Lady*, 3 vols (London 1806), vol. 3, p. 219.
57 Mary Wollstonecraft, *A Vindication of the Rights of Woman* (London, 1792).
58 Mrs West, *Letters*, vol. 3, p. 224.
59 I believe it also had consequences for boys in terms of social class, but this is outside the scope of the present chapter.
60 C. Stray, *Classics Transformed: Schools, Universities, and Society in England, 1830–1960* (Oxford: Clarendon Press, 1998), p. 21.
61 Langford, *Polite and Commercial*, p. 88.
62 Barrow, *Essay*, vol. 2, pp. 111, 114–17.
63 Address delivered at the distribution of prizes in the Liverpool College, 21 December 1872, cited in Maurice Milne, 'Gladstone's Idea of a University', paper presented to the Gladstone Umbrella, St Deiniol's Library, Hawarden, July 2002, p. 10.
64 See especially Hannah More, *Strictures on the Modern System of Female Education*, 2 vols (1799), and Mary Wollstonecraft, *Thoughts on the Education of Daughters* (1787) and *A Vindication of the Rights of Woman* (1792). I do not discuss 'accomplishments' here as the subject requires more extensive treatment than is possible in this chapter. See Cohen, *Fashioning Masculinity*.
65 Bennett, *Strictures*; Hester Chapone, *Letters on the Improvement of the Mind* (1773); Darwin, *A Plan*; James Fordyce, *Sermons to Young Women* (1766); Reeve, *Plans*. A number of these subjects were also part of the recommended curriculum for boys, especially in private academies.
66 Henry Thompson, 'The Life of Hannah More' (1883), quoted in M. Leranbaum, '"Mistresses of Orthodoxy": Education in the Lives and Writings of Late Eighteenth-

Century English Women Writers', *Proceedings of the American Philosophical Society*, 121, 4 (1977), p. 285. Harriet Martineau, *Autobiography* [1877], 2 vols (London: Virago, 1983), vol. 1, p. 53; Irvin Ehrenpreis and Robert Halsband, *The Lady of Letters in the Eighteenth Century*, Papers read at the Clark Library Seminar, (Los Angeles, California, 1969).

67 Revd A.G. L'Estrange, *The Life of Mary Russell Mitford*, 3 vols (London: Richard Bentley, 1870), vol. 1, pp. 12–15.

68 R. Watts, *Gender, Power and the Unitarians in England 1760–1860* (London: Addison Wesley Longman, 1998), especially ch. 3.

69 M. Butler, 'Jane Austen and the War of Ideas' (1987), quoted in A. Richardson, *Literature, Education and Romanticism: Reading as Social Practice 1780–1832* (Cambridge: Cambridge University Press, 1994), p. 183.

70 Jane Austen, *Pride and Prejudice* [1813], (London: Penguin, 1994), ch. 8, p. 33.

71 Watts, *Gender*, p. 20.

72 Darwin, *A Plan*, p. 10.

73 See for example Helena Wells, *Letters on Subjects of Importance to the Happiness of Young Females* (London, 1799), p. 99.

74 Beale does not specify when this conversation took place. D. Beale, *Reports Issued by the Schools Inquiry Commission, on the Education of Girls* (London: David Nutt, 1869), p. 37 (footnote).

75 J.S. Mill, 'The Subjection of Women', in John Stuart Mill and Harriet Taylor Mill, *Essays on Sexual Equality*, (ed.) A.S. Rossi (London: University of Chicago Press, 1970), pp. 194, 198.

76 George Eliot, *The Mill on the Floss* [1860], (London: Penguin, 1985), Book II, ch. 1, pp. 220–1.

77 Clarendon Report, vol. 9, cited in A.J. Meadows and W.H. Brock, 'Topics Fit for Gentlemen: The Problem of Science in the Public School Curriculum', in B. Simon and I. Bradley (eds), *The Victorian Public School: Studies in the Development of an Educational Institution* (Dublin: Gill and Macmillan, 1975), p.102.

78 See Beale, *Reports*.

79 Even when they consider it possible for girls to study Latin, commentators usually have some explanation as to why girls can never learn it quite as thoroughly as boys.

80 John Ruskin, *Sesame and Lilies* [1882], (London: George Allen, 1905), p. 149.

81 W.H.D. Rouse, 'Classical Studies', in D. Beale, L.H.M. Soulsby and J.F. Dove (eds), *Work and Play in Girls' Schools* (London: Longmans, Green and Co., 1898), p. 67.

82 *Report of Her Majesty's Commissioners Appointed to Inquire into Revenues and Management of Certain Colleges and Schools* (Clarendon Commission), 4 vols, (London, 1864), vol. III, Eton evidence, Sir John Taylor Coleridge, p. 187 and John Walter Esq., Eton old boy, QQ 9412, p. 300.

83 Mill, 'Subjection', p. 197.

84 Beale, *Reports*, p. 3.

85 Despite the determination of Frances Buss and Emily Davies that the curriculum of girls' secondary schools should be assimilated to that of boys' public schools, they never seem to have considered that girls' schools should adopt the narrow concentration on the classics. See A. Percival, *The English Miss To-day and Yesterday* (London: George G. Harrap and Co., 1939).

86 See J.S. Mill's analysis of the different mental character of the two sexes in 'Subjection', ch. 3.

87 Charles Darwin, *The Descent of Man and Selection in Relation to Sex* (London: John Murray, 1901), p. 859.

88 Cohen, *Fashioning Masculinity*.

89   On this point, see also S. Skedd, 'Women Teachers and the Expansion of Girls'
     Schooling in England, c.1760–1820', in H. Barker and E. Chalus (eds), *Gender in
     Eighteenth-Century England: Roles, Representations and Responsibilities* (London:
     Longman, 1997), p. 125.
90   My emphasis. This foundation, set up in 1872, aimed to open public collegiate day
     schools for girls. These schools were to become girls' 'high schools'. See R. Aldrich,
     *School and Society in Victorian Britain: Joseph Payne and the New World of Educa-
     tion* (New York: Garland, 1995), p. 171; Percival, *English Miss.*

2

CHANGING THE BOUNDARIES: THE VOLUNTARY SYSTEM, PRIVATE POPULAR EDUCATION AND THE BATTLE FOR USEFUL KNOWLEDGE, c.1830s–c.1860s

Dennis Dean

INTRODUCTION

In the 1860s, the reports of three Royal Commissions – Newcastle (1861), Clarendon (1864) and Taunton (1868) – reflected increasing state concerns about education and indicated a move from private to public responsibility. A century later Richard Johnson, influenced by protest movements of the 1960s, investigated strategies adopted from the 1830s by independent working-class activists anxious to build up resistance to the growing power of a capitalist state. 'One of the most interesting developments in working-class history has been the rediscovery of popular education, the springs of action which owed little to philanthropic, ecclesiastical or state provision. For a long time these provisions had remained hidden.'[1] Johnson defined this response in terms of 'really useful knowledge'. This was in contrast to the 'useful knowledge', emanating from both secular and religious sources, which sought to ensure not only that the poor knew their place in society but also were convinced that this was either divinely ordained or was deeply ingrained in the laws of society uncovered by the political economists. Johnson argued that in the 1830s and 1840s independent working-class thinkers strongly contested this provided knowledge, using their own space such as debating societies, discussion groups, coffee shops and taverns to spread their own alternative knowledge about society.

In the 1970s David Vincent used autobiographical material to investigate nineteenth-century history from below and to explore the working class through its own voice rather than through the refracted vision of other classes. He was particularly concerned with the diffusion of literacy and what this meant to the working-class family. Those who could read and write were usurping an older, oral culture based upon experience and knowledge gained over time. Francis Place was one who acknowledged tensions in his own family. As he prospered, he resolved that his children must have an education that was an improvement on what their parents had received. 'So my wife found herself going far behind in all sorts of school learning and she conceived that as they advanced so they became less respectful to her and at length she became fully persuaded that she was an object of reproach.'[2]

Philip Gardner's pioneering study of private elementary working-class education was published in 1984, at a time when the Thatcher revolution was gathering pace and interest was reawakened in older forms of self-help activity. Gardner uncovered layers of elementary schools, financed from within the working class itself, held in houses and shops and uncontrolled by armies of inspectors. In consequence the 1870 Education Act could be interpreted in a new light, as a means of 'closing down' working-class space and remoulding the working class in a new image. Gardner argued that private working-class education 'produced little documentary evidence of its own existence and has inevitably been passed over in favour of more glamorous, more dramatic, more accessible – though far less numerically impressive – connections between "education, and the working class"'.[3]

Gardner's thesis challenged an older modified Whiggish history of education. For example, G. Lowndes surveyed the progress made by successive governments until the mid-1930s, which he compared to an instalment plan. Thus 'for the first forty years of that century (1833–70) they laid the premium of men of goodwill wherever they might be found who showed themselves ready to undertake the building and the maintenance of voluntary schools'.[4] He went on to discuss failings and concluded that in 1870 'the state itself had to enter the field and pay larger instalments in the education of the whole people'.[5] State intervention secured compulsory schooling and a statutory leaving age. Educational issues of public and private in England, however, were complicated by the role of the churches, and not least by the position of the Anglican Church. As Marjorie Cruickshank noted, 'So numerous and so widespread were the facilities of the Established Church (and to a lesser extent the other denominations) when at last the state intervened in education in 1870 it was impractical to dispossess those already in the field and start afresh.'[6]

Since 1960 Brian Simon had provided another line of challenge to Whiggish history of education. For Simon, educational history was a contested territory and 'mass working-class pressure contributed to ensuring that at least the first foundations of a universal system were laid – that education was no longer a charity but a right'.[7] Landmark legislation in education was conditioned by a perception amongst the ruling classes that limited concessions must be made. Simon warned that 'the story of the working-class struggle for education is itself chequered because it is once more interrupted or forced underground by persecution and intimidation'.[8] Nevertheless, Simon's own destination was never in doubt. His ultimate vision was an egalitarian state educational system. Independent working-class activists were seen as the spearhead of a drive for improved state provision rather than as promoters of an alternative approach to education.

VOLUNTARY EDUCATION: IMPLICATIONS AND CONSTRAINTS

During the first half of the nineteenth century voluntary educational institutions proliferated – ranging from infant establishments through teacher training colleges to adult schools and mechanics institutes. Voluntary schooling meant voluntary attendance. Family circumstances prevailed. Thus Robert Lowery recalled his early departure from education: 'at the commencement of my father's illness I was taken from school at the age of 9 and never had the privilege of returning afterwards'.[9] John Buckley recorded an arrangement made by his father and grandmother that, in return for a weekly payment, she would bring him up and his education would continue. Nevertheless, he 'was frequently kept away from school to mind the bakery, a duty which had hitherto been done by a girl who was discharged on my arrival'.[10] Parental priorities were clear. The value of basic literacy was increasingly accepted. On the other hand parents might be less than enthusiastic about much of the ethos of denominational education. William Cobbett advised the working classes to be wary of teachers in provided schools who sought to extend the scope of education for their own benefit. Indeed, Cobbett created a critical discourse in the independent radical press that challenged most educational initiatives provided from above. This approach contrasted strongly with that of the middle-class radical, Joseph Hume, who envisaged a proper national system of education and deplored the paucity of the first government grant in 1833. Hume declared that 'If it was meant that a system of national education should be established this was seen as too small and without such a system no grant at all should be made.'[11]

Suspicion of powerful central government was a feature of the years following the final defeat of Napoleon in 1815. Feelings of superiority and isolationism were strong. Compulsion in all matters, including education, was to be deplored. In defining Englishness one writer declared, 'There is a natural dislike of dictation, an impatience with anything approaching to interference. We carry our love of personal liberty to a point which seems to our Continental critics resembling anarchism.'[12] Working-class radicals subscribed to this view. They argued that individual freedoms were a feature of the ancient constitution. A Chartist periodical explained the historical source: 'The great moment of our ancient Saxon constitution consisted in this that they allowed every parish, every tithing and every county to legislate exclusively for its own affairs. This is genuine democracy.'[13]

Sunday schools constituted one of the great educational movements of the late eighteenth and early nineteenth centuries. In the early days there was some interdenominational co-operation and some Sunday schools were largely under working-class control. Their main purpose, however, was the salvation of souls. As one pupil from the 1820s remembered, 'Some six hours a week, certainly not one hour of useful knowledge; and certainly what many teachers used to call explaining difficult texts in the Bible but very little else.'[14]

In education, as in other areas of life, the growth of the voluntary principle was strengthened by the rise of Dissent. This was particularly true in the developing urban areas. Dissenters had little attachment to a central government so closely identified with the Established Church, not least in matters of education. Church supporters, in turn, feared the growth of public activity at local level as in 1870. As the *Quarterly Review* enquired:

> What will be the effect of the new system of rate supported schools, backed by the compulsory power of the law on the voluntary system, which has hitherto been thought to be congenial to our national character and which has continuously done considerable work?[15]

Disagreement also existed over the place and nature of religious teaching in schools. In 1839 Lord Stanley argued for the strongest presence of religious teaching. 'He was contending that education was not a thing apart and separate from religion: but that religion should be interwoven with all systems of education, controlling and regulating the whole mind and habits and principles of the persons receiving education.'[16]

Thus by the middle of the nineteenth century the forces of Church and Dissent were engaged in a major struggle to secure the allegiance of the young. In this struggle the voluntary system was firmly defended on both sides, but in different ways. The Anglican Church expected and received aid from the state to uphold its several efforts. When subsidies were dispensed, Anglican schools gained the lion's share. When new types of Poor Law, reformatory or factory schools were created and initiatives in teacher training were suggested, pressure from the bishops ensured that Anglican influences predominated. All this, in turn, encouraged Dissenters to adhere more closely to the voluntary principle. Their goal was a free trade in religion to match the concept of free trade in commerce.

Ultimately the attempt to impose national stability through a closer relationship between Church and state foundered. The Religious Census of 1851 demonstrated that the Established Church no longer commanded the support of a majority of the people. Amidst the plethora of education bills of the 1850s and 1860s, a Whig backbencher summed up the changing mood: 'The real question ... is what religious opinion shall have the favour of the state.'[17] The claims of the Anglican Church to a dominant position in the education of the young underwent a steady retreat. Tory Romantics like Lord John Manners and Lord Lytton wistfully looked back to a pre-industrial age and to a rural society in which everyone knew their place. Manners, addressing a Birmingham audience, maintained that 'there was far more peace, more real happiness and more complete security for all classes than had existed or could exist under such a class system that is prevalent in society'.[18]

This desire to turn back the clock was shared by a range of so-called radicals. Cobbett was probably the most influential member of this group, but it also included others, like Oastler and Stephens, who were often associated with the more aggressive forms of Chartism. In their eyes the spread of industry and of the factory needed to be curbed rather than encouraged, and the emphasis on traditional rural culture should be maintained. They deplored the effects of industrialisation and urbanisation upon children and resisted palliative measures, including more forms of schooling, to ease life in these surroundings. An article in the *Poor Man's Guardian* expressed:

> an insuperable contempt and loathing for those heartless hypocrites who mean by education more book learning and who, while they despise, devour and oppress the poor can discover no other remedy for the wrongs they inflict and the destitution they cause than more bibles and more prisons for their victims.[19]

This view did not go unchallenged. For those children of the eighteenth-century Enlightenment like Robert Owen, the advance of industry was to be welcomed. The task was not to destroy the means of progress, namely the factory and the mill, but to ensure that any benefits were distributed fairly. This entailed new industrial structures and co-operative ventures. It also meant dispelling ignorance, superstition and what Owen saw as the negativism of organised religion, beset as it was, in his opinion, with a view of humanity deep in original sin that made it very difficult to break down hopelessness and despair. Owen's answer was to open minds by schooling. If the young received the right stimulus from a very early age they would free themselves from constraint. The knowledge that was necessary to undertake this task was expanding. Society needed to be armed with the method and the authority of science. As Owen told his fellow industrialists:

> Indeed, after experience of the beneficial effects of due care and attention to the mechanical implements, it became easy to a reflecting mind to conclude that at least equal advantages could arise from similar care and attention to the living instruments.[20]

Science supplied the laws that governed the natural world and Owen was more than convinced that exposure to its methods and techniques would progressively enable humanity to uncover the laws underlying society. For Cobbett, the equation of the care of machinery with that of the human workforce filled him with alarm and horror. Capitalism could in no sense improve the lot of the mass of the population. One of his followers angrily denounced 'the cold and dreary system which represented our fellow creatures as so many rivalries and enemies, which makes us believe that their happiness is incompatible with our own, which builds our wealth upon their poverty'.[21]

Science as knowledge became one of the battlegrounds of this period. Many still concluded that science and revealed religion were natural allies; others did not. Science was widely seen as a means of increasing productivity through the creation of a workforce capable of understanding the processes in which they were engaged. There was concern that science was underrepresented in the great institutions of the state. Thus the suggestion was mooted:

> that we might hope to see if it should ever be determined by our rulers to establish a public office and make a minister of public affairs, being himself a scientific man of the highest character, holding an official seat in the House of Commons and a responsible status in the executive government.[22]

The majority of the men who governed the nation saw science in its various forms and the new industrial and urban world through a very clouded lens. Their world was still that of the rolling acres of southern and western England. In the new urban heartlands they were forced to rely on the knowledge of such urban explorers as Chadwick, Kay and Southwood Smith. These professional men produced a plethora of surveys, statistics and local censuses on such issues as housing, schooling and working conditions. Kay stressed how little the governing classes really knew about what was happening in Manchester: 'Very few of their order reside in or near our large provincial towns.'[23]

In 1974 Harold and Pamela Silver provided a local framework in which to examine the rising level of debate and interest about popular education in a rapidly changing society. In their study of the formation of local National Society schools the Silvers described a sense of urgency:

> The educational movement of which the Kennington schools were a product took shape therefore in a situation such as this, with unparalleled social change and new towns growing without any of the ties of squire and church that had been typical of the small agricultural community and the old market town.[24]

Rapid population increase meant that children, particularly in the burgeoning industrial towns, were not only growing in numbers but also constituting a larger percentage of the population than hitherto. In 1846 the *Quarterly Review* gloomily reported that 'Year after year crowded neighbourhoods become more crowded, moors are covered over with villages, villages condense into towns, towns compress their multiplying denseness into deeper cellars and more airless alleys.'[25] Neglected boys were growing up 'into hordes of thoughtless, ignorant, too often depraved and godless men'.[26] In the new industrial towns where whole households, including husbands, wives and older siblings were often in employment away from the house, how was the working-class family attending to the needs of younger children? Gardner has made much of the presence of a range of dame schools and private educational facilities. In other cases relatives, close friends and older people were drawn into self-help activities that enabled families to survive. This knowledge, possessed by communities themselves, was not easily available to outsiders. Those in authority were often convinced that many families in the larger cities were out of control and hopelessly ill-disciplined. Education was seen as the cure for such ills. Thus the conservative *Quarterly Review* concluded that 'the education of the people will repay the state almost to any amount ... in self-maintained social order, in some check at least in the waste of health and life by intemperance and low vice and gaming and robbing'.[27]

CHARTISM, EDUCATION AND THE SEARCH FOR USEFUL KNOWLEDGE

The Chartist movement originated in 1838. Its supporters drew up a six-point charter for parliamentary reform: abolition of the property qualification for MPs; equal electoral districts; payment of MPs; secret ballot; universal adult male suffrage and annual parliaments. Early writing on the Chartist movement exhibited two approaches. The 'official' approach was to discredit. The events of 1848, when a third petition bearing a supposed two million signatures was presented to Parliament, were ridiculed in an attempt to persuade the population that this was a movement led by fraudsters and adventurers and consequently unworthy of support. The second perspective proceeded from members of the movement themselves. This was characterised by disillusionment and a search for scapegoats.

Re-evaluation in the early twentieth century was spearheaded by such historians as Mark Hovell and R.H. Tawney, figures associated with the foundation of the Labour movement and the activities of the WEA (Workers' Educational Association). Hovell, a former pupil teacher who became an assistant lecturer at Manchester University, was placed in charge of WEA classes in Ashton, Colne and Leigh, a former centre of Chartist activity. Hovell was killed in action, but his study of Chartism was published posthumously in 1918. In a preface to the book T.F. Tout commented on Hovell's 'deep interest in the condition of the people who were successfully working out their own salvation'.[28] R.H. Tawney made similar connections between Chartist pioneers and students in his classes. He saw their fellowship of learning and search for justice as culminating in the labour movement of the early twentieth century. This approach highlighted divisions between the 'knowledge' Chartists and the ethos of the London Working Men's Association on the one hand, and the disaffection of displaced artisans and factory hands under the flamboyant leadership of Feargus O'Connor on the other.

Chartism existed intermittently between 1838 and the late 1850s. In governing circles it was often assumed that a cadre of 'evil' educators were misleading the mindless masses. Thus in 1839 an anxious MP warned against 'the disciples of Thomson, the followers of Stephens and the millions whose creed is Chartism: for such are the instructors to whom you leave the minds of the people'.[29] Chartist lecturers, indeed, travelled the country and addressed a range of meetings both great and small, some in the new adult schools and mechanics institutes. Highly-educated Chartists eked out a living from collections and subscriptions as lecturers and debaters.

Chartist knowledge was frequently displayed in courts of law. For example, Thomas Dunning attended a famous trial at Chester Assizes where:

> McDouall conducted his own case and cross-examined witnesses and addressed the jury for 4 hours in his defence. During his peroration Sir John Jarvis who sat below the dock appeared spellbound with the doctor's eloquence. At the close of his speech there was a great cheer in court for him.[30]

Many Chartists sacrificed both livelihood and liberty. Chartism's major figure, Feargus O'Connor, eloquent and energetic, was a lawyer by background and training. At his funeral in 1855 it was noted that 'He commenced life as a comparatively rich man and was gifted with strong natural talents particularly adapted for achievement in the profession he selected.'[31] Imprisoned Chartists continued to conduct political discussions and to insist on having access to reading and writing materials.

Chartism and Owenism played significant parts in the communications revolution that accompanied the industrial revolution. The several churches and improvement societies such as the Society for the Diffusion of Useful Knowledge poured out booklets, tracts and other forms of literature. Chartists and Owenites responded in kind. The Chartist newspaper, the *Northern Star*, was a major vehicle. National and local events were reported, while articles provided the agenda for Chartist meetings. Additionally, individuals, localities and factions within Chartism were represented in a range of periodicals and tracts. Writers, reporters and distributors were complemented by a cadre of skilled digesters and readers who relayed the information in a variety of ways to their less literate colleagues.

Chartism was the product of a simmering history that went back to the 1790s. Thomas Wheeler recounted that he had absorbed his own radicalism within the family home where 'his father was an adherent of the politics of the noble old man Major Cartwright, of Hunt, Cobbett, Hobhouse and Burdett'.[32] Figures such as William Benbow, who had served his political apprenticeship in Jacobin clubs and societies, were present at the birth of Chartism. These men had survived in a twilight world of clubs, discussion groups and debating societies that government had never totally managed to silence. They encouraged others to emulate their tactics. John Bates recalled, 'I acquired an interest in public affairs through meeting with a company of men on Saturday nights for the reading of a newspaper. ... I was often asked to read aloud. The reports of the national distress and discontent aroused my sympathies.'[33] The early decades of the nineteenth century witnessed a proliferation of mutual learning and improvement societies. Independent learning was a lonely and expensive experience and these societies provided the possibility of fellowship, discussion and exchange of books. Probably they were also places where radical independent ideas were circulated. In spite of the imposition of a tax on newspapers, the 1830s saw the burgeoning of an 'unstamped press'. Many future Chartist leaders were involved in this movement and thereby came to understand the power of the printed word. Thomas Frost recalled that 'No term of approbation was too strong to be applied to these unstamped newspapers. ... Prosecution after prosecution resulting in heavy fines and long imprisonment failed to suppress the pioneers of the penny press.'[34] Radical ideas were spread in a variety of ways. Many younger workers were on the move. Settlement houses served as rest houses and incipient labour exchanges, and also initiated many young men into political activity and trade societies. For example, the nomadic young Robert Gammage abandoned his Tory family background when he 'caught the sound of every voice and took in and compared the various ideas that were expressed'.[35]

Thus Chartism espoused a central educational message and strategy. Knowledge was to be placed at the disposal of the movement. Learning was to be seen as a co-operative venture in which those with education shared their possession of it with those who as yet were dispossessed. Economic arguments were also developed and deployed. Explanations were sought for economic cycles in the theory of under-consumption. Mass production required mass consumption. 'Though the machines – which can be made for money can make the several fabrics of manufactured merchandise they cannot buy them nor wear them nor use them.'[36] Thus the middle classes depended upon the working classes both as producers and as consumers. 'Take away the labour and the support of the lower classes and they must at once fall to the ground.'[37]

For the Chartists the 1830s and 1840s were not only a period of rapid economic changes, they were also characterised by the emergence of an increasingly articulate and resourceful working class. Indeed, 'for the first time in the annals of the world is the working man rising up a class of himself, distinct from all other classes'.[38] Neither the existing government nor the social structure could cope with the ever-expanding economy. Implementation of the Charter would ensure that power would be placed in the hands of the rightful rulers, the people. Whig governments of the 1830s had betrayed the movement for parliamentary reform and further depressed the lot of the poorest in society. A stocking-maker, addressing a semi-clandestine meeting, declared that 'Church and State had entered into a partnership. One said, "You enslave their bodies and we will enslave their minds."'[39]

From the 1790s there was great resentment at the charge made by Burke that any form of democratic government created by the masses would put power into the hands of 'the swinish multitude'. Many of the more educated Chartists were aware of the extent of ignorance among their fellow workers, but argued that such ignorance resulted from deliberate deprivation and degradation. As Henry Vincent proclaimed: 'Punishment, punishment, punishment seems to be the cry of the whole community: but I say educate, educate, educate. Do more for the improvement of the population, not to make them become poorer.'[40] Chartists, indeed, could argue that in spite of their failure to secure major parliamentary reforms, they were the main promoters of social change. Thus Wilson maintained that Chartists had:

> played a leading part in agitating in favour of the ten hours question, the repeal of taxes on knowledge, education, co-operation, civil and religious liberty and the land question, for they were the true pioneers of all the great movements of our time.[41]

Nevertheless, members of the ruling classes continued to insist that their own hours of ease and leisure were 'indispensable to the growth of the Arts, Sciences and Literature', while 'the masses should look and endure a certain amount of privation'.[42]

Both Feargus O'Connor and William Lovett were convinced of the need to broaden access to knowledge. They differed, however, over the role of education in the struggle to secure the Charter. For O'Connor and his supporters the purpose of education was to mobilise the working classes and prepare them for the mass demonstrations that would ultimately bring the government to its knees and force them to concede the Chartist demands. For Cooper, Lovett and Vincent the education of the people went far beyond immediate political ends. They argued that, by themselves, mass demonstrations and petitioning were unlikely to win concessions. Since the British state, unlike the despotic regimes of continental Europe, granted its people certain rights in terms of protest and redress, it was important that Chartism should not be tarred with the rhetoric of violence and threat. Even while standing trial, Lovett believed that rational argument must prevail, for 'Public opinion is the great bulwark of justice to which the poor and the oppressed appeal when wealth and power have denied them justice.'[43] 'Knowledge' Chartists, as they were known, saw their task as being to transform national character. Chartists halls and meeting places provided the opportunity to ensure steady exposure to educative (and temperance) processes. John Bates recorded that 'Some of us, moreover, were soon convinced that no charter could bring much happiness while the people everywhere were so involved with drink.'[44]

Divisions hardened. Lovett and like-minded Chartists came to regard O'Connor as a demagogue. 'Not possessing a nature to appreciate intellectual entities he began his career by ridiculing our moral force Chartism as he was pleased to designate our efforts to create and extend an enlightened and moral public opinion in favour of Chartist principles.'[45] For their part, the followers of O'Connor had deep suspicions about the intentions of the 'moral force' or 'knowledge' Chartists. At best they were likely to be a distraction to the cause, slowing down the pace of change by putting forward grandiose schemes for educational progress before the levers of power had been wrested from the existing rulers. Revolution in Europe in 1848 gave a sense of urgency. George Boun saw these uprisings as the call to action: 'While the most enslaved nations in Europe are progressing can England remain stationary or become retrograde?'[46] Until political change had been achieved it was premature to look too far into the future. There were other undertones in their opposition. Cobbett's distrust of professional teachers, lecturers and educationists lived on into the 1840s: 'like the late Mr Cobbett he feels an insuperable contempt and loathing who mean by education mere book learning'.[47] There was also a suspicion that 'knowledge' Chartists, because of their willingness to debate with other groups, were open to cross-class alliances which would eventually lead to a dilution of the full Chartist demands.

Chartism and the Chartist period produced issues that continued to dominate independent working-class thinking on education for many years. What knowledge was required to challenge the political, economic and social *status quo*? What strategies would ensure that the forces of progress eventually succeeded? Were there periods when a longer educational strategy aimed at raising the consciousness of the workers was to be preferred to a more spectacular mass action programme? Above all, what were the means to ensure that the existing ruling classes would ultimately concede power to the forces of democracy?

EDUCATION AND KNOWLEDGE IN AN AGE OF EQUIPOISE

In a seminal work published in 1964, W.L. Burn characterised the 1850s and 1860s as 'The Age of Equipoise'. Whereas the 1830s and 1840s had witnessed alarms and threats of insurrection, in the following decades economic growth and rising standards of living ushered in a period of relative calm. Local government reforms instituted in the 1830s began to take effect. For example, municipal libraries assisted in a wider diffusion of knowledge. Working-class radicals became wary of physical force tactics and more inclined towards education. Following the failures of 1848, Britain became a refuge for a number of revolutionary figures from continental Europe, including Karl Marx, whose days were spent in the reading room of the British Museum. The message they received was one of moderation. As G.J. Harney advised Friedrich Engels, 'Notwithstanding all the talk in 1839 about "arming" the people, the people did not arm and they will not arm.'[48]

Other issues came to the fore. The Crimean War, 1854–6, and the expansion of empire extended the horizons of the British working classes. The benefits of British civilisation – in terms of the extension of peace, prosperity, good government, railways and Christianity – were widely extolled. By the 1870s a new discourse of aggressive patriotism, imperialism and scientific racism had emerged as a means of re-affirming national identity and securing the loyalty of the working classes. In 1859 the publication of Charles Darwin's *The Origin of Species* cast fundamental doubts upon one of the most sacred of all pieces of public knowledge – the account of creation contained in the Bible.

Many working-class parents came to appreciate the benefits of formal education. A differentiated working class was emerging. Some sections were convinced of the need for schooling and regular exposure to the classroom. Other sections remained sceptical. Alternative, working-class educational provision, such as dame schools, came under attack from government inquiries and inspectors. Questions were also asked about the voluntary system and whether Church enthusiasm and denominational rivalry could reach those groups in the community as yet untouched by the provided schoolroom. Voluntary agencies were competing for those pupils who would attend regularly and follow school rules, and whose parents would pay the school pence. As the shortcomings of private working-class schooling became more apparent, the very principle of voluntaryism came to be questioned. In 1867 Matthew Arnold, who had been appointed an inspector of schools some 15 years before, noted the change in opinion: 'Throughout my district I find the idea of compulsory education becoming a familiar idea with those who are interested in schools.'[49]

The 1850s saw a reshaping of the working-class political experience as the lessons of 1848 were digested. Some of the tactics which had marked earlier radical activity, namely the politics of the mass platform, mass petitioning and demonstrations, were not entirely abandoned, but other forms of activity, for example, co-operatives, friendly societies and trade unions, became more prevalent. These new forms of activity led to a re-examination of the educational forms and knowledge required in promoting the wellbeing of the working class. For all their energy and enthusiasm, Chartist educational activities had clear shortcomings. Resources were spread too thinly to give more than a smattering of literacy to the illiterate who came to meetings. In times of economic hardship Chartist halls found themselves so crowded with the unemployed that sustained teaching became impossible. On the other hand, in periods of prosperity and full employment, numbers rapidly declined. There was a growing awareness that the basic tools of education could no longer be supplied through traditional methods of self-education and collaborative learning. This was coupled with a cautious acceptance of the need for state intervention in education. Debate now concentrated upon the nature of that state intervention and the best means of curtailing control by central government. In 1840, in proposals put forward by William Lovett and others to establish a national education system, stark warnings were issued about the dangers that concentration of power might bring. 'We are decidedly opposed to the placing of such immense power and influence in the hands of government as that of selecting the teachers and the superintendents, the books and kinds of instruction and the whole management of schools in each locality.'[50] The emphasis should be on accountability to the locality through popularly and frequently elected committees. In contrast, Church power and influence should be reduced. Emphasis in the new schools should be on those subjects that would enable the working-class child to survive in a still hostile world. Further educational facilities would continue to be supplied within the working-class movements themselves. Co-operatives, friendly societies and trade unions should provide courses on accounting, bookkeeping, drafting of letters and memoranda, and even a smattering of labour laws. Workers should be encouraged to consider their daily experiences and how to respond to them. Thus a wider system of adult education based on class discussion and access to well-stocked libraries was required.

In the 1850s the issues of education and franchise became more entangled. Although the 1832 Reform Bill was seen as a final solution by the Whigs and by others in Parliament, by the 1850s franchise extension was back on the political agenda. For most parliamentarians the safeguarding of property rights remained crucial, and thus the vote should only be extended to those who already had a stake in society. Disputes arose over the value of property that should be used as a qualification for the vote. Another suggestion was that the vote should be extended to males who could pass an educational test. The *Spectator*, a liberal journal, welcomed this approach: 'The plan meets many of its objectives, by its gradual operation, by the premium which it puts on self-education, by identifying the more intelligent and therefore more influential part of the working class.'[51] Support also came from George Holyoake, promoter and historian of the co-operative movement, who saw the prospect of an educational franchise as an important incentive in the struggle for an educated working class.

Prominent politicians also espoused the cause of education as the best means of avoiding class conflict. In 1841 the Conservative leader, Sir Robert Peel, expressed his anxieties about the growth of a discontented and illiterate population in the manufacturing towns. 'Is it possible', he asked, 'to consider their present habits and the temptations to crime to which they are exposed without feeling deep anxiety?'[52] Repression and the use of coercive law on their own were unlikely to change this situation. Fiscal policies to encourage economic growth and rising prosperity were required. It was also important to ensure that the working class did not regard the government and the agencies of the state with unbridled hostility. Those in authority must convince all members of the population that the government was aware of their needs and willing to consider careful reforms, including the extension of popular education.

Lord John Russell, the leading figure in the Whig–Liberal coalition, was another politician prepared to reduce social tensions by promoting educational reform. He saw education in the context of earlier struggles to secure civil and religious rights, and began to believe that endless disputes concerning conscience clauses and the role of clergy in schools could only be resolved by the introduction of a national, non-sectarian system. His criticisms of the voluntary system increased. In 1869 he looked back on the years of the scheme's operation and concluded 'that while great good has been done by the increased spread of education and more especially by its improved quality, it cannot be said that the plan had been a success as regards the general situation of the country'.[53] Benjamin Jowett, fellow, tutor and from 1870 master of Balliol College, Oxford, was one who congratulated Russell on his advocacy of change. 'I am sending you a few notes on education. I am very glad that you are taking the matter up. There could be no better or nobler ending of a great political career.'[54]

William Gladstone was a third politician whose views on education were to change. A Conservative and staunch supporter of the Church's role in education, Gladstone had been a severe critic of the Whig educational reforms of 1839 which established a committee of the privy council for education and led to the appointment of the first government inspectors. During the following decades his political stance shifted, and by 1868 he was Prime Minister at the head of a Liberal government. Gladstone came to believe that if the Church was to remain a major influence in the life of the nation it must stand more firmly on its own feet. He accepted the need for a rate-supported, non-sectarian system of education that would supplement, but not replace, Church schools. In 1874, in a letter to John Bright, he indicated the extent to which his opinions had altered since the late 1830s. After discussing the position of Nonconformists on the issue of non-sectarian rate education or simple secular teaching, Gladstone explained, 'I have not been against the latter of these two which seems to me impartial and not, if fairly worked, of necessity in any degree unfriendly to religion.'[55]

CONCLUSION

By the 1870s many of the issues concerning private and public in education had been resolved. Most private working-class schools were swept away as the Education Act of 1870 provided for the election of local school boards with the power to levy a rate in areas where there was insufficient school provision. Henceforth, the schooling of the majority of the population would take place under the auspices of three 'public' bodies – central and local government and the churches. Some private schools for children of the middle classes also disappeared, a process that continued when secondary schools maintained by local authorities were provided under the terms of the Education Act of 1902. Many of the leading private schools (particularly boys' public schools), however, would continue to flourish. Indeed schools such as Harrow, Rugby and Shrewsbury discarded their local dimensions and assumed leading places in a national elite of schools, a situation that continues until the present day.

Thus the educational structure became heavily weighted towards class, hierarchy and status. Free elementary education, the preserve of the working-class child, was strongly subject to public control by regulation, inspection and school attendance officers. It would also be shaped by the limited knowledge dispensed in these institutions and the perception that they were very different places from the prestigious private (public school) sector and the more slowly developing secondary school system. After 1870 an independent tradition of education and of knowledge that had existed from the 1830s until the 1860s had to find new ways of surviving in a system that was increasingly under public control.

NOTES

I am grateful to Richard Aldrich for his assistance in the preparation of this chapter.

1   J. Clarke, C. Critcher and R. Johnson (eds), *Working Class Culture: Studies in Working Class History* (London: Hutchinson, 1979), p. 75.
2   Francis Place to John and Anne Meirs, 7 March 1828, in M. Teale (ed.), *Autobiography of Francis Place* (Cambridge: Cambridge University Press, 1972), p. 255.
3   P. Gardner, *The Lost Elementary Schools of Victorian England* (London: Croom Helm, 1984), p. 3.
4   G. Lowndes, *The Silent Social Revolution: An Account of the Expansion of Public Education in England and Wales 1895–1965* (London: Oxford University Press, 2nd edn, 1969), p. 3.
5   Ibid.
6   M. Cruickshank, *Church and State in English Education* (Basingstoke: Macmillan, 1964), p. 14.
7   B. Simon, *The Two Nations and the Educational Structure 1780–1870* (London: Lawrence and Wishart, 1974), p. 365.
8   Ibid., p. 15.
9   B. Harrison and P. Hollis, *Robert Lowery, Radical and Chartist* (London: Europa, 1979), p. 45.
10 J. Buckley, *A Village Politician. The Life Story of John Buckley* (London: Caliban Books, 1902), p. 14.
11 *Hansard* (Parliamentary Debates), vol. XX, col. 733, 17 August 1833.
12 *Contemporary Review*, 18, 24 September 1864, p. 284.
13 '*Poor Man's Guardian* No. 7', in D. Thompson, *Small Chartist Periodicals* (London: Garland, 1986), p. 51.
14 '*Life of John James Beezer*', in D. Vincent, *Testament of Radicalism* (London: Europa, 1979), p. 157.
15 *Quarterly Review*, 131, July–October 1871, p. 265.
16 *Hansard* (Parliamentary Debates), vol. XLVIII, col. 238, 14 June 1839.
17 T.A. Jenkins (ed.), *Trelawney Diaries 1858–1865* (London: Royal Historical Society, 1994), entry for 21 March 1860, p. 111.
18 J. Merrow (ed.), *Young England: The New Generation* (Leicester: Leicester University Press, 1999), p. 67.
19 '*Poor Man's Guardian* No. 2', in Thompson, *Small Chartist Periodicals*, p. 15.
20 Robert Owen, *A New View of Society 1816 with an Introduction by John Saville* (Basingstoke: Macmillan, 1972), pp. 74–5.
21 'Piercy Ravenstone on *Capitalism*, 1821', in T. Benn (ed.), *Writing on the Wall: A Radical and Socialist Anthology* (London: Faber, 1986), p. 41.
22 Harcourt to Brougham, 23 February 1832, in I. Inkster (ed.), *Gentlemen of Science: Early Correspondence* (London: Royal Historical Society, 1984), p. 64.

23 James Phillips Kay, *The Moral and Physical Condition of the Working Classes Employed in the Cotton Manufacture in Manchester* [1832], (Manchester: E.J. Martin, 1969), p. 8.
24 P. Silver and H. Silver, *The Education of the Poor* (London: Routledge, 1974), p. 8.
25 *Quarterly Review*, 78, September 1846, p. 380.
26 Ibid., p. 381.
27 Ibid., p. 418.
28 T. F. Tout preface to Mark Hovell, *The Chartist Movement* [1918], (Manchester: Manchester University Press, 1970), p. xxv.
29 *Hansard* (Parliamentary Debates), vol. XLVIII, col. 557, 14 June 1839.
30 'Thomas Dunning', in Vincent, *Testament*, p. 139.
31 'William Jones Funeral Oration 1855', in D. Thompson, *Feargus O' Connor: Attack and Defence* (London: Garland, 1986), pp. 2–3.
32 'Thomas Wheeler', in D. Thompson, *Chartist Biographies and Autobiographies* (London: Garland, 1986), p. 10.
33 'John Bates', in Thompson, *Chartist Biographies*, p. 2.
34 Thomas Frost, *Forty Years Recollections: Literary and Political* (London: Garland, 1986 reprint), p. 8.
35 W. Maehl, *Robert Gammage: Reminiscences of a Chartist* (London: Society for the Study of Labour History, 1983), p. 38.
36 '*Lifeboat*, 6, 1, 6 January 1844', in Thompson, *Small Chartist Periodicals*, p. 88.
37 Ibid.
38 D. Thompson, *Chartist and Anti-Chartist Pamphlets* (London: Garland, 1986), p. 6.
39 Buckley, *Village Politician*, p. 55.
40 W. Darling, *Henry Vincent: A Biographical Sketch* (London: Garland, 1986), p. 46.
41 'D. Wilson, *The Struggles of an Old Chartist*', in Vincent, *Testament*, p. 210.
42 '*Democrat and Labour Advocate*, 3 November 1855', in Thompson, *Small Chartist Periodicals*, p. 2.
43 D. Thompson, *Chartism: Working Class Politics in the Industrial Revolution* (London: Garland, 1986), p. 9.
44 'John Bates', in Thompson, *Chartist Autobiographies*, p. 13.
45 Thompson, *Chartism*, p. 2.
46 G. Claey (ed.), *The Chartist Movement in England* (London: Pickering and Chatto, 2001), vol. V, p. 27.
47 '*Poor Man's Guardian No. 2*', in Thompson, *Small Chartist Periodicals*, p. 15.
48 Harney to Engels, 30 March 1846, in F. Black and R. Black (eds), *The Harney Papers* (Assen: Van Gorcum and Co, 1969), p. 240.
49 Matthew Arnold, *Reports on Elementary Schools 1852–1882. Report for 1867* (London: HMSO, 1908), p. 137.
50 Thompson, *Chartism*, p. 6.
51 *Spectator*, 33, May 1860, p. 66.
52 *Hansard* (Parliamentary Debates), vol. LVIII, col. 125, 11 March 1841.
53 *Hansard* (Parliamentary Debates), vol. CXCIV, col. 806, 8 March 1869.
54 Jowett to Russell, 27 October 1867, in G. Gooch (ed.), *The Later Correspondence of Lord John Russell*, 2 vols (London: Longman, 1925), vol. 2, p. 362.
55 Gladstone to Bright, 27 January 1874, in C. Matthew and M. Foot (eds), *The Gladstone Diaries 8, 1871–4*, (Oxford: Oxford University Press, 1994), p. 450.

3

FROM INCORPORATION TO PRIVATISATION: PUBLIC AND PRIVATE SECONDARY EDUCATION IN TWENTIETH-CENTURY ENGLAND

Gary McCulloch

INTRODUCTION

Of all the features that have marked secondary education in England since the establishment of state secondary education under the Education Act of 1902, one of the sharpest and most enduring has been the differentiation between private provision on the one hand, and state provision on the other. The divide between the two sectors has survived all the major social and political changes of the past century, and has resisted unscathed even the most determined of educational reforms.[1] This chapter will investigate the seemingly intractable nature of this divide, and focuses on attempts to cross the lines between state and private provision, or to bring them closer together. These initiatives do much to illuminate the relationship between 'public' and 'private' in education over the past century. They also provide an important historical context for recent and contemporary attempts to redefine the relationship between state and private provision, first under the Conservative government in the 1980s and 1990s, and secondly under the Labour government that came to power in 1997.

Private education was provided in schools widely, if confusingly, known in the English context as 'public schools', private schools, or independent schools. The legal definition of the sector was elusive; it included both boarding and day schools, and it embraced a wide variety of schools from the socially elite to the progressive and local. The popular image of the public schools was primarily that of the socially elite, mainly boarding schools that had gained pre-eminence in the previous century. These and other private schools were independent of the administration of the central state and of LEAs (Local Education Authorities), and were administered by their own governing bodies. Parents paid fees to the school attended by their children, although some of the schools received financial aid from the state or from endowments. According to the Fleming Report on the public schools and the general educational system, published in July 1944, the definition of a public school was that it was represented on the Governing Bodies' Association (founded in 1940, with an Association of Governing Bodies of Girls' Schools founded in 1942), or the Headmasters' Conference (founded in 1869), which together consisted of 89 schools that were fully independent and 99 schools that were aided by grants from the Board of Education or from LEAs.[2] The same definition was adopted by a further Public Schools Commission whose report was published in 1968.[3] Included in this was a category of schools known as direct grant schools, which received aid directly from the state rather than from LEAs. This category of schools was phased out by the Labour government of 1974–9, but the Education Reform Act of 1988 reinvented and sought to augment this 'third tier' under the new title of grant maintained schools, which 'opted out' of LEA control and received their grants directly from the central department.

By contrast, the state or maintained sector of secondary education was administered by LEAs, and increasingly became subject to the direct involvement of the central state. In the early twentieth century it catered for only a very small proportion of the age range, and still charged fees to most of its pupils. Under the Education Act of 1944, free state secondary education became a universal right and obligation for all children between 11 and 15 (16 from 1972). After the 1944 Act, the Ministry of Education initially encouraged LEAs to develop three different types of secondary school in a so-called 'tripartite' system: academically selective grammar schools, technical schools, and modern schools. The policy was superseded in the 1960s with the spread of a system of comprehensive schools for all abilities and aptitudes. At the end of the century, the vast majority of children of secondary school age were attending state schools, usually comprehensives, while about 7 per cent were attending private schools.[4]

The separate development of these systems of education has engendered periodic debate. In the 1940s the educational reformer R.H. Tawney criticised the 'co-existence of a public and a private educational system'.[5] In the past decade, this division has continued to encourage vivid comparisons with the

'Two Nations' of nineteenth-century England, the Berlin Wall that symbolised the divisions of post-war Europe, and even the apartheid regime of South Africa. The Conservative MP, George Walden, claimed that an 'educational apartheid' exists which effectively 'severs our educational culture at the neck'.[6] The Labour Party advisers, Andrew Adonis and Stephen Pollard, have also complained of an 'educational apartheid' underlying what they describe as 'a school system which, more than any other in the western world, is founded on a division between state and private'.[7]

At the same time, these two systems have never been totally separate. To begin with, the products of the private system have generally been responsible for administering the state system and the supervision of its reform. This indeed went to the heart of a deeper critique that the educational division between the state and the private system sustained the social superiority of the latter and the political pre-eminence of its products. Tawney commented acidly that many MPs 'have rarely themselves been educated in schools which are directly affected by parliamentary decisions on educational policy, nor do they often send their sons to them'. This being the case, he reasoned, 'They can hardly be expected – apart, of course, from bright exceptions – to regard the improvement of those schools as the urgent issue which it is.'[8] More recently, such association with the private sector has become a common basis for charges of hypocrisy levelled against politicians. According to one leading commentator, for example, 'Conservative MPs claim their intention is to create "excellent" state schools, yet few would dream of sending their children to them.'[9] Such a rebuke was also often extended to the privately-educated Labour Prime Minister, Tony Blair, who sent his two sons to an advantaged Catholic school, the London Oratory.[10] Moreover, as the editor of the *New Statesman*, Peter Wilby, observed, even the London Oratory struggled against the private sector in the competition for entry to the elite universities, which was why Blair also provided his son with tuition from teachers at Westminster, one of the country's most elite private schools.[11] This dilemma of whether to choose state or private provision for one's own children affected many other public figures at the end of the twentieth century and into the twenty-first. These included the black left-wing Labour MP for Tottenham, Bernie Grant, who admitted that with hindsight he regretted not considering the private sector for his children, but that his former position as leader of Haringey Council in north London had made this 'unthinkable'.[12]

The social inequalities that resulted from these educational divisions were often criticised. There were many critics of the public schools, such as T.C. Worsley, himself a former public school master, who in the early years of the Second World War called for a democratic alternative to the 'old school tie'.[13] At the same time, it was widely acknowledged that the public schools had much to offer if their qualities and assets could be shared for the public good.

This was the view, for example, expressed by Fred Clarke, Director of the Institute of Education in London, at the same time that Worsley's ideas were being widely canvassed. According to Clarke, 'The real point of criticism is not that the education they offer is bad, but that it is so good and so much needed that it ought to be more generally accessible.'[14] In other words, how could the benefits of the elite private or independent sector be enjoyed by the mass of the pupils in the state system? It was in these terms that many initiatives developed to attempt to bring the state and private sectors of secondary education closer together.

In the period 1902–44, a strategy of incorporating the private schools into the maintained system was often favoured as the best means of achieving a single national system of education. After the Second World War, significant attempts were made to foster an alliance between the state grammar schools and the private schools, especially in relation to the school curriculum. Scholarship schemes were also developed to try to supply a tangible connection between the two systems. Each of these strategies involved crossing the lines between the public and the private sector, and each was fraught with difficulty due to the in-built resistance of the separate systems to a closer relationship. It is especially important to understand the nature of these problems, both in terms of the historical development of secondary education over the past century, and to address the issues raised in recent and contemporary policies in this area.

INCORPORATING THE ENGLISH TRADITION

A common approach to the problem of bringing the private and state systems of secondary education closer together was the idea of incorporating the private system, or the benefits and values associated with it, into the state system. This strategy took different forms. One such tactic was to seek to define the values of the established public schools and to encourage the maintained schools to adopt them. Another was to find ways to allow pupils in the state system to enjoy the benefits and social prestige hitherto enjoyed by the private schools. All such plans, however, were hampered partly by the social differences of the two systems, and partly by the political difficulties involved in compelling the independent schools to take part.

The social distance between the state and private sectors represented a gulf that was hazardous to attempt to traverse. Private schools, and especially the elite public boarding schools, were widely regarded as socially superior and indeed exclusive. This superiority was often cultivated in a highly conspicuous fashion, marked at Eton College, for example, in school dress, tail-coats, top hats, Eton jackets and Eton collars, in what one former pupil remembered as 'an ostentatious and arrogant defiance of contemporary society'.[15] This social snobbery was compounded by ignorance. For instance, a master at Marlborough College in the early 1920s, Ronald Gurner, applied for the headship of a state secondary school in London, and later recalled:

> I knew, to all intents and purposes, next to nothing about State secondary schools or State schools of any sort. Although I had read papers and taken part in discussions on them, I had never, to the best of my knowledge, been inside one. I understood that elementary schools turned out boys and girls after the same pattern, and I supposed, when I thought about the matter at all, that the secondary schools did the same.[16]

Gurner extolled the virtues of maintained day schools but he was tellingly frank as to the differences between such schools and the private schools. The first difference was social, in that maintained schools included former elementary and working-class pupils which could lead to what Gurner described as 'contamination':

> It is difficult, if you are a country solicitor or doctor of any standing, to contemplate with equanimity the possibility of your son sitting side by side with the son of your junior clerk or chauffeur – better send him to St Cuthbert's on the south coast. The fees are high, and you are not certain as to exactly what is the standard of education which that excellent residential establishment provides – but there are no board-school [sic] boys there, and in the things that matter your boy will be safe.[17]

Board schools had ceased to exist 30 years before, but the ignorance of this suggested here seems to epitomise the Olympian detachment of the private sector. Secondly, Gurner pointed to the loss of independence and the 'degradation of the school by inspector and educational official', in that

> ... inspectors have the right to come and bully the headmaster and staff; that an education officer, or his underlings, can question items of expenditure, or refuse, in the name of the committee, to give sanction for the building of the much-needed swimming-bath or pavilion; that the school is not as free as it was in the good old days before the nation spent hundreds of thousands a year, mainly upon an army of unwanted officials. ...[18]

This was fundamentally a political objection, although also with a social undertone, that reflected the fierce resistance of the independent schools to any attempts at usurping their rights and freedoms.

It was in this context that attempts were made to define the qualities of the public schools and to incorporate these in the maintained sector. A key figure in this regard was Cyril Norwood, from 1906 until 1916 Headmaster of Bristol Grammar School which was aided by the Board of Education, but thereafter a leading public school headmaster at Marlborough College from 1916 until 1926, and at Harrow School from 1926 until 1934. Norwood was also significant for his role as member and then chairman (from 1921 until 1946) of the SSEC (Secondary Schools Examinations Council), which reported to the Board of Education on the School Certificate and Higher School Certificate examinations.[19] As early as 1909, when Headmaster of Bristol Grammar School, he made clear his view that state provision of secondary education should become pre-eminent, but that this provision should incorporate the public schools and the values that they represented. In a work entitled *The Higher Education Of Boys In England*, jointly edited with a Bristol Grammar School master, Arthur H. Hope, Norwood argued that the grammar school was likely to become 'the increasingly predominating type of English higher education', because of 'its combination of liberal study and contact with life'. It should, therefore, be given 'the fullest measure of State and local support'. At the same time, he added:

> The Public School must, willy-nilly, be brought into line and given the leading place it merits in a national system. As a residential school and as a school endowed for learning it is in equal need of inspection, and public control alone can improve the standard of its average intellectual work and break down its caste spirit, without impairing its individuality or that keen spirit of loyalty and that athletic energy which have made its contribution to international education of unique and lasting value.[20]

In such a way, he insisted, the value of secondary education 'will under expert State control become as patent to English, as to foreign, parents and employers', performing an important service in 'bringing different classes together when they are young and generous, and thereby introducing a spirit of union and mutual sympathy into a nation so split to-day by faction that it is risking both its internal prosperity and its outward strength'.[21]

Twenty years later, now as Headmaster of Harrow School, on the other side of the educational divide, Norwood attempted to elaborate on the distinctive virtues of the public schools by invoking what he termed a uniquely 'English tradition' of education. He defined this above all in relation to an ideal of service which he argued should be preserved and also extended into schools provided and aided by the state, concluding:

I put forward the ideal of the highest English tradition, of that education which trains a generation through religion and discipline, through culture of the mind and perfection of the body, to a conscious end of service to the community, as an ideal which shall inspire the whole of our education in every type of school, and create the democracy of the future.[22]

This was an ideal of infusion that envisaged the incorporation of the values of the public schools into the maintained system of secondary education.

During the 1930s, many private schools encountered severe financial difficulties due to the effects of the economic depression and of a low birth rate. In this situation they came under severe pressure to be brought under the auspices of the state, and this pressure continued into the war years. Norwood was again ubiquitous in this debate. He made use of his connections with Board of Education officials to discuss the problems of the public schools and to put forward his own proposals for the future. He argued against the introduction of scholarships to the public schools on the grounds that this would be akin to 'a speculator who is trying to hold up shares in a market out of which the bottom is falling'. Rather, he suggested:

Start after the war a National system of boarding schools, age range 12–18+, take the boys from the elementary schools and sons of clergy and ministers and from other classes on a small payment, and run the public school system yourselves through Boards of Governors as now. Do not let it fall into the hands of LEAs who would not understand it. It may be expensive, but not more expensive than such a system of scholarships as would really save the public schools. And you would really mobilise it without destroying its values. ...[23]

He pursued the issue further in an article in the *Spectator* in February 1940, emphasising the urgent need to address 'the problem of the class-division created by the existence of the public schools and the state-aided schools side by side, and the inequality of opportunity which it thereby created'. It was important now, Norwood asserted, to graft together the traditional boarding school system and the state-aided system that had been developed since 1902, in order to establish 'that single national system of the future which will make democracy not unequal to its task'.[24]

These views raised the prospect of compulsion, and spurred the public schools into protest. Lord Hugh Cecil, Provost of Eton College, wrote to the President of the Board of Education, Earl de la Warr, to denounce Norwood's proposals as 'pure Totalitarianism', and to thunder against any notion of incorporating private schools into the state system: 'Surely the last thing to be desired is educational union. Our educational system should have the variety that belongs to human nature, and should, above all, be filled with the atmosphere of liberty, which is the very opposite of a unified standardised State system.' Moreover, he continued:

> What is wanted is not to assimilate the Public Schools to the State Schools, but on the contrary to try and give to Secondary Schools as much liberty of management, and as much individuality of character, as is consistent with sound financial administration. I should like to liberate Secondary Schools from all educational, as distinct from financial control.[25]

Nevertheless, there was widespread agreement with Norwood's basic contention that some means should be found to incorporate the public schools into the state system of secondary education, as part of a broader reconstruction of the education service. The *TES* (*Times Educational Supplement*), for example, acknowledged the argument that 'a democracy cannot afford the segregation, in youth, of one class from another, and that the opportunities of being trained for responsibility and leadership should not be open only to the well-to-do'.[26] It was soon ready to support the fusing together of the private schools with the state system in clear terms:

> It has been for long a chief pride of the public schools that their main aim is the inculcation of the loftiest ideals of Christian service. They have today the supreme opportunity to put these ideals into practice. Their incorporation into the State educational system would involve for them great sacrifices intangible but none the less real – and the fact that they would in many instances reap correspondingly great material benefits would not necessarily eliminate nor even diminish the pain of sacrifice.

The *TES* recognised the dangers of compelling the public schools against their will, and so proposed a voluntary act of self-sacrifice for the greater good of the nation as a whole:

> By its nature democracy cannot demand this sacrifice of them, but equally because of its nature it knows how to accept and profit by its offer, and the schools would never be more true to their tradition than if they came voluntarily and willingly to the nation and placed themselves unreservedly in its hands, to take and to use as it thought best.[27]

Similarly, the Labour Party intellectual, G.D.H. Cole, in conversation with the new President of the Board of Education, R.A. Butler, suggested that the public schools 'should renounce their proud claim to constitute the method of training our leaders and should simply regard themselves as the boarding element of a national system of education'. According to Cole, such schools 'would have a happy future provided they assimilated themselves in some way to the State system'.[28]

Butler decided to appoint a Departmental committee under Lord Fleming, a Scottish judge, to inquire into how to bring the public schools into a closer association with the general education system, but the outcome was disappointing. The report produced by the committee showed in its introduction an acute understanding of the constraints involved in incorporating or assimilating the public schools, and recommended instead proposals that it hoped would encourage 'the voluntary association with the general educational system of all Public Schools, whatever their financial position, without any sacrifice of educational standards or of reasonable freedom in such matters as school government, curriculum, religion, and general educational principle'.[29] It went on to propose two schemes of scholarships for selected pupils in maintained schools to be given places in approved private schools, which would be known as associated schools. It was, insisted the report, 'vital to our conception that the system should, from now onwards, be regarded as a single whole, with schools of different types'.[30]

However, as Norwood had predicted, scholarships did little to affect the separate characteristics of the private and state systems. Cole was also suspicious of the prescription offered by the Fleming Report. He had originally been included in the membership of the Fleming Committee, but had to withdraw from this position due to illness.[31] Cole would have preferred to attempt to incorporate the day public schools in the state system while leaving the boarding schools to their own devices, rather than introducing scholarships that would strengthen the public school system, 'bolstering it up artificially by apparent reforms which will leave its essential character unaltered'.[32] In retrospect, Butler observed that the Fleming Report was 'sensationally ingenuous' and 'had little influence on the course of events'.[33]

A further attempt to promote a closer association was made through a Public Schools Commission established under the Labour government of the 1960s, this time under the explicit injunction to produce a plan of action to 'advise on the best way of integrating the public schools with the State system of education'.[34] It recommended a scheme of integration by which suitable boarding schools should provide at least half of their places to assisted pupils who needed boarding education. This more radical scheme of scholarships convinced very few, and the government decided not to proceed with it. This episode served indeed to underline the long-term failure of the project to incorporate the private schools into the state system. The social differences of the two systems, combined with the hostility of private schools to any undermining of their independence, had thwarted attempts to legislate or compel the schools to comply. This left the ideal of incorporation either at the lofty, intangible and uncertain level of Norwood's 'English tradition', or consigned to the wishful thinking of voluntary scholarship schemes. A further initiative in the same direction in the 1980s, the assisted places scheme, appeared to confirm this message.[35]

INVESTING IN SUCCESS

In the decades that followed the Second World War further initiatives of a very different kind were developed to foster a closer relationship between the state and private sectors. These centred largely on the school curriculum. In these years the Ministry of Education was assertive in policy issues, but generally unwilling to intervene openly in the curriculum, which was held to be the domain of LEAs and teachers.[36] This situation also created opportunities for private agencies to become involved in sponsoring and encouraging curriculum development. In the 1950s, the so-called 'Industrial Fund', an ambitious plan to sponsor the design and equipment of science laboratories in schools, was at first intended to help bring the state and private sectors closer together. Again, however, such hopes were disappointed due to the entrenched positions of the separate systems.

The Industrial Fund arose from concerns that were widely expressed during the 1950s about a lack of accommodation for science education and a shortage of science teachers. A.H. Wilson, the director responsible for research and development at Courtaulds Ltd, approached the Ministry to discuss how major industries could contribute to improving facilities for science education, such as paying for additions to laboratory space and equipment. He was uncertain as to whether the private schools were more in need of such facilities than were state schools, but emphasised that he would not wish any industrial sponsorship to have the effect of widening the gulf that already existed between the private and state sectors.[37] Wilson developed his ideas further in an interview with a senior Ministry of Education official, Anthony Part. Courtaulds had already given Christ's Hospital School some money to equip new science laboratories and had helped provide new science equipment to some schools in Coventry, but was anxious that such investment should not be haphazard and should achieve the best results possible. Also, as Part noted, Wilson reiterated his concern that 'if possible, any assistance given should not serve to widen any gap which there might be between independent and maintained schools'.[38]

The Ministry was interested in Wilson's ideas, but proved reluctant to involve state maintained schools in such a scheme, despite their lack of science facilities. From the beginning, Part was highly sceptical about the prospects of funding state schools in this way, commenting: 'I cannot myself think of any sensible scheme whereby industry could contribute towards the cost of science facilities at maintained grammar schools, though I suppose there would be no objection to a particular firm or industry helping a particular school.' On the other hand, he was willing to envisage the Ministry giving informal advice about the need for such facilities at particular independent schools.[39] The senior science inspector, R.A.R. Tricker, agreed with this view.[40] Moreover, as discussions continued, the proposal became increasingly confined, first to provision for an academic elite, and then to the private sector. Eric James, High Master of Manchester Grammar School, was invited to advise the Ministry about the possibility of such a scheme, and declared firmly that it should operate on a highly selective basis. This was consistent with James' general view that the education system should cultivate a recognisable social and political elite.[41] James insisted that 'the money should be devoted in the first place to those schools which *already* have large science sixth forms and from which large numbers of boys go to the university to read science'. Indeed, he continued, 'I should regard it as a mistake – unless the money were unlimited – for an attempt to be made to build up science in dim schools with dim staffs and no scientific tradition.'[42] Ministry officials readily agreed that it would be best to 'invest in success',[43] and therefore to concentrate on a limited group of schools that already possessed well established and successful science sixth forms. Such criteria would mean that the scheme would be restricted to a limited number of grammar and public schools, but that there would be at least some involvement from both the state and private sectors.

Nevertheless, it was not long before maintained schools were excluded from the scheme altogether. This was principally on the grounds that since LEAs were responsible for such schools, they should not receive outside support in providing accommodation and equipment. The schools involved 'would have to show that their financial position was such that the necessary improvements could not be made without outside assistance', which meant that only independent and direct grant schools would be able to benefit from the scheme.[44] Another key official, Toby Weaver, expounded at length on the basis for this doctrine. It was, according to Weaver, a 'familiar difficulty' that prevented private funds from being channelled into activities that were the responsibility of LEAs to maintain at a reasonable standard from public funds. Weaver suggested that there was an inherent contradiction in private funds subsidising public authorities to carry out their statutory duty. Moreover, he added, even if such an objection could be ignored, there would be major difficulties in practice in administering private funds for such a purpose:

If you put your money where it is most needed you find yourself subsidising the stingiest authorities. In any case, it would be a gigantic
undertaking to survey the science equipment in maintained schools and
to devise a method of private grant aid which was other than arbitrary.
For these reasons I do not think that we ought to ask for assistance
towards the provision of accommodation or equipment in maintained
schools.[45]

The Ministry therefore preferred to confine its role to discreet and informal
advice on how such investment should be targeted towards independent schools,
rather than involving schools in the maintained sector. It was even happy to
consider encouraging industrialists to turn their attention to subsidising
science education in preparatory schools, also in the private sector, once the
initial scheme was completed.[46]

Having established that the scheme would be directed exclusively to independent and direct grant schools, its planners restricted its scope still further
by giving priority to particular categories of schools within the independent
sector. Alan Wilson was not convinced that only the strongest schools should
be supported: 'If there was a good prospect of the number of pupils taking
advanced courses being increased if assistance were given to some of the
weaker schools, he would certainly be prepared to include them.'[47] Other
industrialists preferred to be more selective, even more so than Eric James'
advice had envisaged. They had little interest in supporting girls' schools,[48]
and it was also decided to consider fully independent schools first before
dealing with direct grant schools, on the basis that 'the Independent Schools
have the greater need'.[49] These priorities were stated explicitly in the terms of
the charitable trust that was set up to administer the fund.[50] Over the following
decade, the Industrial Fund invested over three million pounds for science
laboratories and equipment in these schools on behalf of industrial firms.

Far from helping to bring the state and private systems closer together,
then, the Industrial Fund reflected and maintained the divisions between them.
Both the Ministry and the industrialists involved in the project were acutely
aware of this, and were concerned to forestall political criticism. The introduction of the scheme was actually delayed until after the general election of
1955 in order to avoid it attracting debate during the election campaign.[51] The
nationalised industries decided against contributing to the Fund because it
would only benefit independent and direct grant schools.[52] As Ministry officials
observed, this was a political objection. Similarly, Labour party MPs such as
Austen Albu protested that taxpayers would in effect be providing a large part
of the money which was given to this privileged class of schools.[53]

Such criticisms led to pressure on the Ministry to introduce a parallel scheme
designed for maintained schools. The Minister of Education, Sir David

Eccles, was determined as a matter of general policy to support the public schools, although he acknowledged privately that two separate systems were still in existence.[54] For this reason he was anxious about the likely effects of criticisms of the Industrial Fund, and noted that 'This is of real political importance to the public schools; a howl from left-wing sources that industry is helping only independent schools and we are doing nothing would be bad.' Therefore, Eccles was keen to show 'that our action in the maintained schools is at least in step'.[55] It is unlikely to have been a coincidence that in 1956 the Minister's only request to the Treasury for additional investment in maintained secondary schools was in relation to science buildings in grammar schools.[56] Nevertheless, the grammar schools added to pressure on the Ministry to develop a scheme comparable to that of the Industrial Fund. As F.L. Allan, the President of the IAHM (Incorporated Association of Head Masters), asked in a letter to *The Times*, in March 1957:

> Why does not the Ministry of Education itself move with the boldness displayed by the industrialists, requesting local authorities to conduct an immediate survey of their schools and submit building plans, with the assurance that approved schemes will rank for 100 per cent grant in aid?[57]

The initiators of the Industrial Fund themselves also became anxious about the Ministry's perceived lack of support for science accommodation in maintained schools. At a meeting with Eccles they reported a number of complaints received from the IAHM and from individual grammar school head teachers. In response, the Minister pointed out that the situation of schools in the maintained sector was not suited to a scheme such as the Industrial Fund because they required a much larger level of investment: 'The problem of the maintained system of education was not just that a few holes needed blocking up, as tended to be the case with the direct grant and independent system, but that most of the structure was inadequate.'[58] As Weaver also admitted, 'Most of the short-comings in science teaching, whether they arise from shortage of teachers, accommodation, equipment or laboratory assistants, are now to be found in the publicly maintained schools rather than in the independent schools.'[59] Ironically, therefore, the Industrial Fund served to widen the gulf that already existed between the private and state systems.

Eccles continued to press for expanded provision for science in the grammar schools, partly to promote a better balance in the curriculum between arts and science, and the Ministry encouraged the LEAs to put forward projects in their building programmes that were designed to improve science accommodation in secondary schools.[60] Ministry officials could claim in their own defence that they had provided support to science in the maintained grammar schools similar in scale to that provided for independent schools by the Industrial Fund. It was noted, for example, that one-third of all 17-year-olds who were still in school were in direct grant or independent schools, for which the Industrial Fund had invested three million pounds. At the same time, two million pounds had been included in the building programmes in the last two years to improve science facilities in maintained schools, 'as part of a sustained school building programme lasting over a much longer period and continuously improving science facilities as well as accommodation of all other kinds'. When all of this work was complete, it was calculated, about two-fifths of the grammar schools in the country would be housed in premises that had been built or substantially improved since the end of the Second World War.[61] This did little to appease the Ministry's critics, including Robert Birley, the Headmaster of Eton College and Chairman of the Headmasters' Conference, who pointed out what he called a 'fairly widespread feeling that the state had not kept its part of the bargain which Sir David Eccles had made with the Industrial Fund'.[62]

The Industrial Fund, therefore, further exposed the entrenched nature of the division between the state and private systems of education. Some of those involved were hoping to bring the two systems closer together, and there was a great deal of interaction between them in negotiating the initiative. In the end, though, the Industrial Fund catered only for the private sector, increasing the visible advantages enjoyed by the independent schools. The academically selective grammar schools, which represented less than 20 per cent of state-maintained secondary schools, struggled to compete with this increased provision, and the modern and technical schools fared even worse. *Faute de mieux*, they could still take part in curriculum initiatives such as those developed by the Nuffield Foundation in the 1960s.[63] They could also seek to imitate and adapt innovations developed by teachers and head teachers in independent schools.[64] Nevertheless, they remained unable to benefit from financial subsidies such as those offered by major industrial firms in the case of the Industrial Fund.

PRIVATISATION AND PARTNERSHIP

Since the 1980s, governments of both major parties have made determined attempts to find radical and novel ways of bringing the state and private systems closer together. For the Conservative governments from 1979 to 1997, the most useful way of achieving this was to expose the schools in the maintained sector to the rigours of the free market that had supposedly made the independent schools so successful. This approach, often described as 'privatisation', was at the heart of many of the Conservatives' educational reforms, including the Education Reform Act of 1988.[65] It was most unlike the ideals of incorporating the private schools into an expanding state system that had been current earlier in the century. In a sense, it was reminiscent of the ideas of those who had dreamed of incorporating the key qualities of the private schools into the maintained system, but the notion of what those qualities were had changed fundamentally. For Norwood and his kind, the 'English tradition' associated with the public schools was about service and citizenship. To the Conservatives of the 1980s, on the other hand, the most important values of the private sector were those of competitive individualism and entrepreneurship.

Labour governments from 1997 onwards also sought to find an accommodation between the state and private sectors, but in doing so preferred to talk in terms of 'partnership'. In November 1997, for example, the School Standards Minister, Stephen Byers, established an independent/state school partnerships initiative, with the aim of promoting collaborative working between the independent and state school sectors.[66] David Blunkett, as Secretary of State for Education and Employment, encouraged partnerships involving the government and voluntary, church and business sponsors, and this aim was pursued in a succession of policy reports.[67] Sympathisers such as Ron Aldridge, Executive Chairman of Capita Group plc, saw this as 'a way forward which will enable the public and private sectors to work together to sustain public service values, maximise investment in education, and provide a world-class system that the UK needs, and our children and teachers deserve'.[68] Critics of the policy regarded it as merely a different form of privatisation.[69] In a very limited sense, the Labour government's approach could perhaps be compared to the attempt of the Industrial Fund in the 1950s to forge an alliance between the state and private systems. Yet unlike the Ministry of Education in the 1950s, the initiatives of the 1990s showed no compunction in using private finance and resources to support the statutory duties of the state-maintained system.

In one respect, nevertheless, there was a marked resemblance between the schemes of the Conservative and Labour governments in the 1980s and 1990s, and those of their predecessors earlier in the century. This resemblance was in the limitations of their achievements in overcoming the division between the state and private systems. This can be shown, for example, in the difficult experiences of two key initiatives: the CTCs (city technology colleges) developed by the Conservative government in the 1980s, and the EAZs (education action zones) of the Labour government in the late 1990s. Both schemes were put forward with much optimism as major steps forward in this area, and both were highly disappointing in their effects.

The city technology colleges were introduced at the Conservative Party's annual conference in October 1986 by the Secretary of State for Education and Science, Kenneth Baker. Initially there were to be about 20 of these schools, set up in urban areas including the disadvantaged inner cities. They would be funded by the government but would be independent and not part of the LEA. They would be run by educational trusts, and private sector sponsors would make a substantial contribution towards their costs. This would create 'a new choice of schools', offering a broadly-based secondary education with a strong technological element.[70] However, the CTCs failed to have the impact that was envisaged. Potential sponsors were less willing to invest in them than had been hoped, and it proved to be difficult to establish even the 20 colleges that had been mooted. They also lacked in practice a clear role and identity, becoming fatally vague and diffuse in their purpose, and in 1994 they were quietly abandoned.[71]

For their part, the EAZs were introduced in 1998, hailed by David Blunkett as 'testbeds for the school system of the next century'. They would provide models for a 'Third Way' in education, departing from the traditional divisions of LEA-controlled and independent schools. According to Blunkett, 'This is the beginning of an entirely new way of delivering the education service. It is about partnership based on success rather than outdated dogma on either side.'[72] Extra funding would be provided for such zones, with opportunities to vary the school curriculum and the pay and conditions of teachers, in return for attracting business sponsorship. Like the CTCs, they were intended to be based in areas of social disadvantage. Again, however, they struggled to make a sustained impact, often failed to draw in sufficient private funds, and were widely criticised for their lack of innovation. Within three years these, too, were regarded largely as a failure.[73]

CONCLUSION

Overall, therefore, initiatives to bring together the separate systems of state and private education are far from new, but have been generally unsuccessful. In the earlier part of the twentieth century, hopes of incorporating the private schools into the expanding maintained system proved to be unfounded. Attempts to bring the systems together through scholarship schemes were only superficial in their effects. Plans to promote curriculum developments across the state and independent sectors were often ineffective and, in the case of the Industrial Fund of the 1950s, merely exposed the gulf that existed between them. The recent and contemporary initiatives developed by the Conservative and Labour governments of the past 20 years need to be understood in relation to this longer term historical context. Indeed, it is this history of public and private secondary education over the past century, from incorporation to privatisation, that surely provides the measure of the task to be achieved if these two separate systems are somehow to be united in the century ahead.

NOTES

I should like to thank the Leverhulme Trust for its support for the research project, 'The life and educational career of Sir Cyril Norwood (1875–1956)' (F118AB), on which part of the research for this paper is based.

1 See also, for example, C. Griggs, *Private Education in Britain* (London: Falmer, 1985); B. Salter and T. Tapper, *Power and Policy in Education: The Case of Independent Schooling* (London: Falmer, 1985); D. Johnson, *Private Schools and State Schools: Two Systems or One?* (Buckingham: Open University Press, 1987); T. Tapper, *Fee-Paying Schools and Educational Change in Britain: Between the State and the Marketplace* (London: Woburn, 1997).

2 Board of Education, *The Public Schools and the General Educational System* [Fleming Report] (London: HMSO, 1944), p. 2.

3 The Public Schools Commission, *First Report*, vol. 1: Report (London: HMSO, 1968).

4 For further details see, for example, R. Lowe, 'New Perspectives on the Evolution of Secondary School Education in the UK', in B. Moon, S. Brown and M. Ben-Peretz (eds), *Routledge International Companion to Education* (London: Routledge, 2000), pp. 642–52; and G. McCulloch, 'Secondary Education', in R. Aldrich (ed.), *A Century Of Education* (London: RoutledgeFalmer, 2002), pp. 31–53.

5 R.H. Tawney, 'The Problem of the Public Schools', *Political Quarterly*, 14, 2 (1943), p. 132.

6 'Tory MP sees private sector as the obstacle', *Times Educational Supplement*, 20 September 1996; see also G. Walden, *We Should Know Better: Solving the Education Crisis* (London: Fourth Estate, 1996), and D. Macintyre, 'Time to end classroom "apartheid"', *Independent*, 10 September 1996.

7 A. Adonis and S. Pollard, *A Class Act: The Myth of Britain's Classless Society* (London: Penguin, 1998), p. 37.

8 Tawney, 'The Problem of the Public Schools', p. 32. See also G. Savage, 'Social Class and Social Policy: The Civil Service and Secondary Education in England during the Interwar Period', *Journal of Contemporary History*, 18 (1983), pp. 261–80.

9 Andrew Marr, 'Lessons for Blair from the war of Little Joe', *Independent*, 25 January 1996.

10 B. Hugill, 'Left to rot in schools free-for-all', *Observer*, 4 December 1994; 'Blairs faced with classic dilemma over schools', *Independent*, 2 December 1994; 'Blair relives school dilemma', *Guardian*, 20 January 1999.

11 Peter Wilby, 'My proposal to end classroom strife', *Observer*, 7 July 2002.

12 'Comprehensive education failed my sons, says Bernie Grant', *Independent*, 25 January 1996.

13 T.C. Worsley, *Barbarians and Philistines: Democracy and the Public Schools* (London: Robert Hale Ltd, 1940), and T.C. Worsley, *The End of the 'Old School Tie'* (London: Secker and Warburg, 1941).

14 F. Clarke, *Education and Social Change: An English Interpretation* (London: Sheldon Press, 1940), p. 56.

15 R. Ollard, *An English Education: A Perspective of Eton* (London: Collins, 1982), p. 12.

16 R. Gurner, *I Chose Teaching* (London: J.M. Dent and sons, 1937), p. 58.

17 R. Gurner, *Day Schools of England* (London: J.M. Dent and sons, 1930), p. 15.
18 Ibid., pp. 16–17.
19 For further details on Norwood's educational career and ideology see G. McCulloch, *Philosophers and Kings: Education for Leadership in Modern England* (Cambridge: Cambridge University Press, 1991), especially chs 3–4.
20 Cyril Norwood and Arthur H. Hope, *The Higher Education of Boys in England* (London: John Murray, 1909), pp. 558–9.
21 Ibid., p. 561.
22 Cyril Norwood, *The English Tradition of Education* (London: John Murray, 1929), p. 244. For further details on the idea of the 'English tradition', see G. McCulloch and C. McCaig, 'Reinventing the Past: The Case of the English Tradition of Education', *British Journal of Educational Studies*, 50, 2 (2002), pp. 238–53.
23 Cyril Norwood to G.G. Williams, 3 December 1939, Board of Education papers, PRO (Public Record Office, Kew), ED12/518.
24 Cyril Norwood, 'The crisis in education – I', *Spectator*, 9 February 1940, pp. 175–6.
25 Lord Hugh Cecil to Lord de la Warr, 21 March 1940, Board of Education papers, PRO, ED12/518.
26 'Public schools', leading article in the *Times Educational Supplement*, 9 March 1940.
27 'Public and other schools', leading article in the *Times Educational Supplement*, 10 May 1941.
28 R.A. Butler, interview note, 12 May 1942, Board of Education papers, PRO, ED136/599.
29 Board of Education, *Public Schools and the General Educational System*, p. 4.
30 Ibid., p. 63.
31 R.A. Butler to G.D.H. Cole, 25 June 1942; Butler to Cole, 18 May 1943, Cole papers, Nuffield College, Oxford, B.3/4/C.
32 G.D.H. Cole, draft for BBC broadcast on the Fleming Report, 22 August 1944, Cole papers, B.3/4/C.
33 R.A. Butler, *The Art of the Possible* (London: Penguin, 1973), p. 121.
34 Public Schools Commission, *First Report*, p. vii.
35 See also e.g. T. Edwards, J. Fitz and G. Whitty, *The State and Private Education: An Evaluation of the Assisted Places Scheme* (London: Falmer, 1989).
36 See, for example, G. McCulloch, 'The Politics of the Secret Garden: Teachers and the School Curriculum in England and Wales', in C. Day, A. Fernandez, T. Hauge and J. Moller (eds), *The Life and Work of Teachers: International Perspectives in Changing Times* (London: Falmer, 2000), pp. 26–37, and G. McCulloch, G. Helsby and P. Knight, *The Politics of Professionalism: Teachers and the Curriculum* (London: Continuum, 2000).
37 A.A. Part to R.A.R. Tricker, 22 July 1954, Ministry of Education papers, PRO, ED147/211.
38 A.A. Part, note of interview with A.H. Wilson, 30 July 1954, Ministry of Education papers, PRO, ED147/211.
39 A.A. Part to R.A.R. Tricker, 22 July 1954, Ministry of Education papers, PRO, ED147/211.
40 R.A.R. Tricker to A.A. Part, 9 August 1954, Ministry of Education papers, PRO, ED147/211.
41 E. James, *Education and Leadership* (London: Harrap, 1951). See also McCulloch, *Philosophers and Kings*, ch. 5.
42 Eric James to A.A. Part, 6 December 1954, Ministry of Education papers, PRO, ED147/211.
43 A.A. Part to Eric James, 8 December 1954, Ministry of Education papers, PRO, ED147/211.

44 A.A. Part and J.F. Embling, note of interview with A.H. Wilson, 13 January 1955, Ministry of Education papers, PRO, ED147/211.
45 Toby Weaver, note to R.N. Heaton, 19 November 1957, Ministry of Education papers, PRO, ED147/794.
46 R.A.R. Tricker to Sir David Eccles (Minister of Education), 21 May 1956, Ministry of Education papers, PRO, ED147/654.
47 A.A. Part and J.F. Embling, note of interview with A.H. Wilson, 13 January 1955, Ministry of Education papers, PRO, ED147/211.
48 A.A. Part, note of interview with A.H. Wilson, 8 February 1955; A.A. Part, note, 22 July 1955, Ministry of Education papers, PRO, ED147/211.
49 A.H. Wilson to A.A. Part, 28 September 1955, Ministry of Education papers, PRO, ED147/211.
50 Report of a meeting on the Industrial Scheme for the Encouragement of Science Teaching in Schools, 27 September 1955, Ministry of Education papers, PRO, ED147/211.
51 A.A. Part to A. Wilson, 20 June 1958, Ministry of Education papers, PRO, ED147/211.
52 Sir Miles Thomas (Chairman, BOAC) to Minister of Education, 8 December 1956, Ministry of Education papers, PRO, ED147/654.
53 J.F. Embling, note, 15 December 1956, Ministry of Education papers, PRO, ED147/654.
54 Sir David Eccles, memorandum, 'Secondary education', 18 September 1956, Ministry of Education papers, PRO, ED147/636.
55 Sir David Eccles, note, 7 October 1955, Ministry of Education papers, PRO, ED147/211.
56 Sir David Eccles, 'Secondary education', 18 September 1956, Ministry of Education papers, PRO, ED147/636.
57 F.L. Allen, letter to *The Times*, 7 March 1957.
58 Notes on a meeting between the Minister of Education and Lord Weekes, Sir Graham Savage, and Peter Ashton of the Industrial Fund, Ministry of Education papers, PRO, ED147/654.
59 T.R. Weaver, note to R.N. Heaton, 19 November 1957, Ministry of Education papers, PRO, ED147/794.
60 Ibid.
61 J.R. Jameson, note, 'Science accommodation in maintained grammar schools', 25 March 1959, Ministry of Education papers, PRO, ED147/654.
62 R.N. Heaton, note of meeting with Robert Birley, 1 December 1958, Ministry of Education papers, PRO, ED147/654.
63 See, for example, M. Waring, 'Background to Nuffield Science', *History of Education*, 8, 3 (1979), pp. 223–37.
64 See, for example, G.T. Page, *Engineering among the Schools* (London: Institute of Mechanical Engineers, 1965).
65 See, for example, G. Walford, *Privatisation and Privilege in Education* (London: Routledge, 1990).
66 Department for Education and Skills, 'Independent/state school partnerships' (DfES website, www.dfes.gov.uk/indstatepartner/summary.shtml).
67 See, for example, DfES, *Schools: Building on Success* (London: Stationery Office, 2001).
68 R. Aldridge, 'We all need to work together', *Times Educational Supplement*, 21 September 2001.
69 See, for example, 'Hackney tests school privatisation', *Guardian*, 20 March 1999; George Monbiot, 'Very British corruption', *Guardian*, 22 January 2002.

70   Department of Education and Science, *A New Choice of School: City Technology Colleges* (London: HMSO, 1986); 'Baker's course to put governors at the helm', *Times Educational Supplement*, 10 October 1986.
71   On the CTC initiative, see, for example, G. McCulloch, 'City Technology Colleges: An Old Choice of School?', *British Journal of Educational Studies*, 37, 1 (1989), pp. 30–43; G. McCulloch, *Technical Fix? City Technology Colleges* (Leeds: University of Leeds, 1994); G. Walford and H. Miller, *City Technology College* (Buckingham: Open University Press, 1991); G. Whitty, T. Edwards and S. Gewirtz, *Specialisation and Choice in Urban Education: The City Technology College Experiment* (London: Routledge, 1993).
72   'Schools to be given radical overhaul', *Guardian*, 24 June 1998.
73   See, for example, 'Cold water poured on hotbeds of innovation', *Times Educational Supplement*, 6 April 2001. B. Franklin and G. McCulloch, 'Partnerships in a Cold Climate: The Case of Britain', in M. Bloch, B. Franklin and T. Popkewitz (eds), *Educational Partnerships: Democracy, Citizenship and Salvation in a Globalised World* (London: Palgrave Macmillan, 2003 in press) provide further detail and discussion on the experience of the CTCs and EAZs.

PART 2

4

ROUND AND ROUND THE MULBERRY BUSH: THE BALANCE OF PUBLIC AND PRIVATE IN EARLY EDUCATION AND CHILDCARE IN THE TWENTIETH CENTURY

Helen Penn

INTRODUCTION

In the UK private fee-paying schools (including those commonly designated as public) have long been regarded by the elite as repositories of knowledge, offering a superior education. For children under 7 there has been less consensus, either about knowledge or about education. At the beginning of the twentieth century Froebel and Montessori schools (whose adherents mainly ignored one another) were grouped on the radical end of the private sector, and featured prominently in the radical education journals of the time such as the *New Era* and its supplement, *Home and School*.[1] But their education methods were highly specialised, and either largely disregarded, in the case of Froebel, or privately franchised in the case of Montessori.[2]

At the end of the nineteenth century, more than half of all 3- and 4-year-olds were in state primary schools, and the outcry about the unsuitability of such schools for young children led to demands for separate nursery or nursery/infant schools. These demands centred on concerns for children's health and welfare. State nursery education began in the 1920s and 1930s. State nursery schools (as opposed to nursery classes) only ever reached a tiny minority of children. They did not, for the most part, draw on the Froebelian and Montessori traditions, but they were always well regarded by public and professionals alike, because their standards for staffing, space and equipment were so high, and their handling of educational discourse was sophisticated. For 40 years, from the 1920s to the 1960s, the standard model of nursery education was the nursery school. Nursery schools were typically located in spacious premises, and offered full-time education, with an emphasis on regular habits and good health – exercise in the fresh air, nutritious food, and rests in the afternoon. Nursery education appealed as much to the middle class as to the working class.[3]

But the state was reluctant to fund nursery education directly. It was left to local authorities to decide whether to provide it. A few northern authorities like Bradford and Burnley proudly introduced nursery schools, but not even the welfare conscious London County Council showed much enthusiasm.

The rapid development of nursery education and childcare provision that occurred during the Second World War was not sustained in peacetime. After the 1960s, the model of nursery education changed and, where available, was mostly provided part-time in nursery classes attached to primary schools, without specific healthcare. Only at the end of the twentieth century did central government acknowledge that 4-year-olds were entitled to nursery education but, as at the end of the nineteenth century, most of those children were simply admitted early to primary schools.

As a result of the dearth of state provision, early education and childcare in the UK has always been characterised by a large voluntary and private sector. Day nurseries, playgroups and other forms of voluntary provision could not match the educational rhetoric – and resourcing – of nursery schooling and instead developed their own rhetoric. Nursery nurses working in day nurseries claimed that they were specially trained to work with babies and very young children and offered a more caring environment than could nursery teachers; or, as with playgroups, there were vigorous claims that volunteerism uniquely involved mothers in their young children's development.

The trade unions, often a powerful force for change, and arguably, in one country at least, instrumental in redefining early years education and care,[4] play only a very small part in this history. The NUT (National Union of Teachers) supported nursery teachers,[5] but it could not accommodate the army of non-teachers pressing for recognition. Conversely, other unions representing nursery nurses talked up their contribution, but could not reconcile the status (or the salary) of nursery nurses – or other childcare workers – with those of teachers.[6]

This history of early education and care has also been shaped by, and has to be set against, broader debates and disputes in education and in society more generally. A key question, asked over and over again in the course of the century, concerned the values and function of education. Should the education system focus on delivering and regulating the transmission of the three Rs to the poor; or should it be more ambitious, a universal service for all children based on concepts of self-development and mutual citizenship? In an editorial in 1926 the *Times Educational Supplement* remarked presciently that 'the national love of individual liberty responds to the appeal that children be allowed freedom for development, yet ingrained prudence prompts the demand that proof shall be forthcoming of money spent'.[7]

Another constantly recurring theme was the family, and crucially, the role of women in the family. In 1926 *Nursery World* introduced a Sunday page for the use of parents and nurses and those involved 'in teaching and training young children'. It aimed to provide 'graphic adventures from the Bible, romantic stories of great heroes, tender tales of noble women and little children'.[8] The emancipation and economic independence of women, and the gradual dismantling of gender stereotypes is one of the greatest changes of the last century. The perception of women, their inclinations and capacities – their noble, but submissive character – as mothers, childcarers and teachers, shaped the availability and scope of provision for young children, and continues to do so.

A third theme, especially in the first half of the century, was the 'greatness of our empire'.[9] Maintaining the glory of the empire and servicing its extremities shaped ideas about learning. 'Character-building', learning not to whine in the face of hardship, was a fundamental tenet for those in boys' public schools,[10] but the philosophy of self-control in all circumstances filtered through to, and influenced, childcare policy.[11] The preoccupation with empire was also played out in innumerable discussions about race and eugenics. In a series of reports Sir George Newman, Chief Medical Officer to the Board of Education, argued that 'healthy motherhood, healthy infancy, and systematic medical supervision at school' were essential for the betterment of the nation.[12] Campaigns for improved early education were closely tied to campaigns for medical inspections and school meals. Young children were too unhealthy to learn and the population was not fit enough or upstanding enough to serve the needs of the empire or the armed forces.

There was also concern that the poor might be a degenerate strain of the population whose rights needed curtailing (a eugenic argument that took a different, and terrifying, turn in Germany). In 1938 the National Council for Mental Hygiene organised a conference at Central Hall, Westminster, on the topic, 'Is our National Intelligence declining?' Its liberal organisers concluded that it was, since the more intelligent had fewer children, and the poor bred uncontrollably. They argued (against some prevailing eugenic opinions) that sterilisation was not the only option; improving the environment, they concluded, would make a more significant difference.[13] The empire has vanished but the echoes of this nature–nurture debate, and the problematic unfitness of the poor linger on;[14] so, too, does the racist legacy of the empire builders.

Psychological understandings of childhood, forged in the child-study movement at the end of the nineteenth and beginning of the twentieth centuries, have infused the debate about education, knowledge and epistemology. Many claimed that the child shaped the man, but what sort of child and what sort of man? A.S. Neill and Bertrand Russell, writing about nursery education in the 1920s and 1930s, scandalised their contemporaries with their Rousseau-like notions of freedom and psychoanalytic explanations about the dangers of repressing children's basic instincts. Outraged critics protested. 'If the old fashioned virtue of obedience is to be ruled out of a child's life ... the children of the future will be exterminated by the process of eating what they like, going to bed when they like, playing with fire when they like.'[15] The pendulum has swung, sometimes violently, between behaviouristic, psychoanalytic and Piagetian interpretations of children's psyches, before the contemporary emphasis on cognitive skills and school-based curricula. Nursery education has always claimed to be well informed and led by current thinking in child development; but the voluntary and private sector have been more pragmatic about their sources.

To a lesser extent, the history of nursery education and childcare is also about charismatic or influential individuals, whose rhetoric seized the public imagination. Margaret McMillan was one such platform star, whose showpiece nursery in Deptford was rooted in early socialism, and attracted the attention of government ministers.[16] Donald Winnicott, Susan Isaacs and John Bowlby were influential psychoanalysts, dedicated to extending and popularising the ideas of the British psychoanalyst Melanie Klein. Bryan Jackson made childminders respectable;[17] Bridget Plowden, after first supporting nursery education, then became a powerful advocate for playgroups. Simon Yudkin and Jack Tizard provided a sceptical academic commentary on changing political agendas. The writings and speeches of such protagonists encapsulated and crystallised the knowledge and understanding of their particular decade or decades.

For the most part, such charismatic individuals played out their roles in various voluntary organisations, including the Nursery Schools Association, the National Society of Children's Nurseries and the Pre-School Playgroups Association, the National Childcare Campaign and the National Childminding Association. The smaller voluntary organisations argued amongst themselves, cross-fertilised, and regrouped continuously, although the bigger ones with wider child welfare agendas, such as Barnardo's or Save the Children, continued under their own banners. These organisations lobbied and gave evidence to various parliamentary bodies. They produced their own newsletters, magazines, journals and pamphlets. There were also various independent publications designed to stimulate the growing market of early years practitioners: the Frobelian *Child Life* from 1891 to 1939; and for most of the century, *Nursery World*. These independent magazines also offered a voice to the distinguished activists.[18]

The child-study movement, aimed at parents and professionals, gave way after the 1920s to the more formal study of psychology and child development. Certain academic institutions, such as the Tavistock Institute and the Institute of Education in London were key intellectual bases for the construction and dissemination of knowledge about young children. Training colleges for nursery teachers and nursery workers were set up to incorporate the new knowledge, and tentative hypotheses re-emerged as dogmatic facts further down the knowledge chain. The National Nursery Examination Board, founded in 1945 and based on the efforts of the National Society of Children's Nurseries a generation earlier, was instrumental in systematising and vocationalising this knowledge, turning it into prescriptive practices.[19]

This history was punctuated by Royal Commissions and national and international reports. Since the Second World War, organisations such as UNESCO (United Nations Educational, Scientific and Cultural Organisation), WHO (World Health Organisation), OECD (Organisation for Economic Co-operation and Development), and latterly the European Union, all provided overviews that enabled practitioners and policymakers to locate their knowledge in a wider understanding of theory and practice. The conclusions, recommendations and uptake of such weighty reports could not but reflect their times, and in the UK were as often glossed over as enacted.

This chapter attempts to trace ideas in early education and childcare, and the actions that followed from them. It has been a highly contested history.

NURSERY EDUCATION FOR THE MIDDLE CLASSES

In December 1919, Dr Maria Montessori was invited to take tea with the Lord Mayor of London. She also visited 10 Downing Street, was widely fêted, and invited to lecture to learned societies. Her writings were published in translation and analysed in journals, and her short courses greatly oversubscribed. She was the educational guru of her time.[20] As a doctor, Montessori was originally concerned with the education of 'subnormal' children, and she devised methods and equipment that 'scientifically' supported learning, enabling children to pass through one clearly defined stage to another. Success led her to apply these methods more widely, to all young children. Montessori's methods, however, had to be carefully followed, using her exact formulae, and could not therefore be absorbed into the mainstream, nor easily updated. Montessori schools, as a movement, still exist in the private sector. But the earlier, scientific, reputation of Montessori has faded, an anachronism in contemporary discussions of child development.[21]

Froebel was an earlier cult figure, although he never gained the social and intellectual acceptance accorded to Maria Montessori. His ideas were initially kept alive in the UK by a band of dedicated ladies who, in 1874, formed the Froebel Society. They were inspired by his ideas of 'mother made conscious', a style of teaching which drew on a sentimentalised view of motherhood, but nevertheless offered women new career opportunities. Froebel believed that children should have great freedom to play and to develop their innate spiritual responsiveness to nature, unobtrusively guided by a dedicated woman kindergarten teacher:

> She is in duty bound not only to watch the unfolding of the powers and capabilities of her pupils but also to teach them to love the good and hate the bad, to awaken in them new desires, to develop new interests, to arouse their higher instincts, and then to satisfy these cravings after higher ideals by opening up to them the wonderful world of nature, of art, of literature, and so give them a glimpse of the joys that await them and the rich heritage that may be theirs for the asking. [22]

Froebel devised 'gifts', a set of materials aimed to inspire and awaken higher ideals. These 'gifts' should be carefully used in 'airy bright school rooms'; space and light were necessary conditions for learning.

The Girls' Public Day School Company, established in 1872, whose aim was to 'promote the establishment of good, cheap day schools for all classes', realised the potential career opening for women as kindergarten teachers. By 1878 all of its 17 schools had kindergarten and infant classes based on Froebelian ideas.[23] Froebel had landed on the middle-class map. In 1890, the London School Board even ordered a supply of Froebelian 'gifts' to distribute to children in their infant schools. This was a travesty of Froebelian ideas, since the children were forced to sit in tiered rows in cavernous schoolrooms all day, and anything less free was hard to imagine. By 1902, the Froebel Society offered a Froebel elementary certificate, and directly supported five kindergartens, and subsequently, a network of training colleges.

Although the Froebel Society suffered splits and regroupings, it was generously financially supported, at least until the 1930s, by Claude Montefiore, the well-known philanthropist. The aims of the Society broadened from the provision of Froebel kindergartens and training to endeavouring to 'educate the public on all matters concerning young children' and to 'bring together and promote better understanding between teachers (of all grades), parents, doctors, officials and all others interested in education'.[24] Unlike Montessori, Froebelian ideas were diluted, and reduced to a general prescription about free play – the belief that intellectual, physical and especially spiritual development came about through the child's own actions. Froebelians argue that although Froebel's methods (and his emphasis on children's innate spirituality) have largely disappeared from view, his ideas about childhood play have become widely accepted and incorporated into the mainstream.

In the 1920s and 1930s there were other radical experiments with nursery education in the private sector. Bertrand Russell and his wife Dora set up an experimental school, Beacon Hill, inspired by the new 'science' of psycho-analysis, somewhat contradictorily mixed with behaviouristic ideas about regular training to inculcate good moral habits. But the over-riding idea was that repressing emotions and feelings in children would prove destructive in later life. Sexual repression was particularly deplored: 'education consists in the cultivation of the instincts, not in their suppression'. Russell spelt out his ideas in a book entitled *On Education – Especially in Early Childhood*, first published in 1926 and frequently reprinted over the next 30 years. He argued that the rich were at liberty – in fact had a duty – to pave the way for others in their experiments. He acknowledged his debt to Maria Montessori but argued that Montessori was too strict in forbidding children imaginative play and games. In this very discursive book, he argued the importance of begin-ning with values – the attributes that, as civilised people, we consider should be encouraged and fostered. His values included vitality, courage, sensitivity and intelligence.[25]

Bertrand Russell was part of a wider group of similar radicals, many of whose experimental schools and teaching methods were chronicled in the journal, the *New Era*, co-edited by the arch-radical, A.S. Neill of Summerhill. Beatrix Tudor-Hart, who had trained in Vienna and been on the staff of Beacon Hill, opened her co-operative nursery school at Fortis Green in the 1930s (after an eviction from her first premises, prompted by her irate neigh-bours in Hampstead complaining about the noise). Fortis Green was 'the first school in the country owned and controlled jointly by parents and teachers'. Beatrix Tudor-Hart wrote a delightful book of practical advice for parents and nursery staff which was favourably reviewed in the *Times Educational Supplement*.[26]

Perhaps the most famous of the radical nursery experiments was Malting House School, run by Susan Isaacs. This was also a school for the young children of professionals – mainly academics. One-third of the children were residential. The regime was inspired by the theories of the psychoanalyst, Melanie Klein, about childhood aggression and repression, and the need fully to express emotion. The job of the wise adult was to chronicle every nuanced step each child took on his or her emotional and intellectual journey. The school became legendary for the freedom it allowed to children, and reporters clustered on the doorstep for salacious copy. Susan Isaacs' own tone was more sober. She scrupulously observed the young children under her care, and subsequently wrote two highly regarded books about this experience.[27] She became a columnist for *Nursery World,* and gave authoritative and dignified advice on child-rearing to a generation of its readers, before finally, becoming a Kleinian analyst.

There was also a long established tradition, in the upper and middle classes, of employing nannies for young children. These nannies were mainly working-class girls, for whom looking after children was a form of domestic service, although as Gathorne-Hardy points out, nannies were entrusted with the upbringing and education of the young children in their care.[28] In the 1920s and 1930s the magazine *Nursery World* was mainly directed at nannies and the mothers who employed them. *Nursery World* ran a friendship club, so that nannies working in the same districts could correspond with and visit each other. It carried adverts for 'Babies' Hotels', highly respected and respectable private children's homes that took children from babyhood to school age on a residential basis. They were used mainly by colonial and armed forces families, before children were sent on to preparatory and boarding schools. They also doubled up as training institutions for nannies. Miss Ethel Moon, the matron of a well-known Babies' Hotel, ran an advice column for several years in *Nursery World.*[29] She dispensed advice on looking after young children, and on the proper training of nannies.

NURSERY EDUCATION FOR THE POOR

Whilst Froebelian and Montessori-style kindergartens were becoming established for the middle classes, and the upper classes relied on nannies, the poor were crammed into elementary schools. Three- and 4-year-olds sat alongside their elder brothers and sisters, subject to the same rigid, didactic teaching. Katharine Bathurst, an Inspector for the Board of Education, in a famous report, first published in 1905, castigated this system:

> Let us now follow the baby of three years through part of one day of school life. He is placed on a hard wooden seat with a desk in front of him ... he is told to fold his arms and keep quiet. ... He is surrounded by a large number of babies all under similar alarming and incomprehensible conditions. ... A certified teacher has 60 babies to instruct, many of whom are hungry, cold and dirty ... they are heavy eyed with unslept sleep ... what possible good is there in forcing a little child to master the names of letters and numbers at this age? The strain on teachers is terrific. [30]

The result of this campaigning was at first simply to exclude young children from school. In 1907 funding was withdrawn for children under 5 in infant schools. The ineffectiveness of providing bulk education, without any attention to the physical conditions and social circumstances of the pupils, was raised by many social campaigners, including members of the Independent Labour Party, most notably Margaret McMillan, who argued forcefully for separate nursery schools.[31] In 1918, the Education Act enabled LEAs to provide 'practical instruction suitable to the ages, capacities and circumstances of the children'. Section 19 of the Act gave LEAs:

> the power to make arrangements as may be approved by the Board of Education for a) supplying or aiding the supply of nursery schools for children over two and under five years of age, whose home conditions are such that attendance at such a school is necessary or desirable for their healthy physical and mental development and b) attending to the health, nourishment and physical welfare of children attending nursery schools.[32]

Activists like Margaret McMillan did their best to interpret the Act as a go-ahead for nursery education. But the wording of the Act did not voice the curricular concerns of the Froebel Society or other radicals; rather it reflected the decision, in 1907, to introduce systematic medical inspection in schools. For 27 years the first Chief Medical Officer, Sir George Newman, expressed his robust views in a series of annual reports to the Board of Education. Schools, especially those for young children, should promote good health. Margaret McMillan helped draft the Labour Party response to the 1918 Act, echoing Newman's concerns. 'What young children require is fresh air, play and rest, and this is what the nursery school offers them. The development of nursery schools would tend greatly to raise the standard of physical health among the children.'[33]

Provision, however, was sparse and by 1939 even the London County Council had provided only five nursery schools and given financial assistance to 18 others maintained by voluntary organisations.[34] A few northern authorities made a splash. In February 1932, Accrington Road Nursery in Burnley was opened by George Newman himself. The building (which is still in use) was beautifully designed with spacious classrooms, large windows leading onto verandas where children could rest, a large walled garden and a smart kitchen.[35]

In 1923 the NSA (Nursery Schools Association) was formed to campaign for more nursery schools. It produced a series of pamphlets on nursery education, some of which sold more than 200,000 copies, such was the popular demand. In an authoritative policy statement of 1927 the NSA argued that children of nursery school age (2–7) 'should be put into the immediate care of fully qualified teachers specially trained for their work'. The essential of the curriculum was free activity:

> Underlying all mental and bodily development lies the need for free activity. Without it neither healthy growth of body and spirit, nor training in self-control is possible. ... Free activity involves the provision of spontaneous and purposeful activity in spacious open-air conditions ... as well as an atmosphere of love, joy and freedom ... the daily routine must provide for the right alternation of rest and activity through the day ... it is undesirable to accept the hours of the ordinary school day as the limit for Nursery school.[36]

The NSA also famously commissioned the *avant-garde* architect, Erno Goldfinger, to design a model nursery school as a prototype; his modernist building design is still referred to in architectural circles.[37]

Despite this vigorous campaigning, by 1933 there were still only 55 nursery schools, catering for some 4,500 children. Thirty of these were provided directly by LEAs, and 25 by voluntary organisations which received some public financial support. The Hadow Committee on Infant and Nursery Schools which reported to the Board of Education in 1933 also emphasised the importance of growth, nutrition, a proper balance of exercise and rest, and open air play. It concluded that: 'it seems highly desirable that (nursery education) should be developed separately (from school) and be left free to perfect its methods and to fulfil its special purpose'. However, times were hard, and nursery schools were expensive, so the Committee cautiously recommended expansion only for poor urban areas.[38] This provoked an outcry from the NSA. Its members had long argued that nursery education should be for 'every child'; it should not be seen as a special remedial service for the poor.[39] The numbers of nursery schools crept up. By 1939 there were 118 nursery schools; together with under-5s in infant schools they catered for 180,000 children.

WORKING MOTHERS AND WARTIME

The NSA campaigned vigorously for state nursery schools but there was an older, rival organisation, with a different campaigning focus. The NSDN (National Society of Day Nurseries) had been founded in 1906 to set standards and register day nurseries and crèches. It described itself as 'the only voluntary body specifically devoted to the problem of the care of young children whose mothers go out to work'.[40] By 1914, 80 day nurseries were recognised, many of them mill nurseries. The Board of Education gave grants of 4 pence per child per week, but in 1919 the Ministry of Health assumed responsibility and gave 50 per cent block grants. The officers of the Society met in the drawing rooms of Piccadilly, and held fund-raising balls at the Carlton Club, the bastion of the Establishment. Despite their fashionable charitable image, members of the NSDN made serious efforts to support the training of girls for nursery work, and to raise standards of private day nurseries and crèches. They were seriously threatened by the NSA. In 1932 the Society realised that 'it was losing ground to the Nursery Schools Association ... it was felt that the Ladies on the Committee, although deeply interested in Child Welfare work, could not be considered as expert authorities'.[41]

By 1932 the NSA, the Froebel Society, the Home and School Council, and the *New Era* magazine all shared premises at 29 Tavistock Square in London. The NSDN lodged around the corner in Russell Square. Despite their differences there was considerable coming and going; their members attended the same conferences, and lobbied the same MPs. At a big conference in London's County Hall in 1936, Lilian de Lissa, Chairman of the NSA, argued (as many have done since) that:

> Clearly the time has come for the creation of a new Ministry. We need a Ministry for Childhood. We have a Ministry of Education, a Ministry of Health, a Ministry of Labour (Employment) and a Home Office. All these are concerned in one way or another with the Welfare of Children. ... But the child is one. Is it possible, by means of uncoordinated separate agencies to develop a far seeing policy for the welfare of the children of the nation as a whole?[42]

The war brought these organisations closer together, but also exacerbated their differences. At the beginning of the war, a joint statement by the Ministry of Health and the Board of Education urged the provision of nursery centres for billeted mothers and evacuee children – to be staffed if possible by voluntary workers. The Treasury, fearing demands for a massive expansion of nursery education, withheld funding. By 1941 it was obvious that more needed to be done to encourage women workers in industry. There was (familiar) confusion between the various ministries as to who should fund and supervise the expansion of provision. It was finally agreed that local authorities should make provision, while the Ministry of Health would fund and regulate the expansion. Once funds were agreed by the end of 1941, 194 nurseries were set up, and another 284 were in the pipeline. By the end of the war there were 1,450 wartime nurseries, each open for children from birth to 5, from 7 am to 7 pm. Their cost was estimated at £10 million over the course of the war.[43]

What should these nurseries be doing with children? 'Strong and divergent views were held on the scope of a nursery's work, its aims and its methods,

and on the complementary question of how a nursery should be staffed.'[44]
Both the NSA and the NSDN, which changed its name to NSCN (National
Society of Children's Nurseries) to cover wartime residential nurseries, were
asked to prepare expansion plans, and make suggestions about staffing and
curriculum. The work of the NSCN in training nannies and nursery workers
led to the establishment in 1945 of the NNEB (Nursery Nurse Examination
Board). The NSA, supported by the NUT, resolutely demanded that trained
teachers should be in charge of any nursery. During the war the chairman of
NSCN agreed to work with NSA providing they signed a joint memorandum
of co-operation: 'Neither NSA nor NSCN will in public or in private attack
the policy of the other.'[45] The respective chairmen signed the memorandum
but the quarrels continued. The division between nursery nurses and nursery
teachers, and their respective remits and remuneration, has never really been
resolved.

RETURNING TO NORMAL: PUTTING WOMEN BACK IN THE HOME

Wartime disputes about nurseries had been as much about mothering as about
children. 'Although the war saw acceptance of the day nursery system in public
provision for the under fives, the nursery school became the basis of post-war
construction.'[46] The priority for social policy after the war was to re-establish
and support family life. As Denise Riley pointed out, this meant taking a con-
ventional view of women's role.[47] A plethora of organisations, the National
Council of Maternity and Child Welfare, the Socialist Medical Association,
the NUT, the Fabians, as well as the NSA, argued that nursery schools would
make a positive contribution to family life. They could provide mothers with
the break they needed from full-time housework, and offer young children an
opportunity to work off their aggressive instincts. The *British Medical Journal*
declared in an editorial in 1944 that 'Destructive impulses let loose in war
may serve to fan the flame of aggression natural to the nursery age.'[48] The
psychoanalyst Melanie Klein, her disciple Susan Isaacs, and psychiatrists at
the Tavistock Clinic, Donald Winnicott and John Bowlby, popularised the
idea that children's aggressive instincts needed expression. Skilled teachers
working with knowledgeable mothers could help redirect these dangerous
instincts into safer channels.[49] Bowlby also put forward his theory of attachment
– that children needed a warm continuous relationship with a mother-figure
and without it they would be emotionally damaged. This was widely
(mis)interpreted to mean that it was wrong for mothers to work.

At the end of the war, the Ministry of Education agreed that it would take
responsibility for administering nurseries, although the Ministry of Health
stipulated that some nurseries, at least, should be kept open for working

mothers. Local authorities received some grant aid, but became directly responsible for their upkeep. By 1947, predictably, 700 nurseries had closed. Some of the remainder became nursery schools; others continued as social services day nurseries. Authorities like Hertfordshire and Lancashire, which had heavy munitions industries, and had therefore provided many day nurseries, kept them as nursery schools; other local authorities without a critical mass, simply closed them.

Lilian de Lissa, still at the helm of the NSA, argued in a pamphlet that nursery schools exactly fulfilled the social reconstruction agenda: 'the way of life organised for the children is simple and childlike and is planned in relation to the physical and psychological needs of children. ... Aggressive dominating "toughs" discover the happiness that comes from friendly co-operation with others.' [50] An article in the *New Era* by Frank Bodman, writing from the Bristol Child Guidance Clinic, put it more romantically:

> We must remember that the child's inner world is a romantic one, peopled like a Breughel Canvas with a crowded population of shining angels in armour wielding swords of justice on a host of goblins, dragons and bat-like figures with yawning mouths and scaly tails.[51]

Nursery education increasingly concerned itself with providing outlets for emotion and instinctual expression in young children. Percy Nunn, a member of the Hadow Committee, and Director of the University of London Institute of Education, had appointed Susan Isaacs in 1934 to run the Institute's Department of Child Development. Her successor, Dorothy Gardner, argued in 1956 that:

> we cannot educate a very unhappy child, or one who is even temporarily in the throes of jealousy, anger or mourning. We are also coming to realise that emotional satisfactions lie at the root of all intellectual inter- ests and that feelings are the driving force between all intellectual effort.[52]

Winnicott tried to distinguish between the functions of day nurseries, which he saw as an aid to paediatric care, and the nursery school, whose function was to wean the child socially, and introduce him or her to company after the fundamental but claustrophobic relationship with the mother had been estab- lished. In 1951 he joined in avuncularly to a flurry of letters about nursery education in *The Times*, arguing that:

> Behind the day nursery is urgent need, so that the question of quality is secondary. Behind the nursery school on the other hand, is not so much need as value. Here the idea is to enrich the lives of children who have

good homes of their own. The mothers have made a good start and they begin to make use of help … the nursery school justifies its existence only by being well-equipped and by having an enlightened staff trained to meet the individual needs, physical, emotional and educational, of growing small children.[53]

Winnicott also served on a UNESCO committee, which in 1951 published a report entitled *Mental Hygiene in the Nursery School.* This international committee of experts concluded that 'it is to such schools that we must look in future for the majority of theoretical and practical advances in nursery education as a whole'.[54] The UNESCO report was taken seriously by some of the contributing experts – from Denmark, France, Sweden and Switzerland – and there was a sustained effort to develop free-standing nursery schooling in those countries. The UK was more reluctant. But by now there was a new theoretical giant on the scene – Jean Piaget. At the 1960 NSA conference, W.D. Wall (previously working for UNESCO, then, successively Director of the National Foundation for Educational Research, and Dean of the University of London Institute of Education) gave a speech entitled 'The Enrichment of Childhood'. He argued that intellectual stimulation of young children was the proper role of nursery education: 'if we could raise by as little as five per cent the average operational intellectual effectiveness of our population, we would have no further immediate troubles in terms of shortage of highly skilled manpower'.[55]

Working mothers and their children were an unpopular cause. Simon Yudkin, a paediatrician, working closely with NSCN, tried to raise the issue, first in a book entitled *Working Mothers and Their Children* and secondly in a committee report entitled *The Care of Pre-school Children,* which was supported by some 30 organisations concerned with children.[56] Yudkin detailed the large numbers of (mainly working-class) women who worked and the lack of childcare they faced. He said that there was no evidence for the common view ascribed to Bowlby, that working mothers harmed their children. The report gave comparative statistics of different kinds of provision. In 1965 there were 448 LEA day nurseries offering 21,396 places; 2,245 private nurseries (mainly small factory and other workplace nurseries) offering 55,543 places; and 3,393 registered childminders offering an estimated 27,200 places. Only 30,000 places were available in nursery schools (although another 200,000 4-year-olds had started school early), and a further 4,500 children were in independent nursery schools – Montessori and other kinds of kindergartens. Only 2 per cent of children aged 3 and 4 had access to state nursery education; and out of a total population of 2,750,000 under-5s, only 11 per cent of all children had any kind of out-of-home care. Yudkin and his committee recommended a proper government investigation into what they considered was an intolerable situation, which weighed heavily upon poor families; and in particular upon black children. The proportion of black working mothers, particularly from Afro-Caribbean backgrounds, was far higher than that of any other group.[57]

THE RE-LAUNCH OF NURSERY EDUCATION

Shortly after Yudkin's report was published, the Government commissioned the Central Advisory Council for Education to produce a report on *Children and Their Primary Schools*. Bridget Plowden, the wife of a senior civil servant, was appointed chairperson. The Plowden Report, as it became known, included nursery education. It endorsed the theories of Jean Piaget about the child as an individual, self-propelled scientist experimenting with the world. It highlighted educational inequalities, except that working-class children were not characterised as physically stunted or unable to control their fierce emotional lives. They were now intellectually stunted, and the job of the nursery and primary school was to reawaken intellectual curiosity.[58] But Plowden was hostile to working mothers, and the report maintained that it was no business of the state to provide services for working parents. Nursery education, from then on (as it still is today) became a part-time service, with the more limited objective of fostering children's intellectual development. The hours of nursery education became shorter than those of any other comparable European country – between 12 and 15 hours per week.

In 1972 Margaret Thatcher, Secretary of State for Education and Science, issued a white paper that firmly endorsed the educational approach and commitment to nursery education set out in the Plowden Report. In Circular 2/73, the Government committed itself to providing 250,000 new nursery places within ten years, for 35 per cent of 3-year-olds and for 75 per cent of 4-year-olds and, surprisingly, an additional 15 per cent of full-time places. Urban aid would be used to fund the first tranche of nursery places, and some local authorities drew up plans for expansion.[59]

Whilst the Government had been deliberating, the shortage of nursery education places had prompted a mother, herself a teacher, called Belle Tutaev, to set up a campaign for more nursery education by encouraging mothers to start their own schools or playgroups.[60] Various organisations such as Save the Children already provided playgroups, that is small local groups partly run by volunteers for two or three mornings a week for local children. The PPA (Pre-school Playgroups Association), founded in 1961, is an example of an uncomfortable alliance between those pressing for better state provision and those advocating self-help, even if self-help meant accepting lower standards and operating outside the state sector. The relationship of the playgroup movement with nursery education was always difficult. In 1970, an editorial in the PPA monthly magazine *Contact* stated that 'it was once feared that PPA might weaken the case by providing nursery education on the cheap. In fact PPA may have helped shame the Government into its first activity for years.'[61]

By the late 1970s, the PPA had commandeered the good and great to argue its case for being better than nursery education. Leading educationists, including Bruner,[62] Halsey[63] and Wall praised the contribution of playgroups to community life. Bridget Plowden was the most famous supporter of PPA, declaring in 1982 that 'if I knew then what I know now' her report would have supported playgroups rather than nursery education.[64] Playgroups, she argued, offered mothers an opportunity to contribute to the daily life of their children in a way that nursery schools could not (although Plowden herself had used nannies and boarding schools like any respectable upper-class parent). This assumption of maternal involvement through volunteering was implicitly – and sometimes explicitly – based on a traditional view of domesticity, in which women stayed at home to look after their children. Indeed looking after children was their prime – if not always fulfilling – function. As one contributor to *Contact* reported: 'I seem to be fighting a battle between the part of me that is determined not to be a domestic cabbage and the part that wants to do well the job of looking after husband, children and home.'[65] For such middle-class, full-time housewives playgroups fitted the bill exactly. For the working classes, especially employed mothers, they were more problematic.

THE LIMITS OF STATE RESPONSIBILITY

The domestically centred self-help rhetoric of the playgroup movement gained in popularity despite formidable criticism. Most notably Tessa Blackstone wrote a Fabian pamphlet in 1972 arguing the case for nursery education.[66] Then, as a prime mover of a government think-tank, the Central Policy Review Staff, she argued that the Government should also consider seriously what kind of support it should offer to working women.[67] Paradoxically, as Tessa Blackstone was arguing the case for more day nursery provision, the NSCN finally gave up its struggle for existence, and sadly amalgamated with the NSA. In 1973, the executive of the NSCN sent a letter to all local authorities stating that:

> it is with mixed feelings that we report to you the passing of a great voluntary society which has led a continuous existence from 1906 to the present day ... we have persistently endeavoured to publicise the value of nurseries to the public ... we hope that day nurseries, whatever form they take, will be given due place in the future planning of provision for the pre-school child.[68]

The NSA also gave up the campaign for free-standing nursery schools, and re-launched itself as BAECE (British Association for Early Child Education).

The economic crisis of 1973 continued under the new Labour government. Widespread cutbacks in public expenditure were needed. David Owen, Minister for Health, advanced the view that nursery education – and any other form of childcare – could be achieved through 'low-cost daycare', that is reliance on playgroups and childminders. At a notorious seminar in Sunningdale in 1976, he praised the 'non-professionals'. Playgroups and childminders were now portrayed, for the first time officially, as warm, homely and mothering, just the qualities a young child needed. Nursery education expansion was finished; day nurseries were an unnecessary expense on the public purse.[69]

There were protests. Jack Tizard, a paediatrician and professor at the Thomas Coram Research Unit and the University of London Institute of Education, and the distinguished team of researchers he gathered around him, produced a steady stream of research that argued that the Sunningdale approach was fundamentally wrong. 'Low-cost daycare' was no more than a euphemism for poor quality provision, and an evasion of state responsibility for a necessary public service.[70] Tizard was a leading contributor to an OECD report, published in 1982, which carefully dismantled ideas about 'low-cost' and argued for sustained investment in co-ordinated education and care provision – a report which many contributing countries (but not the UK) took to heart.[71] The NUT and a few Labour LEAs continued arguing against the grain for nursery education. [72]

Meanwhile Lady Plowden, as patrician as ever, decided to set up a new organisation – VOLCUF (Voluntary Organisations Liaison Committee for Under Fives).[73] She met with the organiser of Save the Children playgroups and announced that 'I thought we all know the same things, and should get together: we need a place where people who wanted to do new things could share ideas.' Forty organisations joined VOLCUF, including major voluntary childcare agencies. Plowden had clout in Whitehall, and VOLCUF was seen as an important contributor to government policy. It was launched in 1977 with a well-attended series of seminars. Addressing the opening seminar, Plowden portrayed 'parents' (meaning mothers) as lacking in confidence and in need of learning how to accept 'responsibility' for their children, a responsibility that they might otherwise cede to professionals:

> it's no large overall system which is needed ... only in the last resort is there need to provide a substitute for those who are completely unable to manage themselves. ... When we are planning for the care of our young children we must also enable care in its widest sense to be given to those who have the day to day responsibility, their parents and in particular, their mothers.[74]

Plowden's analysis fitted neatly with the new Thatcherite Conservative government thinking. It also received academic endorsement from Jerome Bruner, a distinguished American psychologist leading a research team at Oxford University, who extensively reviewed the kinds of early years provision available. Bruner was critical of the relatively limited resourcing of playgroups and childminding, but added his weighty opinion to the position that support should be given to the voluntary sector rather than to a professionally delivered system of nursery education. 'No long term benefit could accrue by making early pre-school care seem like the domain of professionals. It would surely have a corrosive effect on the self-confidence of parents and reduce volunteer efforts.'[75]

FEMINISM HITS BACK

In 1980 a group of feminists launched an organisation called the NCCC (National Childcare Campaign). Building on the work of local grass-roots campaigns, the NCCC argued that if women had the same access and entitlements to work as men, and the same income, then the problem of depressed and un-self-confident mothering would largely disappear. Men did not automatically become depressed and lacking in self-confidence by dint of being fathers. Gender inequalities (and racial inequalities) had been blurred or ignored; the problems of mothering, whilst real enough, had been mostly misdiagnosed and mistreated. Financially supported by the EOC (Equal Opportunities Commission), NCCC argued that the answer was a more comprehensive childcare system, funded, if not directly provided by, the state. In a closely argued discussion paper, *Childcare for All*, it outlined the case for a system which would benefit children – good nurseries, offering both education *and* care for the children of working parents, and staffed by well-trained women and men. Such nurseries would be flexible, community run, and would involve volunteers or work sharing if that seemed appropriate to the communities involved.[76] NCCC produced a booklet entitled *The Do-it-Yourself Nursery* but, unlike the playgroup movement, they made no assumptions about the willing availability of mothers, and insisted that no system could work without adequate funding. 'Do-it-Yourself' did not mean 'do it on the cheap'.[77] NCCC also worked with the CRE (Commission for Racial Equality) to draw attention to the racial inequalities that nursery provision would have to address in an increasingly diverse and multi-cultural society.

Community nurseries began to spring up, grant-aided by a few enterprising local authorities, most notably the GLC (Greater London Council). Strongly influenced by the NCCC, the Women's Committee of the GLC adopted a policy of supporting and encouraging community nurseries. They received hundreds of applications for grants. But like so many of the initiatives to increase provision for young children, it foundered as the political situation once again changed. In 1986 the GLC was abolished by the Thatcher government, and with it the programme of community nurseries. The GLC's own waterfront nursery was turned into an aquarium when County Hall was sold. The DHSS (Department for Health and Social Security) which still held responsibility for all non-education provision for young children, had become interested in the community nursery idea, as a token towards the new gender agendas. As part of a wider voluntary sector programme, it financed a reluctant NCCC to establish a group of community nurseries.[78] The NCCC felt its radical campaigning stance might be jeopardised by this offer, and set up a parallel organisation, the DCT (Daycare Trust) to run its DHSS programme. DCT, toned down from its NCCC days, has since become one of the most influential advocacy groups of the late twentieth century.

The Thatcher and Major governments were pursuing other changes in education. The Plowden Report was disgraced, because of its support for 'progressive teaching'.[79] A more formal curriculum was re-introduced and a new inspection regime, Ofsted (Office for Standards in Education) established. Education was marketised, and made internally competitive; league tables were produced to compare schools' performance. Within this marketised framework, a voucher system was introduced entitling all 4-year-olds to nursery education. Nursery education was defined minimally in terms of a set number of hours, a prescribed curriculum anticipating the 3 Rs of formal schooling, and a satisfactory Ofsted inspection.[80] Nursery education did not have to be delivered within the education system; private and voluntary bodies could equally well provide it. The voucher system resulted in primary schools rushing to admit 4-year-olds to reception classes, in order to claim the voucher monies. The overwhelming majority of 4-year-olds are now admitted directly to primary schools, a similar situation to the one to which Katharine Bathurst had so objected 100 years earlier.

In 1997 the Labour government abolished the administrative rigmarole of nursery vouchers, but enthusiastically endorsed the education initiatives of the previous government. Four-year-olds in schools take part in literacy and numeracy hours; free play and free movement, the *sine qua non* of the nursery movement, has been reduced mainly to scheduled playtime breaks.[81] But at the same time as endorsing marketised educational reform, the Government accepted the gender equality arguments. Women could and should work. The Daycare Trust's arguments about the need for more childcare, and for closer integration of care and education services, resulted in the transfer of all formal responsibility for the administration of education and care services to the Department for Education and Employment (now Department for Education and Skills). But in its enthusiasm for the market, the Government considered that the private and voluntary sector could be stimulated to provide the extra childcare places necessary, rather than rethink nursery education yet again. This policy worked in that the number of private day nursery places has grown enormously. Many childcare places are now provided by market chains, whose shares can be bought on the stockmarket.[82] But the number of playgroup, childminder and nursery school places has collapsed.[83]

CONCLUSION

Thus, as this chapter has shown, the intertwined history of early education and childcare in the twentieth century has been a history of advances and retreats, muddle and reversals within a context of private and public provision. Over the century, ideas and initiatives have been introduced, dropped, then re-introduced as new and untried. This history is, to borrow Kessen's (1965) phrase, 'a history of rediscovery … with some modest advances towards truth'.[84] The European Union[85] and the OECD[86] have recently issued reports comparing the system of early education and childcare in the UK adversely with other European and economically advanced countries. The essence of these criticisms is that in order to be equitable, the system has to be publicly funded (if not publicly provided) and deliver a separate and coherent system of education and care – neither watered down schooling nor a commercial baby park. In the UK we have seen a century of intense but unsuccessful effort towards such goals.

NOTES

1   J. Liebscher, *Foundations of Progressive Education. The History of the National Froebel Society* (Cambridge: Lutterworth Press, 1991).
2   The organisation, Montessori International, developed by Montessori, and her son, runs a private training organisation, Maria Montessori Training, a trading arm, Montessori Trading Co, and a monthly magazine, *Montessori International*.
3   See, for example, L. de Lissa, *Essentials in Nursery School Education* (London: Nursery School Association, 1935).
4   H. May, *The Discovery of Early Childhood* (New Zealand: Auckland University Press, 1997).
5   The NUT and NSA issued a joint pamphlet entitled *The First Steps in Education* in London in 1943. The NUT has since issued several pamphlets on nursery education.
6   For example, for many years NUPE (National Union of Public Employees) had a Nursery Nurses Committee, chaired by Rodney Bickerstaff, that claimed the work of nursery nurses was commensurate with that of teachers. (UNISON archives). See also TUC (Trades Union Congress) Working Party, *The Under Fives* (London: TUC, 1976).
7   *Times Educational Supplement*, 23 January 1926.
8   *Nursery World*, 9 June 1926.

9   An organisation calling itself 'The Order of the Child' was set up by Sir Murray Hyslop, Basil Peto and others to campaign for the general welfare of the nation's children, and in particular to maintain 'the greatness of our empire' through appropriate character training. It advertised regularly in *Nursery World*. Even the National League for Health, Maternity and Child Welfare issued a film in 1926 about the work of infant welfare centres, entitled *Empire Builders*.

10 D. Leinster-Mackay, *The Rise of the English Prep School* (London: Falmer, 1984).

11 N. Middleton, *When Family Failed: The Treatment of Children in the Care of the Community during the First Half of the Twentieth Century* (London: Victor Gollancz, 1971).

12 *Times Educational Supplement*, 5 January 1915.

13 *Nursery World* report, 52 (1938), p. 237.

14 The Department for Education and Skills and the Treasury currently run a multi-million programme, Sure Start, aimed at supporting mothers in poor areas to improve their parenting and other skills, in order to give their children a better chance of educational progress.

15 A.S. Neill's book, *The Problem Child*, was favourably reviewed in *Nursery World* by Ethel Mannin in June 1926, which led to an angry correspondence for the rest of the summer. The quoted letter was published on 18 August. Bertrand Russell's book, *On Education*, was also published in 1926, and reviewed in the *Times Educational Supplement* on 27 February. A similar correspondence ensued.

16 C. Steedman, *Childhood, Culture and Class in Britain: Margaret McMillan, 1860–1931* (London: Virago, 1990).

17 B. Jackson and S. Jackson, *Childminders* (London: Routledge and Kegan Paul, 1979). For a discussion of Jacksons' claims see B. Mayall and P. Petrie, *Childminding and Day Nurseries – What Kind of Care?* (London: Heinemann, 1983).

18 L. Gurjeva, 'Everyday Bourgeois Science: The Scientific Management of Children in Britain, 1880–1914', University of Cambridge, PhD thesis, 1998, p. 243.

19 B. Wright, *A History of the National Nursery Examination Board* (St Albans: CACHE, 1999).

20 Accounts of her activities regularly appeared in *Child Life, New Era, Nursery World, Times Educational Supplement*, and *The Paedologist* (later *Child Study*) the journal of the child-study movement.

21 See note 2 above.

22 C. Steedman, 'Mother Made Conscious: The Historical Development of a Primary School Pedagogy', in M. Woodhead and A. McGrath (eds), *Family, School and Society* (London: Hodder and Stoughton, 1988), pp. 82–95.

23 R. Smart, *Bedford Training College: A History of a Froebel College and its Schools* (Bedford: Bedford Training College Publications Committee, 1982), p. 7.

24 Liebscher, *Foundations of Progressive Education*, p. 80.

25 B. Russell, *On Education, Especially in Early Childhood* (London: Allen and Unwin, 1926).

26 B. Tudor-Hart, and E. Landau, *Play and Toys in the Nursery Years* (London: Country Life, 1938).

27 S. Isaacs, *The Nursery Years: The Mind of the Child from Birth to Six Years* (London: Routledge, 1929); *Intellectual Growth in Young Children* (London: Routledge, 1930).

28 J. Gathorne-Hardy, *The Rise and Fall of the British Nanny* (London: Hodder and Stoughton, 1972).

29 See *Nursery World*, 25 August 1926, for a justification of Babies' Hotels.

30 K. Bathurst, 'The Need for National Nurseries', *The Nineteenth Century and After*, May 1905, pp. 812–24.

31 Steedman, *Childhood, Culture and Class in Britain*. This book describes Margaret McMillan's lifelong campaign for nursery education.
32 Reproduced and discussed in the minutes of NSCN, BLPES (British Library of Political and Economic Science), BAECE archives.
33 *Nursery Schools*. Extract from the memorandum prepared by the Advisory Committee on Education, Labour Party, 1919.
34 E. Jackson, *Achievement: A Short History of the LCC* (London: Longmans, 1965), p. 46.
35 County Borough of Burnley, *Procedures for the Official Opening of Accrington Rd Nursery School*, 26 February 1932.
36 NSA, *Nursery School Education. Statement of Policy* (London: NSA, May 1927).
37 NSA, *Description of a Model of a Nursery School* (London: NSA, 1935); NSA, *Buildings Advisory Committee: Designing the New Nursery School* (London: NSA, 1950). These publications are discussed in M. Dudek, *Kindergarten Architecture* (London: E. Spon, 1998).
38 Board of Education, *Report of the Consultative Committee on Infant and Nursery Schools* (Hadow Report) (London: HMSO, 1933).
39 NSA, *Open Letter to the Public* (London: NSA, April 1927); NSA, *Memorandum on the Educational Needs of Children Under Seven Years of Age* (London: NSA, 1935).
40 NSCN, *Address to the First International Conference on Day Nurseries*, 1923, BLPES, BAECE archives.
41 NSCN minutes, Extraordinary General Meeting, 24 November 1932, BLPES, BAECE archives.
42 NSA conference proceedings (London: NSA, 1935). Reported in *New Era*, 1, 1 (1936), p. 168.
43 S. Ferguson and H. Fitzgerald, *History of the Second World War: Studies in Social Services* (London: HMSO, 1954), p. 203.
44 Ibid, p. 193.
45 Major Nathan, NSCN, to Lady Allen, NSA, 30 June 1943, BLPES, BAECE archives.
46 Ferguson and Fitzgerald. *History of the Second World War*, p. 193.
47 D. Riley, *War in the Nursery* (London: Virago, 1983). This book describes shifting attitudes towards mothers and other women throughout the war and post-war period.
48 Ibid., p. 1.
49 In the 1950s Winnicott gave a series of BBC radio broadcasts about childcare which attracted large audiences. Bowlby wrote a report for the World Health Organisation, *Maternal Care and Mental Health* (Geneva, 1952), later popularised as *Childcare and the Growth of Love* (London: Penguin, 1953).
50 L. de Lissa, *Education up to Seven Plus* (London: NSA, 1945), p. 3.
51 F. Bodman, 'Aggressive Play', in *Play and Mental Health* (London: New Era/New Education Fellowship, 1945), p. 17.
52 D. Gardner, *The Education of Young Children* (London: Methuen, 1956), p. 11.
53 *The Times*, 8 September 1951.
54 UNESCO, *Mental Hygiene in the Nursery. Report of a Joint WHO–UNESCO Expert Meeting* (Paris: UNESCO, 1953), p. 11.
55 W. Wall and A. Halsey, *No Man is an Island: Two Speeches from the 17th Annual Conference of the Pre-school Playgroups Association* (Reading: Southern Region Pre-school Playgroups Association, 1978).
56 S. Yudkin, *A Report on the Care of Pre-school Children* (London: NSCN, 1967); S. Yudkin and A. Holme, *Working Mothers and Their Children* (London: Michael Joseph, 1963).
57 Community Relations Council, *Who Minds: A Study of Working Mothers and Child-minders in Ethnic Minority Communities* (London: CRC, 1975).

58 *Children and Their Primary Schools: A Report of the Central Advisory Council for Education* (England) (London: HMSO, 1967).
59 Department of Education and Science, *Nursery Education*, DES Circular 2/73, 31 January 1973.
60 Tutaev wrote a much-quoted letter to the *Guardian's* 'Woman's Page', 25 August, 1961.
61 *Contact*, October 1970.
62 Wall and Halsey, *No Man is an Island*.
63 J. Bruner, *Under Fives in Britain* (London: Grant McIntyre, 1980).
64 Plowden's presidential address on the twenty-first anniversary of the founding of PPA received wide press coverage and comment.
65 Letter to *Contact*, October 1965.
66 T. Blackstone, *First Schools of the Future* (London: Fabian Research Series 304, 1972).
67 Central Policy Review Staff, *Services for Children with Working Mothers* (London: HMSO, 1978).
68 NSCN, *Letter to Directors of Social Services*, BLPES, BAECE archives. September 1973.
69 Department for Health and Social Security, *Low Cost Day Provision for the Under Fives*. Papers of a conference held at the Civil Service College, Sunningdale Park, 9–10 January 1976.
70 Ibid.
71 Centre for Educational Research and Innovation, *Children and Society: Issues for Pre-school Reform* (Paris: OECD, 1982).
72 NUT, *The Needs of the Under Fives* (London: NUT, 1977).
73 Now renamed the National Early Years Network and taking a more radical stance on government policy.
74 B. Plowden, 'Opening Address: Children and Parents: Self Help and the Voluntary Role', in *0–5: A Changing Population: Implications for Parents, the Public and Policy Makers* (London: Voluntary Organisations Liaison Committee, 1977), p. 9.
75 Bruner, *Under Fives in Britain*, p. 196.
76 National Childcare Campaign, *Childcare for All* (London: NCCC, 1985).
77 NCCC, *The Do-it-Yourself Nursery* (London: NCCC, 1980).
78 Department of Health, *Under Fives Initiative: Final Report* (London, DoH, 1988).
79 'Plowden's Progress', *Economist*, 20 June 1998, pp. 31–5.
80 School Curriculum and Assessment Authority, *Desirable Learning Outcomes for Children's Learning on Entering Compulsory Education* (London: DfEE/SCAA, 1996).
81 The numbers of places in different forms of provision have been set out in DfEE (DfES) annual statistics. As from 2002, for the first time nursery school education places would not be listed as a separate category.
82 *Nursery World* now provides a regular supplement on the development of nursery chains.
83 See DfEE and DfES annual statistics.
84 W. Kessen, *The Child* (New York: John Wiley, 1965), p. 2.
85 EU, *Quality Indicators in Services for Young Children* (Brussels: EU, DV5, 1997).
86 OECD, *Starting Strong: Thematic Review of Early Childhood Education and Care* (Paris: OECD, 2001).

5

BIRDS, BEES AND GENERAL EMBARRASSMENT: SEX EDUCATION IN BRITAIN, FROM SOCIAL PURITY TO SECTION 28

Lesley A. Hall

INTRODUCTION

This chapter deals with the long and vexed history of sex education of children and young people within the British education system. It is far from being a coherent and continuous narrative. Long periods of neglect have been punctuated by occasional moments of crisis and flurries of moral panic with an effect of *déjà vu*. This is perhaps understandable since the subject falls not only in the delicate liminal zone between the public and the private, but also on a boundary, which has had significant administrative repercussions, between medical and educational concerns. The subject has been intricately bound up with questions of national as well as personal health, in particular the issue of sexually-transmitted diseases, and thus has tended to surge to prominence during wartime, only to become quiescent once more when peace arrives. The sorry tale reflects the persistent reluctance of all political parties in Britain to intervene in sexual matters: whatever the party in power, the same evasions and cautious expedients have been deployed.[1]

THE BEGINNINGS

The idea that children should receive some enlightenment about sex from responsible guardians dates back at least to the 1870s, as the social purity movement evolved from the campaign against the Contagious Diseases Acts of the 1860s. These Acts were aimed at counteracting the venereal diseases rife in the Victorian army and navy: any woman in the designated garrison and port towns believed to be a prostitute could be forced to undergo medical examination and incarcerated in a 'Lock' hospital until 'cured' if diagnosed as diseased.

These Acts, which penalised women but not men, violated civil liberties, offended Christian morality by endeavouring to make 'vice' safe, and caused a great outcry from women, religious bodies, working-class organisations and champions of civil liberties. An organised movement rose up against them. This initially concentrated on rousing public feeling and lobbying for their repeal. Increasingly a wider crusade (though one by no means monolithic in its aims) developed, aimed at the moral regeneration of British society.[2]

One of its tenets was the belief in the necessity of giving children healthy and moral information about sex. Previously childhood innocence had been assumed and considered to be its own best protection. Warnings might be needed at puberty, especially for boys; but children, it was believed, had no sexual instincts or curiosity. Rejecting the idea that instruction would contaminate innocence, social purity advocates argued instead that children were liable to pick up wrong ideas and behaviour from untrustworthy servants or nasty-minded companions. Giving children the 'right' information would protect them against the sort of misinformation conveyed by 'dirty talk', as well as preparing them to withstand lurking sexual dangers.

However, right from this early stage, arose the three big and problematic questions which would haunt sex education, both in discussion and in practice. Who tells the children? When do they tell them? What do they tell them? In this early phase advocates of sex education aimed at encouraging parents to provide their children with healthy and accurate information about sex. 'How' (and what) 'to tell the children' was a problem, however desirable it might seem that they should be told something. Miss Agnes Cotton, founder of the first Moral Welfare Home for Children, suggested the line 'Every little bit of our bodies is given to us by God our father, to be used for the work he made it for, and for nothing else.'[3]

An important work in providing acceptable ways of talking about 'the birds and the bees' was Patrick Geddes and J. Arthur Thomson's *The Evolution of Sex* (1889) aimed at average intelligent adult readers. It approached sexual phenomena by gradually working up the evolutionary ladder from the amoeba, via plants, invertebrates, insects, and mammals, to man. This seems to have stimulated an explosion of the deployment of botany and the 'lower animals' as a discursive model suitable for the sexual instruction of children.

The mid-1890s appear to have been the critical period for the emergence of the stamens and pistils school of sexual enlightenment. In 1894 *The Human Flower* appeared from 'Ellis Ethelmer' (pseudonym of the radical, Ben Elmy, husband of Victorian feminist, Elizabeth Wolstenholme Elmy) and in the following year its sequel, *Baby Buds*. Edith MacDuff wrote in the same year to the socialist and sex-reformer Edward Carpenter (1844–1929) describing how she had drawn her children's attention to 'Nature's infinitely varied and beautiful schemes for the fertilisation of flowers'.[4] A correspondent wrote in a similar vein to the feminist journal, *Shafts*, in 1895. Following discussions of sex education in its columns, she had decided that she 'would no longer be a coward, and shrink from my clear duty' and thus, 'by the aid of simple botany' prepared her children's minds 'for the revelation, and then I talked of birds and their young, and animals'.[5] This may well have been an approach which parents found spared themselves embarrassment.

By the early twentieth century a few progressive educational establishments incorporated some form of sex education into their curriculum, and there were even occasional experiments in public elementary schools. The National Council of Public Morals included sex education in its moral crusade for the regeneration of the race.[6] Its moving spirit, Revd James Marchant, solicited Sir Patrick Geddes to provide a volume on sex education for children for his series of 'New Tracts for the Time', using botany, 'on scientific lines' to 'lift these subjects out of the sentimental rut'.[7] The feminist National Federation of Women Teachers advocated a rather similar approach, which Hilda Kean has characterised as 'a mixture of homily, religion, science, botany, and soap and water cleanliness'. The emphasis was heavily on sex as reproduction, and the biological analogies – plants, birds' eggs, salmon spawning – safely distinct from humanity. Kean comments that 'the natural world ... was moralised to carry the significations of goodness, health, and social harmony'.[8]

While the great and good who subscribed to the tenets of social hygiene believed that the enlightenment of children in the ways of 'racial health' was essential, this was not uncontested by communities to whom such ideas were introduced, as the 1913 case of Miss Outram, Headmistress of Dronfield Elementary School, reveals. Responding to queries raised in scripture class, she gave a small group of senior girls information which to present-day eyes seems innocuous if not obfuscatory, but was described by one local mother as 'too disgusting for the children to know: they have not the same respect for their parents when they know that'. Local resistance to her dissemination of 'race hygiene' caused press furore and the case was investigated by the Board of Education.[9] Theodora Bonwick, however, in her work with the National Federation of Women Teachers and at the Enfield Road Elementary School, Hackney, stressed involving parents and explaining what was intended. She achieved considerable success, but her enterprise was unique. The London County Council's 1914 Commission of Inquiry on the Teaching of Sex Hygiene found most teachers 'averse' to discussing the subject and concluded that it should not be taught in class.[10]

'THE ROYAL COMMISSION RECOMMENDS ...'

In 1913, after many years of campaigning for a government investigation into the prevalence of venereal diseases and existing measures for their treatment, a Royal Commission on Venereal Diseases was set up. From 1913 to 1916 it heard evidence from a wide range of experts. Many of these urged that one long-term approach to this major problem of national health should be sex education, though exactly what this should consist of, who should give it and how, and at what age, remained very open questions. However, probably as a result of the publication of the Commission's First Report in 1914, the Board of Education issued a procedure minute, 'Sex Hygiene', in October that year concerning 'Courses for parents intended to assist them in the intelligent supervision of boys and girls in the matter of Sex and the like ... if carried on under proper conditions.' Such courses were eligible for Board recognition if organised for mothers attending a School for Mothers, and also if given under the educational direction of the Local Education Authority as part of evening school programmes.[11]

However, there was no official committee of investigation into sex education. As with the similarly touchy topic of the birth-rate, the NCPM (National Council of Public Morals) took up the task. The NCPM's National Birth Rate Commission (established in 1913) investigated *Youth and the Race: The Development and Education of Young Citizens for Worthy Parenthood* between 1920 and 1923. Its report delineated various themes and approaches which were already, and were to remain, standard motifs. The Commission addressed the perennial questions:

> Should instruction in regard to sex be given to young people? At what age should it be begun? What should be its content? By what method should it be imparted? What is the agency which it is practicable to employ?

As a result of the evidence they received, they were convinced that:

> *however difficult and delicate the task may be, it is one that cannot with due regard to the moral safety and welfare of youth, be shirked but must be undertaken, and should be therefore considered, not as an irksome duty, but as a privilege* [italics in the original].[12]

The Commission was convinced that it was desirable to begin the task well before the onset of puberty, with children's questions being answered honestly and traditional legends eschewed, and should take into account appropriateness to different stages of development. Teaching on sex hygiene should not be isolated from 'moral education generally', and should be positive rather than negative, a point which was emphatically stressed: 'dwelling on the ideal of marriage and parenthood rather than on the peril of illicit intercourse'; 'the motive of fear of the consequences of any abuse of the function should not be stimulated by the instruction given'.[13]

However, although this might be a worthy agenda, the recurrent issues of the practicalities of implementation surfaced. As usual, the general view was that 'the duty of instruction rests first of all with the parents', but, unfortunately, 'not less general was the opinion that many parents are not competent to give that instruction',[14] while 'the majority of the teachers are not yet competent to give instruction, as they have not themselves been taught in the Training Colleges'.[15]

By the time the Commission took up this problem in 1920 there had been some 40 years of arguments in favour of sex education, and a modest flood of handbooks for parents, teachers and youth workers, and simpler tracts for children and young people to read themselves. Letters to Marie Stopes (1880–1958), author of the best-selling marriage manual, *Married Love* (1918), and other contemporary sources, illustrate the enormous amount of sexual ignorance which continued to prevail in the inter-war years. Mothers either thought that girls 'should learn all that is necessary when ... married',[16] or simply told them of 'certain things your husband will require from you. It's not nice and you'll just have to put up with it.'[17] There was enormous mutual embarrassment: a member of the Women's Co-operative Guild confessed to Virginia Woolf that 'she had to get a friend to explain the period to her own daughter'.[18] Men were usually somewhat better informed, though any formal sex education was most likely to have consisted of cautions against self-abuse, and perhaps some warning about venereal diseases and the dangers of resorting to prostitutes.

Following the Final Report of the Royal Commission on Venereal Diseases, the Government had established a network of clinics for treatment, but there was much less direct action over the Commission's recommendations on sex education. Instead of making the Board of Education responsible, the Government gave a Treasury grant to the voluntary NCCVD (National Council for Combatting Venereal Diseases), to undertake propaganda and educational work in liaison with the Ministry of Health. The NCCVD organised courses for teachers, parents and youth leaders, encouraged the teaching of biology in elementary schools and arranged visiting speakers for schools. In 1925 it was renamed the BSHC (British Social Hygiene Council) to reflect this broader interest in sexual health education. The low official priority their work enjoyed, however, was indicated when the direct Treasury grant was withdrawn in 1929 and replaced by discretionary allotments from local authorities, many of which declined to contribute.[19]

Some local and institutional initiatives went forward, but with no obligation and no centralised co-ordination. Provision, when it existed, too often consisted of occasional visiting lecturers, rather than the ongoing, integrated, programme which had been recommended for decades. Some notes by the veteran social purity campaigner, Dr Helen Wilson, prepared for a conference of the International Federation of Medical Women in 1930, indicated that it was not Board of Education policy to encourage the direct teaching of sex hygiene in elementary schools, because of large class size, the youth of the pupils (leaving at age 14) and the anticipation of parental opposition. In secondary schools, however, biology and nature study were found useful as a basis for more direct teaching to the later years. In training colleges the teaching of sex hygiene was at the discretion of the college authorities; the subject was not compulsory but instruction was not discouraged. Some instruction, via 'a short course of lectures', had become a general feature in most colleges. Some local authorities were taking their own initiatives in the matter in spite of Board apathy: Hertfordshire County Council held a conference on sex instruction in 1933, while Cardiff Local Education Authority arranged for classes to the final year in elementary schools by lecturers from the Welsh National Council of the Alliance of Honour, a leading social purity organisation. However, central direction was woefully lacking: in 1935 a civil servant at the Board of Education informed a counterpart at the London County Council who had hoped for guidance, that he had 'not been able to find anything here which would be likely to help you very much'.[20]

'Large numbers of teachers, social workers, youth leaders' were feeling 'that something serious should be done about sex education' by the time of the outbreak of the Second World War. However, they were frightened off by two factors. First, as both the Ministry of Education and the principal teaching unions were opposed to it (or perceived as being opposed), there was a fear that 'they wouldn't get any backing if they ran into trouble'; second, 'they didn't know how to set about it'.[21]

A FALSE DAWN IN THE 1940s

As concerns about venereal disease had stimulated earlier attention to the subject, the recurrence of these concerns with the outbreak of the Second World War and the sharp upturn in previously declining figures of venereal infections, led to renewed preoccupation with the need for sex education. In 1942 the responsibility for social hygiene education was removed from the British Social Hygiene Council, and reassigned to the Central Council for Health Education, a quasi-official body with widespread support from central and local government.[22]

In 1943 the Board of Education finally gave cognizance to the subject of sex education by issuing its pamphlet 119, *Sex Education in Schools and Youth Organisations*. The tone of this pamphlet does not suggest authoritative guidance. It pointed out that such instruction had not 'generally been undertaken in schools', and in 'no sense [was] it the accepted practice to include in the work of schools ... either instruction in the facts of sex, or specific guidance on the moral aspects of personal conduct or sex relationship'. Indeed, 'ways and means are still matters for careful exploration'. The Board felt it 'not possible to lay down specific principles, or to recommend specific methods'. Issues which the pamphlet reiterated were the continuing reluctance of parents to undertake the enlightenment of their own children and the 'diffidence' of teachers about embarking upon it.

Statistics of what was being done were 'by no means complete': in about half of the local education authorities, at least a few schools were undertaking 'carefully planned instruction' (though little detail was given as to what this consisted of). More attention was given overall in girls' schools than boys'. While the fear of giving offence to parents restrained many educators, there was considerable evidence that in fact parents welcomed initiatives by teachers. Although there was strong theoretical agreement in favour of the integrated approach, for example covering matters relevant to sex education as an incidental part of biology lessons, religious instruction or civics classes, it was noted that the system of special lectures by outside experts, or talks to school leavers, remained prevalent. The Board pointed out that there was increasing advocacy of the desirability of introducing the basic biological facts prior to puberty, 'before strong emotions develop', rather than at that tricky developmental stage. However, the reiteration of the sensitivity and difficulty of the task, and the importance of the essentially personal qualities of the individual teacher, who was exhorted to 'draw upon his own wisdom and experience of life', does not seem calculated to encourage teachers to undertake sex education with any confidence.[23]

When the Mass Observation organisation undertook its 'Little Kinsey' Sex Survey during 1947–49, one of the questions it asked was how respondents had acquired knowledge of sex. Very few (mostly from the younger age-groups) mentioned formal sex education through school or youth organisations. A mere 6 per cent had learnt from a teacher. Twice as many said it 'came naturally', four times as many had 'picked it up'. The information thus acquired was extremely haphazard. The views of 'leaders of Opinion' (doctors, clergymen, educators) were deliberately solicited. While few argued that children should not receive some kind of instruction concerning sex and reproduction, opinions differed considerably as to whether this should be given formally and outside the family: many continued to consider it the mother's prerogative. And 'even where it is attempted', the conclusion was that 'Sex instruction ... would still seem to be of a very timid and limited nature.'[24]

A more active approach was initiated in the mid-1940s. The CCHE (Central Council for Health Education) appointed a Special Advisor for Sex Education, Cyril Bibby, who had been working for the British Social Hygiene Council following dismissal from his post at Chesterfield Grammar School because of his actively pacifist opinions. Bibby's background was in education, not medicine, and he had been involved for several years with the Woodcraft Folk (the pacifist, co-operative, co-educational, alternative youth organisation). Prior to joining the BSHC, he had 'never given any special thought to sex education'. Reading everything he could find on the subject, he 'didn't think anything of it': approaches were either 'sacramental ... sex is so beautiful, in effect we mustn't tell you anything about' or 'the anatomy and physiology of sex', rather than what Bibby thought important, 'attitudes and sentiments ... a feeling of responsibility ... self-discipline'.[25]

His reports on the explosion of interest in sex education strike a very gung-ho note. In 1943 Bristol Education Committee closed all its schools so that all teaching staff could attend a lecture and discussion, followed by a week's vacation school for teachers. In the following year the Associations of Assistant Masters and Assistant Mistresses (representing most secondary school teachers) passed AGM resolutions in favour of sex education, and the National Union of Teachers (representing most elementary school teachers) issued a statement, 'Sex Teaching in Schools', which was generally favourable. The Board of Education held its first teachers' summer school on the subject in Cambridge, and Roman Catholic archbishops and bishops of England and Wales issued a statement recommending instruction of children by parents. In 1945 the first really thorough (ten lecture) course in sex education for parents was arranged by the CCHE at Chiswick Polytechnic. Figures collected in 1944 from schools and LEAs (Local Education Authorities) which had circularised parents asking their consent to their children receiving sex education, showed almost unanimous support, and many were so convinced of the general approval of the subject that they did not even bother to seek parental permission. Increasing numbers of courses were being given by the CCHE to teachers, parents, youth leaders, young people, and schoolchildren.[26] To some extent this was presumably a result of the publicity being given to venereal diseases and the general sense of social and moral upheaval during the war years which comes over strongly from the Mass Observation material. In 1946 Bibby reported that:

> It is now widely accepted in Britain that sex education should not be treated in isolation, but as part of health education generally; that it is to be regarded not as a new 'subject' but rather as a new orientation of

existing teaching; that it is not mere anti-venereal disease propaganda but preparation to live a rich and joyous life. ... Clearly there is much yet to do in Britain ... When, however, the overall structure is compared with that existing only five years ago, there is room for sober satisfaction.[27]

His sanguine summation of the situation was that 'it seems that the general battle for the recognition of the importance of sex education is over in Britain'.[28]

The 1944 Education Act paid lip service to the need for sex education in schools. However, the onus of provision still lay very much with the individual school, and there was little government support apart from the purely guidance function of pamphlet 119, subsequently absorbed into a more general pamphlet on health education.[29] In practice, therefore, sex education continued to be extremely haphazard.

'THIS HOPEFUL EXPECTATION HAS, UNFORTUNATELY, NOT MATERIALISED'

Nearly 30 years later Bibby reported sadly that although in 1946 'a wide programme of sex education was well-established ... and it seemed likely that within a decade or two it would be thoroughly integrated within the total educational picture', it was clear, as he looked back, that 'This hopeful expectation has, unfortunately, not materialised, and in some respects the situation today is less satisfactory than it was 20 years ago.' Bibby considered that several factors were involved. Funding for the CCHE had been reduced, with consequent restructuring, while the implementation of the 1944 Education Act and the 1948 National Health Act absorbed central and local government agencies in the educational and health fields. There was a general slackening of tension after the strain of the war years. But the study of sex education continued to suffer from neglect and lack of interest. Bibby commented that his own manual remained the accepted standard text for some 25 years, even though it had become 'sadly dated',[30] and he deplored the 'total lack of basic thinking in this field by everybody else for a quarter of a century'.[31] He did not mention, though it may have played some part, the rapid decline in public concern over venereal diseases as a result of the development of effective antibiotic treatment. Although 1946 was actually a peak year in terms of numbers of cases, little attention was given to provisions for these ailments when devising the National Health Service.[32] He also later wondered whether his youthful and perhaps rather brash approach (he was only 27 at the time of the initial appointment), while it worked 'in those circumstances in those times', was something which was only effective in the wartime situation. Bibby was 'not much of a respecter of positions', which might have militated against him once government departments shook back down into normal peacetime routines.[33]

By 1955, according to journalist Audrey Whiting of the *Sunday Pictorial*, 'the majority of our fourteen-year-old schoolgirls are completely in the dark about babies' while 'the Ministry of Education dumps the responsibility for sex education in schools on local authorities and leaves it entirely to their whim'.[34] The failure of the Ministry of Education to provide guidance was acknowledged by its civil servants: 'all these matters are left to the discretion of local education authorities, head teachers, and other bodies responsible for the running of schools',[35] and it was conceded that there was 'no direction from the centre on sex education'.[36]

Some schools did run successful programmes and a good deal was being done by certain LEAs. Some issued their own printed guidelines, although these were not necessarily any great advance: in 1969 a journalist described the Inner London Education Authority's book for London teachers, first issued in 1949 and revised in 1964, as 'devious and tedious'.[37] Others appointed Health Education Officers to take responsibility.[38] In some schools, individual biology or religious studies teachers might take the task upon themselves. Elsewhere, if there was any provision at all, this continued to rely on the old expedient of occasional outside lecturers – doctors, nurses, health visitors, clergymen, and representatives of sanitary protection manufacturers – who did not necessarily have any particular qualifications or training. Indeed, there were no standard requirements for the job, although Tampax Ltd did employ trained nurse lecturers in its Educational Service, and also provided materials for teachers themselves to use. But this, of course, was at root an innovative marketing strategy.[39]

Throughout the 1950s and 1960s sexual behaviour slowly changed. Premarital intercourse for both sexes became more widespread and less stigmatised. The darker side of this loosening of inhibitions was a rise in unmarried motherhood and venereal disease. The 'Sexual Revolution' of the 1960s brought the contraceptive pill, the legalisation of abortion and the decriminalisation of homosexuality. But the amount of media attention given to sex did not mean that finally a paradise of enlightenment had come about. Many still floundered in confusion and ignorance, only made worse by media messages which both titillated and obfuscated.

The 1960s saw increasing articulation by various groups and individuals of the need for a more coherent approach to sex education. In 1962 a BMA (British Medical Association) Report on Health Education advocated teaching the 'basic facts' in primary school.[40] In 1964 this message was reiterated when the Association published its Report on Venereal Diseases and Young People, claiming that sex education was mostly inadequate or misdirected. An article on this report in *The Medical Officer* argued that 'sex education needs complete overhaul'.[41] In 1963 the council of the National Union of Students passed a motion in favour of compulsory courses in secondary schools.[42] A member of the national executive of the National Union of Teachers was reported as saying 'questions on sex better in class than toilets'.[43] In the same year the Church of England Board of Education produced a pamphlet, *Sex Education in Schools*, in which, while the responsibility of parents was yet again emphasised, it was claimed that 'it remains important, and even urgent, that the schools should accept some responsibility'.[44]

In 1966 representatives of the Ministry of Health and the DES (Department of Education and Science) discussed the implications of the BMA Report on VD (venereal disease) and Young People. It had 'quickly been realised that the DES would have to be the prime mover'. Little was known about the existing extent of instruction on the subject, but in spite of all earlier efforts, many teachers still left training college ignorant and thus reluctant to give instruction.[45] As a result, and given increasingly pervasive concerns on the matter more generally, in 1967 the DES embarked on re-drafting their booklet, *Health in Education*, to include a more substantial chapter on 'School and the future parent'.[46] In the same year Dr Julia Dawkins, Medical Officer in the DES, in a memorandum on sex education to the Royal Commission on Medical Education, referred to the demand from schools for advice on the subject.[47] The main impetus behind these initiatives came from the medical rather than the educational side of the equation, while there seems to have been a greater demand by schools for guidance than leadership imposed by the DES.

In 1969 an unprecedented furore arose with the production of a BBC educational film on sex education. Opinions were violently polarised. On the pro-sex education side, it was maintained that ignorance, fear and misinformation were prevalent and that as a result, sex was regarded as dirty and degrading, leading to problems and maladjustment. On the anti-side, it was argued that children should be left to enjoy their innocence; knowledge about sex came naturally; there was too much sex around already; children would try it out. Those in the middle ground believed that while it might be advisable for children to be enlightened, this was not something which could appropriately be undertaken in a collective classroom setting, and that there was no set age which could be recommended for the communication of 'the facts', because of differing levels of maturity.[48] Statistics cited in favour of a more active approach included the claim that 'more than 360,000 boys and girls who will leave school next summer will have had no formal sex education. Most of the rest will have had little scant instruction.' It was alleged that 'the Ministry of Education unofficially approves of sex education but officially gives no guidance'.[49]

There was clearly massive variation between different localities as well as widely divergent individual views. On Merseyside Jill Kenner of the National Marriage Guidance Council was successfully providing lessons in local primary schools, whereas a student teacher at Nottingham College of Technology who gave an impromptu talk to a class of 15- and 16-year-olds (who claimed that they had never had a sex education lesson) was dismissed.[50] In Sussex one headmaster took 400 pupils to a special showing of the German sex education film, *Helga*, whereas there were complaints that girl students at a college of domestic science in one unnamed city were being taught about 'sexual deviations, drug addiction, birth control and alcoholism'.[51] Most of the reported pleas for better sex education were attributed to Medical Officers of Health rather than to Education Officers. The problem that parents were either unable or unwilling to tell their children the facts recurred yet again. Though mostly expressed in terms of a sense of personal lack of information, there were occasional comments such as 'I think there's something indecent about a woman talking to her child about subjects like that. It would be degrading for both of us.'[52]

'PERMISSIVE SOCIETY' VERSUS 'BACKLASH'?

In the 1970s the FPA (Family Planning Association) finally achieved its 50-year-old aim, the incorporation of birth control into the provisions of the National Health Service, and moved on to develop even further its existing sex education projects. As early as 1967 the FPA had designated health education as one of its major tasks, conceptualising its role as 'educating the educators', working with local authorities to train teachers and other health educators. Its activities in this capacity included special training sessions for sex educators, and the path-breaking Grapevine initiative, which aimed at providing informal peer sex education by young people themselves. Rather than laying down rigid and inflexible rules, the ideal was to encourage a greater sense of responsibility in young people.[53] A widely disseminated handbook was Jane Cousin's, *Make It Happy* (1978). Sex education was apparently gaining more attention within the education system, though still with major local variations. Birth control was featuring more, and many parents expressed approval of adolescents receiving accurate information. However, fewer boys than girls were exposed to it, suggesting a tendency to conceptualise protection from pregnancy and personal relationships as female issues.[54]

During the 1980s a 'moral backlash' by vociferous individuals and groups gained a good deal of media attention and political support in the changed climate of Thatcherism. In spite of growing international evidence that effective sex education correlated with low rates of teenage pregnancy and venereal infection, there were recurrent allegations that sex education (unless tightly tied to 'family values' and prohibitive teachings) encouraged promiscuity.[55]

In the era of AIDS, sex education continued to remain a battlefield. Throughout the 1980s and early 1990s there was discernible tension between the agenda of the Department of Health and that of the Department of Education. Health was strongly committed to a pro-active campaign of health education around preventive measures. However, the Department of Education granted sex education low priority. The devolution of powers to schools and their governors meant that many innovative programmes by local education authorities bit the dust, while head teachers were nervous of upsetting the susceptibilities of governors. The subject was increasingly eroded from the National Curriculum, taught only at the discretion of school governors, and parental rights to withdraw children increasingly strengthened.

Wider anxieties around children and sexuality were expressed in arguments over this still-debated territory. It is sometimes claimed that the breakdown of morals perceived as occurring within present-day society (rising illegitimacy, especially among teenage mothers, rise in STDs (sexually transmitted diseases), instability of families, 'promiscuity' and so on) is contemporary with and caused by the massive spread of sex education since the 1960s. In fact, as both the first-person accounts by Carol Lee of her experiences as a sex-educator, and the 1987 Policy Studies Institute report by Isobel Allen on *Education in Sex and Personal Relationships* make clear, sex education provision within the school system has been very far from universal and very uneven in quality. Often it stuck to basic biological facts and cautions about potential dangers. Isobel Allen's research revealed both children and parents expressing over-whelming support for sex education within the school context, in spite of the persistent rhetoric claiming that educators were usurping the parental role and contravening family values.[56]

However, the place of sex education in the curriculum and its content continue to be contested. 'Clause 28' of the Local Government Act, 1988, forbade local councils to 'promote' homosexuality or teach its acceptability as a 'pretended family relationship'.[57] Medical, pedagogic and moral values, as ever, clashed. In 1994 a Health Education Authority guide to sex, commissioned specifically to be understandable and acceptable to teenagers, employing slang in common usage, was withdrawn following objections from the Department for Education that its terminology and style were 'smutty and not suitable'.[58]

In October 2000 the sexual health charity, Marie Stopes International, reported that although 90 per cent of people believed that parents should have the main responsibility for the sex education of their children, one in six parents had not discussed sex with their teenage children. Parents 'felt embarrassed about the subject ... [they] did not feel equipped with the information they needed'. Seventeen per cent of parents of 15-year-olds were still 'intending' to discuss sex with them. There was a gap between good intentions and the reality of what parents could or would discuss.[59] The government sex education initiative during the same year aroused major media furore, misleadingly presented and sensationalised as a costly campaign to convince teenagers of the benefits of virginity.[60]

In June 2002 the *British Medical Journal* published two articles casting doubt on the claim that sex education programmes had any influence on modifying behaviour amongst adolescents. However, questions of what these programmes consisted of and the context in which they were provided raise some of the old troubling questions about what sex education is and when it should be given. There was 'some evidence that prevention programmes may need to begin much earlier than they do' (that is well before puberty). They still tend to be framed in negative rather than positive terms, focusing on the prevention of sexually-transmitted diseases and adolescent pregnancy. Adolescents themselves (who, it was noted, seldom get a chance to have any input into programmes deployed for their supposed benefit) argued that 'sex education should be more positive with less emphasis on anatomy and scare tactics' and that sexual health interventions should concentrate more on 'negotiation skills ... and communication'.[61]

The control group in the Scottish survey suggests what is presumably the usual standard. The training of the teachers involved in sex education was 'generally limited'. The schools provided seven to twelve lessons for third and fourth years, primarily supplying information with some discussion. Only two schools included demonstrations of how to handle condoms, and none of them 'systematically developed negotiation skills for sexual encounters'. However, the theoretically-based SHARE (Sexual Health and Relationships: Safe, Happy and Responsible) programme, involving active learning in small groups, development of skills and role-playing, had little better success. While pupils who had participated reported some beneficial effects on sexual relationships, and demonstrated better knowledge about sexual health, there was little impact on actual condom use for the third of the group already engaging in intercourse by the age of 16. However, longer-term effects may emerge in planned future follow-ups. The report on this study in the *British Medical Journal* also asks a question which has underlain the whole issue of sex education and continues to be troubling: what is likely to be the impact of a time-limited educational programme in the adolescent years, 'compared with long term and pervasive influences from, for instance, family, local culture and the mass media'?[62]

CONCLUSION

It is clear, therefore, that who should be talking to whom about it, when they should start talking about it, what they should be saying and whether the approach should focus on mechanics or emotions, still remain contested topics around sex education in the new millennium.

Why has sex education been such a problematic issue? For one thing, while it may be viewed as a desirable public health measure, actual implementation has been in the hands of education authorities rather than health services. Teachers are already under pressure to teach required subjects and to ensure that pupils pass the necessary exams, and sex education, being a non-examination subject, tends to get pushed down the list of priorities. This pressure also affects pupil response: 'in UK secondary schools personal and social education is perceived by pupils to require little attention or effort because there are no exams'.[63] This low priority within the educational scale of values emerges even before the sensitivity of the topic is taken into account and the concomitant reluctance to undertake classes by many teachers, who feel ill-equipped to tackle the subject and may well experience personal embarrassment at the prospect of dealing with it in front of a class.

It is also a politically touchy issue. For more than 100 years there have been many causes for anxiety over issues concerning children, sexuality and changing social mores. Nevertheless, very few of these are felt to be matters about which the individual can do anything. Sex education, however, is publicly funded through rates levied on private citizens, while it is compulsory to send children to school or else make demonstrably satisfactory alternative arrangements. This not only renders the provision of sex education a delicate area, it makes it particularly susceptible to pressures from concerned individuals and groups. It can, in fact, be seen as forming a 'soft target' for anxieties generated by wider and far less easy to influence factors in society at large, just as it has sometimes been seen as an easy-fix solution for problems generated by complex social changes. The continuing ambivalence of British attitudes towards sexual matters, which reflects wider cultural concerns over the place of sex in society and the individual, and where the boundary between public and private lies, has been an underlying element throughout.

NOTES

1   L.A. Hall, 'No sex please, we're socialists: the British Labour Party closes its eyes and thinks of the electorate', *Territoires Contemporains, Cahiers de l'IHC*, no. 8 (Dijon: L'Institut d'Histoire Contemporaine, 2003).
2   P. McHugh, *Prostitution and Victorian Social Reform* (London: Croom Helm, 1980), and J.R. Walkowitz, *Prostitution and Victorian Society: Women, Class and the State*

(Cambridge: Cambridge University Press, 1980), are two excellent accounts of this legislation and the campaign against the Acts. For a broader study of social purity and moral reform movements, see E. Bristow, *Vice and Vigilance: Purity Movements in Britain since 1700* (Dublin: Gill and Macmillan, 1977).

3 Miss Agnes Cotton, founder of the first Moral Welfare Home for Children, to Miss L.M. Hubbard, 16 July 1880/1, Autograph Letters Collection, The Women's Library, London Guildhall University.

4 Edith MacDuff to Edward Carpenter, 7 April 1894, Sheffield City Archives MSS 271/51.

5 *Shafts: A Journal for Women and the Working Classes*, edited by Margaret Shurmer Sibthorp, issues of January/February and April 1895.

6 Bristow, *Vice and Vigilance*, pp. 144–5; S. Hynes, *The Edwardian Turn of Mind* [1968], (London: Pimlico, 1991), pp. 281–7; F. Mort, *Dangerous Sexualities: Medio-moral Politics in Britain since 1830* (London: Routledge and Kegan Paul, 1984), pp. 174–6.

7 James Marchant to Patrick Geddes, 13 June 1911, 4 December 1912, 8 February 1914, Geddes papers T-GED 9/1015, T-GED 9/1124, T-GED 9/1245, University of Strathclyde.

8 H. Kean, *Deeds not Words: The Lives of Suffragette Teachers* (London: Pluto Press, 1990), p. 59; Mort, *Dangerous Sexualities*, p. 156.

9 Mort, *Dangerous Sexualities*, pp. 153–63; Board of Education file 'Health and Sex Education', PRO (Public Record Office, Kew), ED50/185.

10 Kean, *Deeds not Words*, pp. 60–2.

11 Board of Education file 'Sex Hygiene', PRO, ED22/57.

12 Sir James Marchant (ed.), *Youth and the Race: the Development and Education of Young Citizens for Worthy Parenthood; being the Fourth Report of and the Chief Evidence taken by the National Birth-rate Commission, 1920–1923* (London: Kegan Paul, Trench, Trubner, 1923), p. 2.

13 Ibid., pp. 3–8.

14 Ibid., p. 12.

15 Ibid., p. 14.

16 Mrs AW to Marie Stopes, 'ML-Gen' correspondence, Marie Stopes papers, Archives and Manuscripts, Wellcome Library for the History and Understanding of Medicine, PP/MCS/A.245.

17 M. Sutton, *'We Didn't Know Aught': A Study of Sexuality, Superstition and Death in Women's Lives in Lincolnshire during the 1930s, 40s and 50s* (Stamford: Paul Watkins, 1992), p. 48.

18 Virginia Woolf, *The Diary of Virginia Woolf: Volume 1: 1913–1919*, (ed.) A.O. Bell (Harmondsworth: Penguin, 1979), entry for Thursday, 18 April 1918, p. 141.

19 Archives of the British Social Hygiene Council, Archives and Manuscripts, Wellcome Library for the History and Understanding of Medicine, SA/BSH; Ministry of Health file 'British Social Hygiene Council: financial contributions by local authorities', PRO, MH53/1328.

20 PRO, ED50/185.

21 Transcript of a video interview with Cyril Bibby on 23 August 1981, 'History of the Central Council for Health Education', transcripts of oral history interviews by Dr Max Blythe, Archives and Manuscripts, Wellcome Library for the History and Understanding of Medicine, GC/196.

22 Cyril Bibby, 'Memorandum on Sex Instruction in Great Britain', probably for Ministry of Information, Bibby papers, Cambridge University Library Manuscripts Department, Add Ms (Additional Manuscript) 8320 II/B.

23 Board of Education Educational Pamphlet no 119, *Sex Education in Schools and Youth Organisations* (London: HMSO, 1943), PRO, ED50/185.

24 The records of Mass Observation, including those of this survey, are held in the University of Sussex Library. The report of this so-called 'Little Kinsey' was published in its entirety for the first time in L. Stanley, *Sex Surveyed, 1949–1994: From Mass Observation's 'Little Kinsey' to the National Survey and the Hite Reports* (London: Taylor and Francis, 1995).
25 Bibby/Blythe interview, GC/196.
26 Cyril Bibby, 'Memo on Sex Instruction in GB', typescript article, probably for Ministry of Information, Cambridge University Library, Add Ms 8320 II/8.
27 Cyril Bibby, 'Sex Education in Great Britain', typescript article, probably for *Health and Public Welfare Yearbook* c.1946, Cambridge University Library, Add Ms 8320 II/8.
28 Cyril Bibby, typescript article on sex education for Ministry of Information, c.1946, Cambridge University Library, Add Ms 8320 II/8.
29 F.A. Harper, 'Notes on sex education in schools' (Brief for the Minister of Housing and Local Government), 25 August 1964, PRO, ED50/862.
30 Cyril Bibby, 'Sex Education, an *Education* Digest', *Education*, 21 July 1972; correspondence with Kevin Crossley-Holland of Macmillan, 1968, Cambridge University Library, Add Ms 8320, VIII/49.
31 Annotation by Bibby on letter from Kevin Crossley-Holland of Macmillan, 7 June 1968, Cambridge University Library, Add Ms 8320 VIII/49.
32 L.A. Hall. 'Venereal diseases and society in Britain, from the Contagious Diseases Acts to the National Health Service', and D. Evans, 'Sexually-transmitted Disease Policy in the English National Health Service, 1948–2000: Continuity and Social Change', in R. Davidson and L.A. Hall (eds), *Sex, Sin, and Suffering: Venereal Disease and European Society since 1870* (London: Routledge, 2001), pp. 120–36, 237–52.
33 Bibby/Blythe interview, GC/196.
34 Audrey Whiting, 'They all funk telling schoolgirls', *Sunday Pictorial*, 30 January 1955, Bibby papers, Cambridge University Library, Add Ms 8320 III/15.
35 G. Sturrock of the Ministry of Education to Miss J. E. Ockeen, 28 November 1961, 'Sex education', PRO, ED50/862.
36 Harper, 'Notes on sex education', PRO, ED50/862.
37 Katharine Hadley, *Daily Express*, 28 March 1969, Family Planning Association archives, Archives and Manuscripts, Wellcome Library for the History and Understanding of Medicine, 'Press cuttings: sex education', SA/FPA/A.17/122.
38 Harper, 'Notes on sex education', PRO, ED50/862.
39 Danda Humphreys, 'Careers extraordinary: One over the Eight of a team of travelling teachers', *Nursing Times*, 68, 19 (11 May 1972), pp. 578–80. I am indebted to Anne Caron-Delion for bringing the Tampax Educational Service to my attention.
40 *Guardian*, 6 April 1962, SA/FPA/A.17/117.
41 *The Medical Officer*, 1 May 1964, SA/FPA/A.17/117.
42 *The Times*, 26 November 1963, SA/FPA/A.17/117.
43 *Shrewsbury Chronicle*, 15 November 1963, SA/FPA/A.17/117.
44 *The Times*, 2 October 1964, SA/FPA/A.17/117.
45 'Note of meeting held in the Ministry of Health on 15th March on VD health education', Ministry of Health file 'Sex education: venereal disease', PRO, MH151/76.
46 'Health education training: pamphlet 49', PRO, ED50/864.
47 'Royal Commission on Medical Education: Draft report: suggested passage on sex education', PRO, ED128/18.
48 SA/FPA/A.17/122.
49 Colin Mackenzie, *Daily Express*, 10 October 1969, SA/FPA/A.17/122.
50 James Kelsey, *Pulse*, 16 August 1969; *Nottingham Evening Post*, 28 March 1969, SA/FPA/A.17/122.

51 *Crawley Observer*, 21 February 1969; *Scottish Daily Express*, 15 March 1969, SA/FPA/A.17/122.
52 *Daily Mail*, 10 June 1969, SA/FPA/A.17/122.
53 P. Ferris, *Sex and the British: A Twentieth-Century History* (London: Michael Joseph, 1993), pp. 239–43; A. Leathard, *The Fight for Family Planning: The Development of Family Planning Services in Britain, 1921–1974* (London: Macmillan, 1980), pp. 148–56.
54 I. Allen, *Education in Sex and Personal Relationships: Policy Studies Institute Research Report No. 665* (London: Policy Studies Institute, 1987).
55 Carol Lee, an FPA sex educator, gives a fascinating if saddening account of her work in *The Ostrich Position: Sex, Schooling and Mystification* (London: Writers and Readers, 1983), and discusses the wider issues around the politics of sex education and the 'moral right' backlash in *Friday's Child: The Threat to Moral Education* (Wellingborough: Thorsons, 1988).
56 M. Durham, *Sex and Politics: The Family and Morality in the Thatcher Years* (London: Macmillan, 1991), pp. 99–122; A. Wolpe, 'Sex in Schools: Back to the Future', *Feminist Review*, 27 (1987), pp. 37–47; Allen, *Education in Sex and Personal Relationships*; Lee, *The Ostrich Position, Friday's Child*.
57 Durham, *Sex and Politics*, pp. 111–18; D. Monk, 'Beyond Section 28: Law, Governance, and Sex Education', in L.J. Moran, D. Monk and S. Beresford, *Legal Queeries: Lesbian, Gay, and Transgender Legal Studies* (London: Cassell, 1998), pp. 96–112; S. Reinhold, 'Through the Parliamentary Looking Glass: "Real" and "Pretend" Families in Contemporary British Politics', *Feminist Review*, 48 (1994), pp. 61–79.
58 *Guardian*, report and leading article, 24 March 1994.
59 'One in six parents shirk sex education', *Guardian*, 25 October 2000.
60 Mary Riddell, 'Oops, they did it again', *Observer*, 15 October 2000.
61 A. DiCenso, G. Guyatt, A. Willan and L. Griffith, 'Interventions to Reduce Unintended Pregnancies among Adolescents: A Systematic Review of Randomised Controlled Trials', *British Medical Journal*, 324 (15 June 2002), pp. 1426–30.
62 D. Wight, G.M. Raab, M. Henderson, C. Abraham, K. Buston, G. Hart and S. Scott, 'Limits of Teacher-delivered Sex Education: Interim Behavioural Outcomes from Randomised Trial', *British Medical Journal*, 324 (15 June 2002), pp. 1430–3.
63 Wight *et al.*, 'Limits of Teacher-delivered Sex Education'.

6

DOMESTIC SCIENCE: THE EDUCATION OF GIRLS AT HOME

Susan Williams

INTRODUCTION

There is no shortage of books and articles about girls and women at school and at university. Historians of education in Britain, especially feminists, have written with energy and enthusiasm about women's entry into formal education – their struggles and their achievements as students and as teachers.[1] This work has uncovered many important strands in the history of female education, which are necessary for our understanding of the past and for the development of plans for the future. But there are other important strands that have been neglected. These strands relate to the kinds of knowledge transmission that have taken place over the centuries within the family and the home.

Up to now, historians of education have focused almost exclusively on the 'public' domain: on schools, colleges and other institutions. They have largely ignored those domains of activity that traditionally have been at the centre of women's lives. This is an odd phenomenon, given that the private sphere itself has received so much attention recently from historians. Tremendous efforts have been made to render visible the strands of life that have previously been hidden from view: the life of 'ordinary' people within the home. This work has been given authority in the academic world by the establishment over the past few decades of a field of enquiry called 'social history' and also by the concerns of sociology with the detail of domestic life.

But nobody seems to have looked at *education* within the home. Even Deirdre Beddoe, whose imaginative approach to women's history is nothing less than pioneering and who warns her reader against neglecting the less obvious strands of women's history, fails to acknowledge that any kind of education takes place in the domestic arena. Her book *Discovering Women's History* (1983) has a substantial chapter on 'The education of girls' – but this chapter is entirely devoted to 'formal' education.[2]

The almost exclusive interest of historians of education in schooling, rather than knowledge transmission in the home, may be an outcome of their own experience. For as successful academics, they must have performed well at school and university – and so they may value these worlds highly. Those who have done less well at school may feel that they learned more from their home environment – but they are unlikely to find themselves working as historians in an academic setting, writing scholarly accounts of the history of knowledge and knowledge transmission. It is important to bear this kind of self-selection in mind when reading the work of historians of education.

One book on the history of educating girls that *has* explored the role of education within the home is Carol Dyhouse's study of *Girls Growing Up in Late Victorian and Edwardian England* (1981). One of her major purposes in writing the book, she explains in the introduction, was 'to show that the majority of girls living in the period 1860–1920 received at least a crucial part – if not the major part – of their education in the family, and not through schooling of any kind'. As she points out, 'This work differs from most histories of women's education.'[3] But Dyhouse finds little of value in the domestic sphere – of anything that might qualify as 'education'. In her view, it serves simply to reinforce concepts of 'femininity' and feminine behaviour, representing economic and intellectual dependency. These concepts are associated by Dyhouse with the suppression of ambition, of intellectual courage or initiative, and of any desire for power or independence.[4] She is right to present these concepts as complicated and problematic. But this is not the whole story. Many women today and in the past might take issue with her assumptions and conclusions. They might regard the teaching of women and by women, in the home and the community, as an appropriate kind of education for their girls – whether in combination with schooling, independently of it, or even despite it. And would it be right to accuse these women of false consciousness?

MOTHERS AND EDUCATION

The meanings of the terms 'private' and 'public' in relation to education, as well as 'formal' and 'informal', have been explored in the introduction to this book. So, too, have the characteristics of 'education', 'teaching' and 'schooling'. It is not therefore necessary to pursue those definitions here, except to draw attention to the fact that very often one's understanding of these terms is informed by issues of gender. For it is a historical fact that whereas the traditional centre of women's lives has been the home and the 'private' sphere, the centre of men's lives has been the 'public' world. This is a generalisation and there are many exceptions and variations, but it represents a basic truth.

Today it is assumed that 'education' takes place outside the home, in the public world. But for most of history, as Averil Evans McClelland has observed in a history of the education of women in the United States, 'mothers have been considered important teachers'. One of the consequences of the emergence of the school as the central agency of education and the professionalisation of teaching, she adds, is a diminution of the perception that mothers have valuable knowledge to offer their children. Rather, beliefs centre now on expectations that the mother would prepare her children to behave well in school, but avoid trying to 'teach' them anything that they might learn in the classroom. But this has only recently become the case. Indeed, she adds, 'the role of the mother in the education of her children has been one of the most important rationales for educating women at all'.[5]

Female knowledge, which has been handed down between grandmothers, mothers and daughters over generations, and between female members of a community, has been fundamental to the processes of human and social survival. The kind of teaching traditionally performed by women in the home fits largely into three categories. The first category is reading, writing and arithmetic, which in more privileged households may extend to languages, geography and other subjects. The second category is domestic management and economy, which is clearly class-specific. Working-class girls learnt how to manage a home – shopping, cooking, cleaning, mending, making clothes, gardening, baby and child care. Middle-class and upper-class girls learnt from their mothers (or their governesses) how to run a household, manage servants, organise a dinner party, follow etiquette, draw and play the piano. The third category relates to values, morality and sometimes religion – a kind of education that was found in every class, though not every home. The Duchess of Atholl, who was the first Conservative woman MP and the Parliamentary Secretary at the Board of Education from 1924 to 1929, asserted the importance to society of this kind of education. 'Have we realised', she asked, 'how much the simple day to day lessons of the home, which bring so many women in contact with the big realities of life, moral, physical, and economic, *can guide us to wise decisions in national affairs*?'[6]

In *Middlemarch* (1871), George Eliot's novel of provincial life in the mid-nineteenth century, we are presented with a mother who is a teacher of all things to her children – moral values and also grammar. This mother is Mrs Garth, who assumes her educating role in the midst of a busy kitchen:

> Mrs Garth at certain hours was always in the kitchen, and this morning she was carrying on several occupations at once there – making her pies at the well-scoured deal table on one side of that airy room … and giving

lessons to her youngest boy and girl, who were standing opposite to her at the table with their books and slates before them. A tub and a clothes-horse at the other end of the kitchen indicated an intermittent wash of small things also going on.

Mrs Garth, with her sleeves turned above her elbows, deftly handling her pastry – applying her rolling-pin and giving ornamental pinches, while she expounded with grammatical fervour what were the right views about the concord of verbs and pronouns with 'nouns of multitude or signifying many', was a sight agreeably amusing. ...

She takes this role seriously. When asked by one of her children to justify these lessons, she explains severely that it is 'To teach you to speak and write correctly, so that you can be understood.'[7]

But from the last decades of the nineteenth century, Britain was evolving into a society where learning at home was relegated to the bottom of the pedagogic hierarchy. 'Public' knowledge – that is knowledge dispensed in institutions – moved to the top. Increasingly, too, 'public' knowledge was associated with progress and science and was regarded as 'scientific'. One moment in this evolution is captured in Molly Hughes' childhood memoirs, *A London Girl of the 1880s* (1945). Here, Hughes described the clash of cultures between the kind of education dispensed at home by her mother, and her schooling at the North London Collegiate School. She recalled that not long after her first term began, she went home and told her mother about the new subjects she was going to learn. 'Mother was properly impressed by the title "Political Economy" of which she had never so much as heard', she recorded. But she was puzzled by the subject called 'Domestic Economy'. At first she assumed that this was an area she knew about – but 'she became meeker', records Hughes, 'when I began after a time to talk familiarly of hydrogenous foodstuffs and carbohydrates. "Foodstuffs!" exclaimed her mother, "what a funny word!"' In fact, Hughes learnt far more about cooking from her mother at home than she ever did from her teachers at school. In the family kitchen she learnt how to make a rice pudding blindfold:

'You take a pie-dish.'
'What size?'
'Oh, the ordinary size. Put some well-washed rice in it.'
'How much?'
'Enough to cover the bottom. Then add a bit of butter.'
'How big a bit?'
'As big as a walnut. Then add salt and sugar.'
'How much?'
'Oh, as much as you think will do. Then bake in a *very slow* oven.'

'For how long?'
'Until it seems to be done.'

The lessons at school, on the other hand, were wasted. 'Nothing whatever remained to me of those recipes at school', wrote Hughes, 'nor of the elaborate menus for a family of seven, and I never had any idea whether my sons were consuming carbon or what'.[8]

ON THE BRIDGE

Discussions of the history of education today tend to privilege formal education over non-formal education. But this has not been inevitable. Rather, it has involved a set of choices. One key moment for making such choices, at least for girls and women in Britain, was the inter-war period. For in the 1930s, many women found themselves entering new territory – the world of public life, which had previously been dominated by men. Up to that point, they had been confined to a private world within the home and the community. Now, however, the passing of various laws had changed their status and rights. Chief among these was the Sex Disqualification Removal Act, which in 1919 made women eligible for the professions and for the holding of any civil or judicial post. Then, in 1928 (following the extension of the vote in 1919 to women aged 30 and over), women won the vote on an equal basis with men. Women were still second-class citizens, because their rights were limited in comparison with men. Most women still had to depend on men for financial support, and even when they were able to work their pay was far below that of men. But now at least they were no longer confined to the domestic sphere. 'The door of the private house', wrote the feminist author Virginia Woolf in her essay, *Three Guineas* (1938), 'was thrown open'.[9]

However, many women did not regard these new rights simply as an opportunity to give up women's ways of doing things and to have a slice of men's cake. Rather, these rights were seen as an opportunity to decide on the best way of enhancing the quality of women's lives and of enabling them to contribute to society. Women were now living in a 'moment of transition', observed Virginia Woolf – 'on the bridge which connects the private house with the world of public life'.[10] It was perceived as a unique historical moment, in which nothing was certain and everything seemed possible. 'A whole world', wrote the Duchess of Atholl in *Women and Politics* (1931), 'is waiting to see what we make of it'.[11]

A particular concern for Woolf and other feminists of the time was education: what kind of education should be developed for women and girls? There was a consensus that girls and women should have access to well-funded education and to the resources needed for this – but this was not the same as assuming that the education established for boys and men, by men, was the best way forward for girls. Woolf explored this issue in *Three Guineas*, which is about education, exclusion and war, and in *A Room of One's Own* (1928), which is about education, exclusion and writing. 'It would be a thousand pities', argued Woolf, 'if women wrote like men, or lived like men, or looked like men, for if two sexes are quite inadequate, considering the vastness and variety of the world, how should we manage with one only? *Ought not education*', she added, '*to bring out and fortify the differences and similarities*?'[12]

Woolf saw an advantage in the maintenance of separate spheres, because she was sceptical about the values of the public – male – world. 'There they go', she observed with some contempt, 'our brothers who have been educated at public schools and universities, mounting those steps, passing in and out of those doors, ascending those pulpits ... a caravanserai crossing a desert. Great-grandfathers, grandfathers, fathers, uncles – they all went that way. ...'[13] Speaking as a representative of the newly enfranchised women of Britain, caught up in a moment of transition on the bridge between the private and public worlds, she set out the following challenge:

> We are here, on the bridge, to ask ourselves certain questions. And they are very important questions; and we have very little time in which to answer them. The questions that we have to ask and to answer about that procession during this moment of transition are so important they may well change the lives of men and women for ever for we have to ask ourselves, here and now, do we wish to join that procession, or don't we? On what terms shall we join that procession? Above all, where is it leading us, the procession of educated men?[14]

Woolf urged her women readers to ask themselves whether they *really* wanted to join the 'procession' of men and, if so, on what terms? With a scornful reference to the regalia and costumes of the public world, she asked, 'Who can say whether, as time goes on, we [too] may not dress in military uniform, with gold lace on our breasts, swords at our sides, and something like the old family coal-scuttle on our heads?'[15]

SCHOOL VERSUS HOME

Woolf's perspective is a limited and a particular one, because it reflects the position of an upper-middle-class woman and does not take into consideration the relevance of social class. However, her concerns about how best to organise the entry of girls into the world of 'public' education are apparent also in the reaction of many other people to the introduction of universal schooling in the late nineteenth century. Ever since the passing of W.E. Forster's Elementary Act in 1870, there have been various kinds of struggle between the state and the private life of the home. Many parents in the late nineteenth century were hostile to the principle of compulsory education. Some regretted the loss of their children's income and help in the home, but many also resented the interference of the state in their private lives. The School boards employed attendance officers or School Visitors, many of whom were retired policemen or ex-non-commissioned officers from the armed forces, to make sure that children went to school. 'What a business it was', observed the preface to *Recollections of a School Attendance Officer* by John Reeves (1913), 'to get the children into the schools'.[16]

The children affected by Forster's Act were largely working class. One stated aim for getting them into school was to influence them with middle-class values – not simply to impart knowledge, but to integrate them into 'civilised' society and to help them to acquire 'culture'. In an essay called 'The Elementary Schools of London', which was appended to the London County Council's *Annual Report* for 1925, a District Inspector, P.B. Ballard, described the elementary school as a gateway to culture – 'a sensitiveness to higher and nobler things and the acquisition of some of the graces and refinements of civilised life'. In some quarters of London, he said, it was 'part of the teacher's work to turn uncouth boys and girls, grimy and inarticulate, into decent members of society, with some small measure of grace of speech and charm of manner'. [17] The school was seen as a place where 'proper' values were taught, compensating the child for the unsatisfactory values learnt in the family.

The Care Committees of London, a network of voluntary committees that were created by the London County Council to care for children's welfare needs at school, saw their role as one of 'rescuing' the child from its family. On the one hand, the Care Committees aimed to provide a bridge between home and school. 'We must unite the home with the school education', insisted Miss Margaret Frere, the pioneer of the system, in 1909. 'Education', she added, 'means growth in grace and in the formation of character, and this cannot be if the home and the school are opposed.' But on the other hand, she insisted that, 'We must ... build up homes where the virtues taught in schools can flourish.' [18] She did *not* say that schools must be built up where the virtues taught in *homes* can flourish. In her view, 'Unwholesome surroundings and overwork out of school hours were *partly* to blame for the condition of the children, but *indolent, incompetent mothers far more so.*'[19] One function of the elementary school, therefore, was to remove children for at least a few hours a day from the negative influence of the home and the mother.

Some feminists of the inter-war period took a different position. They chose to support mothers in their care of children in the home, not to find ways of taking the children away. Once the struggle for the franchise had been won, many women campaigners concerned themselves with women's welfare in the home, in a movement called New Feminism. A major strand of this movement was the Family Endowment Society, which had been set up years before by Eleanor Rathbone, a feminist and social reformer who was an Independent MP. The chief objective of the Family Endowment Society was to put public funds in the purses of working-class mothers, to help them in their efforts to care for their families. 'The endowment of motherhood', argued a campaign leaflet, is 'the most urgent question of the hour'.[20] The campaign for family allowances led finally to the introduction in 1945 of a regular and universal payment of family allowances, which was paid directly to the mother. This was a real success for the support of women in the home, but a fairly isolated one.

BACK TO BASICS

The moment of transition between the private and public worlds, as defined by Woolf, is over. As it turned out, women *did* adopt the regalia of the public world that so far had been the prerogative of men. Women university students, just like men, can be seen wearing the equivalent of something like Woolf's coal-scuttles on their heads at graduation ceremonies all over Britain. Of course, these are only clothes and costumes, but they are symbolic of an overall acceptance of the principles of the 'male' values in education described by Woolf.

And today, at the start of the twenty-first century in Britain, there is barely any recognition of the educative role of the home. National policy on education reflects this in every way. Instead of supporting mothers to look after their children at home and to complement the work of the teacher at school by teaching them domestic arts and other skills needed for survival, mothers (and especially single mothers) are expected by the state to go out to work. Resources are put not into the purses of mothers, as campaigned for by Eleanor Rathbone. Instead, they are put into the creation of After School Clubs, to baby-sit the children until their mother finishes work. The home does not seem to matter much any more, writes the feminist sociologist Ann Oakley, 'except as a retreat from the public world'.[21]

Mothers continue, of course, to educate their children on a daily basis. Almost any journey on a bus or train, outside commuter hours, serves as a reminder of this work. Mothers are heard reading to children and teaching them values (like consideration for other passengers) and skills (how to juggle pocket money). But has the teaching of recipes and other specialised forms of education in the home continued in the homes of British families into the twenty-first century? Probably not, because mothers increasingly need to spend their time earning an income. There are few hours left over, once work is finished and the family are fed, to concentrate on teaching children how to cook or how to knit a sock.

This may explain the best-selling success of Delia Smith's cookery books – a set of three volumes entitled *Delia's How To Cook*, which purport to teach 'back to basics' cooking. Book 1 is specifically dedicated to 'the young cooks of Britain' and the introduction of Book 3 observes that:

> What I sincerely hope for now is that, collectively, the three volumes of *How To Cook* will provide a sound basis for any young person (or, indeed, older person) who wants to begin to cook well but lacks the knowledge.[22]

So very 'back to basics' is Delia Smith's cookery course that she covers topics like the selection of saucepans and knives. This is the kind of information that a daughter might have expected to pick up in her mother's kitchen in previous generations. A high level of ignorance is assumed and the first book even includes careful instructions on how to make toast, with such obvious advice as, 'A toast rack is absolutely necessary if you want to avoid soggy toast; failing that, prop the slices up against a jar for a minute or so before serving.' The instructions given are precise and straightforward, but are dressed up in a language that is reassuringly mum-like and recalls the recipe for rice pudding learnt by Molly Hughes: 'if the bread is slightly wonky'; 'nasty black smoke signals'; 'keep an eye on it and don't wander far away'.[23]

CONCLUSION

We need to develop a thoughtful and rigorous historical account of girls' and women's education in the home, based on reliable evidence. We need to identify the forms of this type of education, the ways in which they have been delivered, the hierarchy of teachers, the evolution of these learning activities and the ways in which they have changed over time. We also need to unpick the implicit theories that served as a framework for these learning activities. All this will be difficult to investigate. Not surprisingly, as Beddoe has pointed out, 'there are few documentary sources which throw light on women's home lives'.[24] But as she also observes, there *are* ways of finding out more, so long as one is determined and imaginative. These include oral testimony, journals and diaries, paintings, fiction, recipes, women's magazines and photographs.

Further work on methodology includes *Researching Women's Lives from a Feminist Perspective*, edited by Mary Maynard and June Purvis (1994),[25] and there is a large body of sociological literature that may prove useful to this kind of study.

Once a start has been made to unearth the history of education within the home, an attempt can then be made to explore its relationship with education in the public world. Did these forms of education complement each other? Did they compete? Or was the story far more complicated than such simplistic questions suggest? Did the relationship change over time? These questions can also be applied to *boys'* education: what did they learn in the home, from their fathers and their mothers? What did they learn from their sisters? What did they *not* learn? Are there lessons to be learned about the positive influence of the domestic sphere, which could be usefully applied to the raising of boys? This is an obvious question to ask, given that at the start of the twenty-first century girls are now outperforming boys in public examinations. It is surely no longer adequate for feminists simply to describe the traditional world of men as best and desirable; it is time to look without bitterness at our own history and to identify and trace those aspects of our upbringing that are uniquely female.

This work should not be simply descriptive. Of course, it will be exciting to celebrate the history of our mothers and our grandmothers. But a rigorous and analytical approach needs to be taken – one which examines the nature of interactions between women and men, girls and boys, and the relationships between the 'public' and 'private' domains of society and between formal and informal education. The study of women's education, both at home and in the public world, offers an ideal opportunity to develop this kind of research. Only by looking for – and looking at – the whole spectrum of women's education, will we come close to a real understanding of the relationship between the history of the past, the nature of the present and the possibilities for the future.

NOTES

1   For example: M. Bryant, *The Unexpected Revolution* (London: University of London Institute of Education, 1979); D.M. Copelman, *London's Women Teachers: Gender, Class and Feminism* (London: Routledge, 1996); C. Dyhouse, *Girls Growing Up in Late Victorian and Edwardian England* (London: Routledge and Kegan Paul, 1981); C. Dyhouse, *No Distinction of Sex? Women in British Universities, 1870–1939* (London: UCL Press, 1995); F. Hunt (ed.), *Lessons for Life: The Schooling of Girls and Women* (Oxford: Blackwell, 1987); F. Hunt, *Gender and Policy in English Education, 1902–1944* (London: Harvester/Wheatsheaf, 1991); J. Purvis, *A History of Women's Education in England* (Milton Keynes: Open University Press, 1991); J. Purvis, *Hard Lessons: The Lives and Education of Working Women in Nineteenth Century England* (Cambridge: Polity Press, 1993).

2   D. Beddoe, *Discovering Women's History* [1983], (London: Longman, 3rd edn 1998).
3   Dyhouse, *Girls Growing Up*, p. 1.
4   Ibid., p. 2.
5   A.E. McClelland, *The Education of Women in the United States. A Guide to Theory, Teaching and Research* (New York: Garland, 1992), p. 21.
6   Katharine, Duchess of Atholl, *Women and Politics* (London: Philip Allan, 1931), p. 4. Emphasis added.
7   George Eliot, *Middlemarch* [1871–2], (Harmondsworth: Penguin, 1972), pp. 276–7.
8   M.V. Hughes, *A London Girl of the 1880s* [1946], (Oxford: Oxford University Press, 1978), pp. 42–3. There is no mention of milk in the rice pudding recipe.
9   Virginia Woolf, *Three Guineas* [1938], (London: Hogarth Press, 1986), p. 19.
10 Ibid., p. 22.
11 Katharine, Duchess of Atholl, *Women and Politics*, p. 177.
12 Virginia Woolf, *A Room of One's Own* [1928], (London: Penguin, 1945), p. 87. Emphasis added.
13 Woolf, *Three Guineas*, p. 70.
14 Ibid., p. 72.
15 Ibid., pp. 71–2.
16 Stewart Headlam, 'Preface', to John Reeves, *Recollections of a School Attendance Officer* (London: Arthur H. Stockwell, 1913), p. v.
17 P. Ballard, 'The Elementary Schools of London', Appendix I of LCC Annual Report 1925, *Education*, p. 38.
18 Margaret Frere, *Children's Care Committees* (London: P.S. King, 1909), p. 2.
19 LCC Education Committee – General Purposes Subcommittee, 'Report (22 March 1961). For members' information only – S.O.', p. 24. Private collection. Emphasis added.
20 Quoted in S. Fleming, 'Introduction', 1986, in Eleanor Rathbone, *The Disinherited Family* [1924], (Bristol: Falling Wall Press, 1986), p. 70.
21. A. Oakley, *Man and Wife. Richard and Kay Titmuss: My Parents' Early Years* (London: HarperCollins, 1996), p. 4.
22 D. Smith, *Delia's How To Cook*, Book 3 (London: BBC, 2001), p. 9.
23 D. Smith, *Delia's How To Cook*, Book 1 (London, BBC, 1999), p. 83.
24 Ibid., p. 144.
25 M. Maynard and J. Purvis (eds), *Researching Women's Lives from a Feminist Perspective* (London: Taylor and Francis, 1994).

7

FAMILY HISTORY AND THE HISTORY OF THE FAMILY

Richard Aldrich

INTRODUCTION

Family history is no doubt as old as history itself, indeed it has been argued that just as the family was the oldest and most basic unit in society, so family history was 'the ancestor and root of all other forms of historical enquiry'.[1] Nevertheless there has been no single historical model of the family. Indeed, a recent estimate identified 'as many as two hundred different arrangements that Europeans and Americans now regard as legitimate "family"'.[2] Nor should families be placed exclusively within the private sphere. In 1973 Barbara Laslett adduced a considerable amount of evidence in support of the hypothesis that in the USA the private family 'is a modern development which has only occurred within this century'.[3]

Families are not only concerned with history, the doings of their contemporaries and forbears, but also, as the previous chapter demonstrates, with education and knowledge, both private and public. Over the centuries children have learned their first social and cultural skills, from toilet training to speech, within a family context. During the modern period, however, in England as in many other parts of the world, the concept of the educative family was complemented or replaced by the rise of the schooled society. This chapter locates family history, including its dimensions of knowledge and education, within a variety of contexts, both private and public. It is divided into three parts. The first deals with the 'public' dimensions of what is here referred to as 'the history of the family'. The second examines the 'private' sphere – family history as represented by research undertaken by individuals into their own families. The third section provides a case study by means of an examination of an aspect of the author's family history. Finally some conclusions are drawn. These relate to the problems and possibilities of reconciling private and public knowledge in respect of family history and to its potential role in histories of education and of knowledge.

PUBLIC: THE HISTORY OF THE FAMILY

Examples of family history in England can be traced from the later middle ages. The major era for the formation of hereditary English surnames has been placed between 1250 and 1450.[4] This chronology has a general acceptance in the 'Western' world. Thus a conference on surnames that took place at Lyons in France in December 1998 was 'limited to those European and North American societies in which surnames were established, according to codified rules, before the sixteenth century; and which had records allowing for the study of the transmission of surnames over generations'.[5] In England in the fifteenth century, John Rous made a collection of more than 50 genealogies, while William Worcester listed the pedigrees of ancient Norfolk families. Such lists of names and dates were soon complemented by more substantial studies. In the sixteenth century, the Elizabethan Society of Antiquaries, which included leading historians, William Lambarde and John Stow, provided an impetus to further work, for example the production of county histories.[6] Another famous Elizabethan scholar, the antiquary and historian, William Camden, best known for his survey, *Britannia*, first published in 1586, provided an important account of the formation and development of surnames. Motives were mixed. While some scholars sought to produce objective works of reference, other studies were conducted by, or on behalf of, family members for the specific purpose of legitimising power and influence, enhancing their family status and of confirming (sometimes spurious) claims to land and property. In England during the later sixteenth century, a fashion arose not only of constructing elaborate family trees, but also of displaying them as works of art.[7]

The late nineteenth and early twentieth centuries saw significant advances in historical study in England. Amateur and antiquarian approaches to the study of the past came under attack. The recognition of history as a public discipline, conducted in accordance with generally recognised rules and conventions, was aided by such developments as the foundation of the *English Historical Review* in 1886 and the establishment of important schools of history at the newer universities, most notably London and Manchester. Some prospective school teachers received training in the teaching of history, which from the 1870s became an accepted subject in the higher classes of elementary schools. Government regulations of 1904 made it a compulsory subject at secondary level. The Historical Association, founded in 1906, provided a forum in which members from these different constituencies could pool their professional historical expertise. Its first council included eleven university staff, nine from secondary schools and four from training colleges.

Prior to the 1960s, practitioners of the public discipline of history dealt mainly with public events and public figures. Biographical studies might encompass both the 'life and work' of such public figures and even, on occasion, as with Lytton Strachey's *Eminent Victorians* (1918), highlight some of their foibles. In general, however, the lives of ordinary people and of their families were not believed to be appropriate subjects of study for professional historians. Nor was the family itself. This was partly because such matters were considered to be essentially private, and of private interest. Concerns also existed about the nature and extent of possible sources. In 1960 the situation changed dramatically with the publication of Philippe Ariès, *L'Enfant et la vie familiale sous l'Ancien Régime*.[8] Henceforth childhood and the family, two of the most private dimensions of human existence, would become legitimate subjects of study for professional historians. They would also become part of the public discipline that is history. Thus following an international conference held at Clark University in November 1985, Tamara K. Hareven, editor of the *Journal of Family History*, could not only look back with some pride at the contributions made by the journal during the first ten years of its existence, but could also declare that 'The time has come, therefore, to assess twenty years of research in this field, and to identify the main goals of future research.'[9]

Although on occasion the term, 'family history', was employed to describe the work of both amateur and professional historians, a division was also apparent between what came to be known as 'family history' on the one hand and 'the history of the family' on the other. For example, in 1980 in a short work entitled, *Approaches to the History of the Western Family 1500–1914*, Michael Anderson, Professor of Economic History at the University of Edinburgh, noted that 'Over the past twenty years family history has been one of the main growth areas in the development of social history.'[10] As his title indicated, however, for Anderson family history did not mean the investigation of an individual family by one of its members, but rather research by university-based professionals into the family as an historical phenomenon. Other academic writers stressed the interdisciplinary nature of the history of the family. Thus in a contribution to an important collection of essays of 1973, all of which had originally appeared in the *Journal of Interdisciplinary History*, Hareven argued that 'the history of the family utilizes the tools of demography and the conceptual models of anthropology, psychology, and sociology'.[11]

Anderson identified four broad approaches to the history of the western family in the modern era – psychohistory, 'the demographic, the sentiments and the household economics'.[12] He also associated each of these approaches with particular groups of professional historians and their publications.

Thus the work of the psychohistorians, to which Anderson gave very short shrift indeed, was exemplified by *The Journal of Psychohistory* and Lloyd de Mause's edited volume of 1974.[13] The demographic approach to the history of the family was traced to family reconstitution studies emanating from France from the mid-1950s. This approach, which was based upon the accumulation of data from such sources as parish registers and tax returns, was associated with the *Société de Demographie Historique*, established by Louis Henry in 1966. It was exemplified in the United Kingdom by the Cambridge Group for the History of Population and Social Structure. Peter Laslett and other professional historians associated with this group were not particularly interested in the details of individual families. Their prime aim was the collection and analysis of banks of data in order to pose and answer questions about the size and composition of households and families in general.[14]

As Anderson acknowledged in 1980, data collected by the demographers clearly provided a much sounder basis for the historical study of the family than previous unsystematic and impressionistic accounts that drew upon very limited evidence. Nevertheless, sophisticated interpretation of these statistics would require them to be located within appropriate socio-economic settings. Members of the household economics group, including Anderson himself, sought to interpret data about households and families 'in the context of the economic behaviour of their families'.[15] Anderson used the themes of inheritance, peasant family economy and the proletarianisation of labour to review the work of these scholars.[16]

The sentiments approach, which concentrated upon continuities and changes within the meaning of families, was not so readily identified with groups of historians or particular projects. Matters of sentiment such as modes of child-rearing, attitudes towards love, sex and illegitimacy, the very concept of privacy within the family itself, were less susceptible to statistical accumulation and analysis. Nevertheless, the key texts identified by Anderson as representative of this school, for example Philippe Ariès, *Centuries of Childhood* (1962),[17] and Edward Shorter, *The Making of the Modern Family* (1975),[18] also emanated from professional historians.

Both books proved to be highly contentious and generated a series of responses. Ariès gained support from those who agreed that there was no real concept of childhood in the middle ages and that childhood was subsequently 'invented', for example in the late eighteenth and early nineteenth centuries by writers such as Rousseau and Blake who replaced the concept of original sin with that of children's innocence. An alternative view was that there were many concepts of childhood across the centuries, while parents' attitudes towards their children were governed as much by individual circumstance and temperament as by general concepts.[19]

Shorter's work provoked even more controversy. Few doubted its importance. Ariès declared it to be 'truly excellent ... a powerful synthesis presented with a logical rigor and grace rare among historians',[20] while Anderson referred to it as 'an immensely stimulating book'.[21] Nevertheless Anderson also declared *The Making of the Modern Family* to be 'marred by a distracting style, some grossly inflated generalisation on the basis of minimal data (sometimes used out of context) and an over-emphasis on vaguely conceptualised cultural causation'.[22] In the preface to the paperback edition Shorter, Professor of History at the University of Toronto, noted that he had expected his work, conceived in 'the frosted glass of my ivory tower', to have been read by 'a somnolent audience of historians picking away at minute quarrels in the remoter reaches of the library stacks'. Instead, to his surprise, he found that he had 'landed in a hornet's nest of feminists, Marxists and caretakers of academic prose'.[23]

Over the last 20 years interest among professional historians in the history of the family and of childhood has continued. Further levels of sophistication have been introduced. For example, in an important volume published in 1989 Carol Dyhouse examined feminist thinking about the family during the period 1880 to 1939. In the introduction she noted that historical studies of feminism in England in the late nineteenth and early twentieth centuries had tended to concentrate on public issues such as the suffrage movement and educational reform rather than on the private domain of the family. Her examination of women's experiences of family life, their economic independence within the family, domestic organisation and marital relationships was based upon exhaustive research into a wide range of sources. Nevertheless, the private nature of family history or the history of the family continues to pose considerable challenges for professional historians. Dyhouse concluded that 'large areas of women's experience in the family remain shadowy'.[24] The relationship between women's history and the history of the family is an intriguing one and too substantial to be considered in detail here. Nevertheless Dyhouse's analysis of the different historiographical trajectories of these two fields in respect of private and public has been confirmed by other studies. For example, Louise A. Tilly conducted a systematic analysis of the content of articles published in the period between 1976 and 1985 in the *Journal of Family History*, three 'self-defined feminist or women's studies journals' and four general historical journals. She concluded that 'women's history, unlike family history, is movement history: it is closer to more central historical fields'.[25]

The professional historian who contributes to the public discipline of history is also a private individual, a member of a family. For example, Edward Shorter dedicated his book to the memory of his grandparents. At first sight, *A World of Their Own Making: Myth, Ritual, and the Quest for Family Values* by John R. Gillis, although dedicated to his wife, sons and a daughter-in-law, is also a public piece, a history of the family rather than family history. The first of the book's three parts surveys the meanings of family and home 'before the modern age'; the second, the 'Victorian origins of modern family cultures'. Part three is entitled 'mythic figures in the suburban landscape'; the conclusion is devoted to 'remaking our worlds' in the context of 'myths and rituals for a global era'. Yet, as Gillis explained in a prologue, as a professional historian he had no intention of writing such a book: 'I did not seek out the subject; it was something that found me.'[26] At Christmas 1991 the death of a son in a flying accident confronted the Gillis family, who had no religious affiliations, 'with the task of creating and performing a ritual entirely of our own making, a remembrance of Ben that would recall the dimensions of his life and spirit'.[27] It also left Gillis, himself, who belatedly recognised his lack of family involvement and many deficiencies as a parent, with an acute sense of guilt. *A World of Their Own Making* ranged widely over time and space, but it did so in order to examine the appropriateness or otherwise of current myths and rituals. The book was Gillis' 'way of contributing to a process of cultural reconstruction that I regard as vital to our future as families and to the creation of more caring communities'.[28]

No doubt the majority of scholarly publications in the field of the history of the family proceeded from the academic or personal interests of their authors. Others, however, were written in support of specific courses. For example, *From Family Tree to Family History* (1994), edited by Ruth Finnegan and Michael Drake, was produced as part of an Open University course (DA301) entitled 'Studying family and community history: 19th and 20th centuries'. This was an honours level undergraduate course designed for part-time adult distance learners. The prime purpose of this volume, which served both as academic text and 'active workbook', with short questions, exercises and questions for research, was to equip such students with the skills and understanding required to enable them to complete a project in family or community history.[29] With Finnegan and Drake's definition of family history as 'something wider than genealogy', the very title, *From Family Tree to Family History*, might usefully serve as an epitome of the history of family history in England across the centuries. In the context of this chapter and volume, however, its principal significance lies in the editors' attempt to bring private and public dimensions together by encouraging students to link 'work on a single family into findings about families in general'.[30]

Thus in England from the 1960s academic historians, principally located within institutions of higher education, were to the fore in historical studies of the family. By the 1970s interest in the history of the family had been extended to schools and institutions for the training of teachers. Curriculum innovations flourished at this time, many of them under the auspices of the Schools Council, which between 1964 and 1978 funded 172 curriculum development projects. In the preface to their influential volume, *Family History in Schools* (1973), Don Steel and Lawrence Taylor acknowledged the contribution of several of these projects to studies of the contemporary family. Although less emphasis had been placed upon its history, on the basis of their research with teachers in six primary and five secondary schools in Berkshire and Hampshire, Steel and Taylor made substantial claims for the value of family history in schools, arguing that:

> Family history has important implications for interdisciplinary work and for the relationship of the school to parents and the community at large. History is about people and for the child we have found no better approach to the past than through the study of his own people, his family.[31]

Steel and Taylor acknowledged that developments in history in schools, as for example with social history, often followed a generation after they had achieved credence in academic circles. They were also aware of academic studies of the history of the family.[32] Nevertheless, their emphasis upon educational justifications for family history in schools led them to question whether the normal sequence of events would be reversed and that in this instance 'it will be the teachers who will show the historians the validity of the approach?'[33] For many teachers in schools, family history was seen as being consistent with contemporary educational philosophy and psychology. Steel and Taylor argued that family history provided motivation and relevance for children, in that it proceeded from their own experience. It was also comprehensible, because it dealt with a small unit over a recognisable time span, or series of time spans, which began in the present. Educational and historical benefits would go hand in hand. Children would no longer be mere recipients of historical facts handed down by teachers and textbooks. Nor would they simply engage in projects of historical research into topics to which answers had already been provided. Family history would provide a curriculum element in which the pupil 'is not only an authority, but can be a unique authority, an idea which has great appeal for children'.[34] Thus, in addition to its general educational rationale and benefits, family history was advocated as the most appropriate means of introducing school pupils to the skills of the historian and to an appreciation of the relationships between historical evidence and historical facts.

Developments from the 1960s and 1970s in the history of the family in higher education and of family history in schools may be situated within two broad contexts. The first was a general democratisation and liberation of British society. Traditional institutions and hierarchies were questioned as never before and family life was revolutionised by the contraceptive pill and divorce legislation. The second context was the establishment of new universities (including the Open University) polytechnics and comprehensive secondary schools. Many staff in these institutions were keen that the study of history should reflect contemporary social changes, both in terms of curriculum content and of teaching methods. In 1964 social and educational changes were complemented at the political level when, after 13 years of Conservative governments, the 'fourteenth Earl of Home' was replaced as Prime Minister by the 'fourteenth Mr Wilson'.[35]

PRIVATE: FAMILY HISTORY

The private dimensions of family history are to be found principally in the numerous individuals who engage in research into their own families. As indicated in the previous section, such amateur studies of family and local history can be traced back to the early modern period. They received a boost in the nineteenth century when historical societies flourished at county, town and other local levels, often producing their own journals or annual transactions. The Society of Genealogists was founded in 1911.

Writing in 1973, Steel and Taylor identified a post-Second World War surge in interest, with a sharp rise in the numbers of 'do-it-yourself' genealogical manuals from 1953 and an increase in membership of the Society of Genealogists, from some 650 members in 1948 to more than 3,000 in 1972.[36] The main growth of family history in the United Kingdom, and elsewhere, however, occurred during the last quarter of the twentieth century, so that by 1987 David Hey could claim with some justification that 'family history has become England's fastest-growing hobby'.[37] He also noted that 'Genealogy used to be a rather snobbish pursuit but nowadays all that has changed.'[38] By the start of the twenty-first century the Federation of Family History Societies, formed in 1974 and granted charitable status in 1982, had a membership of some 200 societies throughout the world, including national, regional and one-name groups.[39]

Explanations for the growth of interest in family history and in the numbers of family historians may be divided into two broad categories. The first relates to interest and context; the second to means.

Why are we interested in our ancestors? In some cultures the veneration of ancestors is marked annually, as in Mexico on the Day of the Dead, or in Vietnam on the Day of Lost Souls. No doubt many people experience a natural human curiosity about their origins and forbears. There is a pioneering excitement in discovering information which no one has known before. The search for a family past may also be interpreted as a search for oneself. Whether such a concern about family identity, both past and present, has been increased or diminished by late-twentieth-century modern society is more difficult to determine. In our contemporary, highly mobile, globalised world, people are less likely than in previous ages to live all their lives in traditional locations within an immediate family context. They may, therefore, research their family history for the particular purpose of securing an increased awareness of their own location both in time and space – 'roots within the unending cycle of the past, and something to hold on to in the confusions of the present'.[40] There is no conclusive evidence, however, that highly mobile, modern societies have a greater interest in family history than traditional populations. For example, those who occupied the same houses and tilled the same soil over the centuries might have had just as keen an interest; an interest expressed in a private and less visible way by the recounting of family tales and the recording of names in the family Bible.

Contextual features, therefore, must also be taken into account. The democratisation of English society in the 1960s and 1970s, referred to in the previous part, was one factor. Genealogy and family history were no longer regarded as being the exclusive (or predominant) preserve of the nobility and gentry. A second was the decline in the influence of other institutions – religious, communal and national – which had supplied the myths and rituals which constrained and supported individuals in previous times. A third was the increased amount of leisure time enjoyed by some groups in society, including those retired from paid employment and others for whom the management of a house and/or household no longer occupied as much time as formerly.

As for means, a vast array of facilities, both public and private, has been generated in support of family history and family historians. As David Hey has argued, 'The sheer bulk of the archives in national and local repositories gives English people and those of English descent a decided advantage over the inhabitants of most other lands. These immense collections are now available for everyone to consult.'[41] For example, the FRC (Family Records Centre) in Myddelton Street, London, EC1, is a joint facility and service provided by the ONS (Office for National Statistics) and the PRO (Public Record Office). The plethora of PRO publications produced to assist family historians include a newsletter, *The Family Record*, and glossy magazine, *Ancestors*. These are supplemented by fact sheets, pocket guides, specialist works, for example William Spencer's *Air Force Records for Family Historians* (2000), and general guides such as Amanda Bevan (ed.), *Tracing Your Ancestors in the Public Record Office*, which reached a sixth edition in 2002. Another indication of the numbers of family historians and the range of available support is provided by *The Family and Local History Handbook*, edited by Robert Blatchford. The 2002 edition listed more than 300 national, local, genealogical, specialist and one-name family history societies within the United Kingdom alone. Australia supplied a further 126, Canada 107 and New Zealand 29.[42]

The *Handbook* also included more than 150 advertisements from individuals, companies and other organisations offering to assist family historians in their research.

Family historians have also benefited greatly from the more general developments in communications. Between them the computer and the internet have revolutionised the capacity to acquire and transmit information. The computer provides both access to archives and other sources, and the facility for the rapid reception and transmission of large amounts of information. Even the circular letters chronicling the family deeds of the past year which have increasingly come to accompany Christmas cards can now (like the cards themselves) be instantly transmitted to family and other members around the globe.

An indication of the potential value (and problems) of the internet for family historians occurred in 2002. On 2 January, the 1901 Census, a complete list of the 32.5 million inhabitants of England, Wales, the Channel Islands and the Isle of Man who were at home on 31 March 1901, comprising 1.5 million pages of census enumerators' books, was placed online. Over a period of five days no fewer than 1.2 million users per hour attempted to access the census website.[43] Not surprisingly, the system crashed. No doubt numbers of visitors to the site were swollen as a result of major features about the 1901 Census which appeared in national newspapers. Many family historians were furious, and reacted angrily to the Public Record Office's pleas for understanding and patience. Their anger was directed at prohibitive online costs, 'a tax on knowledge', 'just another tax on genealogy, something else for the family historian to pay for', and at the chronic underestimate of interest and demand. A British Telecom spokesman described the situation as 'selling 20 million tickets for a stadium with 20,000 seats'.[44] Correspondents to the *Family Tree Magazine* for February 2002 condemned 'a typical British cock-up which just about everybody except those offering the service foresaw', wondered at the failure to appreciate 'the keen interest that would be generated', and called on those responsible to be sacked or at least have the courage to resign.[45] This incident shows that, as yet, the fastest-growing hobby in the land continues to grow.

PERSONAL: GEORGE ALDRICH

This section examines a brief fragment of the work of an amateur family historian whose elder son is an historian by profession. Its purpose is to provide further perspectives on the relationships between private and public with reference to the construction of family history and the acquisition and ownership of knowledge and education.

My father, George Arthur Aldrich (hereafter George), was born in February

1910 and died in January 1999. The eldest of three boys, his second brother, Charles, died tragically in Guy's Hospital in 1922 at the age of 9 following an accident while playing football. His youngest brother, Arthur, died from cancer in 1967 at the age of 52. George's wife, Kathleen, also born in 1910 whom he married in 1934, predeceased him in October 1995. George was a survivor in every sense. Supremely self-sufficient in mind and body until suffering a stroke a few months before his death, in his final years George took it upon himself to become the family historian. He compiled an elaborate family tree, listed family photographs and memorabilia and produced a short draft autobiography.[46]

George's father, also George, was born in 1886 and killed in action in Belgium in November 1917. The eldest of six brothers and a 'Saturday night soldier', as the members of the Territorial Army were known, he joined up when war was declared. Three other brothers, Fred, Arthur and Benjamin, also served in the army during the First World War and another, Charles, in the navy. Jack, the youngest, was not of military age. George grew up with but hazy memories of his father. There was not much to remind him – a couple of faded photographs and a few cards sent home from the trenches. The last one, a '*Souvenir de Belgique*' embroidered with the year 1917 composed of the flags of the allied nations, said simply 'To George from Dad 12/9/17 B.E.F..' Enclosed in the card pocket was a smaller card printed with the words 'Forget me not.' On the reverse, the young soldier had written 'With my Best Love and Wishes to you all, George.' On an embroidered card to his wife, 'A Kiss from France', bearing the same date, he had written 'To Annie From George. With Best Love'.

Early in December 1917 Annie received official notification that her husband, Gunner G. Aldrich of 279 Siege Battery, Royal Garrison Artillery, had been killed in action on 12 November 1917.[47] A separate brief letter written by Major Allen, George's commanding officer, informed her that 'he was struck by a shell splinter and was rendered unconscious so he suffered no pain. We are all sorry to lose him. May he who protects the widow and orphan assist you in your great grief.'

Prior to her marriage in 1909 Annie Smith, like her mother before her, had been in service. The remainder of Annie's life would consist of a perpetual struggle against poverty and hardship, making ends meet on a war widow's pension supplemented by a mere 6d a week from her husband's former employers, the Civil Service Company, where George had worked in the grocery department. Her main stay in this struggle would be her eldest son, George, who at the age of 7 became the 'man of the family' and an important breadwinner.

In 1917 Annie and her three young sons were living at 22G Peabody Buildings, in Southwark Street at the junction with Southwark Bridge Road.[48]

The 12 Peabody blocks were four stories high. Each level comprised four or five flats, a large wash/drying room, two lavatories and two sinks with cold taps. The buildings were lit by gas, the mantles on the landings being turned on by the porter from a control on the ground floor. Two boys were employed to light the lamps from a taper, with each boy responsible for six blocks. For several years George was one of these boys and bounded up and down stairs every evening, seven days a week, 365 days a year. Fitness and speed were essential because by the time he reached the sixth block the residents would be complaining of the smell and fumes from the gas. Not surprisingly George attributed his subsequent prowess as an athlete and gymnast in large part to this daily 'training'. His lamplighting duties made him well known to the Peabody Buildings' residents, many of whom needed immediate access to the City or West End at the beginnings or ends of the normal working day. These included market workers, office cleaners and entertainers, even music hall and opera singers, who were markedly unpopular with other tenants on account of their 'practising scales all day'. George's other money-making activities included helping the men with teams of tow horses who assisted drivers of heavy vehicles struggling to surmount the steep rise on the south side of London Bridge. His main Saturday job, however, when slightly older but still at school, was to deliver *The Handy Shipping Guide*, a publication showing the movement of ships for the coming week, to City of London offices concerned with imports and exports. This was hard physical work, staggering under a heavy kitbag loaded with books, but the job was well paid and generous tips could be expected at Christmas time.

George's early formal education was at Christ Church School in Blackfriars Road. In 1922 he passed entrance and scholarship examinations for St Olave's Grammar School, then at the south side of Tower Bridge, and for the Borough Polytechnic School in the Borough Road. He chose the latter, taking a three-year, full-time day course and obtaining a first-class diploma in electrical engineering with distinction in workshop practice.[49] He remembered the strict discipline at Christ Church School where the cane was liberally used, and the influence of a number of outstanding teachers at the Borough Polytechnic, including his form master and mathematics teacher, Dr W.N. Rose. The author of mathematical text books and a keen motor cyclist, Rose believed in setting practical exercises, for example problems based on results in the annual Tourist Trophy motorcycle races in the Isle of Man. Practical activities in woodwork and metalwork included the making and maintenance of tools, some of which George retained throughout his long life. On leaving the Polytechnic, George began work as an instrument maker for GEC at their factory in North Wembley. The expense of fares combined with the impossibility of travel during the General Strike of 1926, however, soon convinced George to seek employment nearer to home. Thus he became a telecommunications engineer, his first job being at the Royal Manual Telephone Exchange in Cheapside where he worked a 48-hour week exclusive of meal times. On finishing his full-time course at the Borough Polytechnic George had been awarded an 'Evening Exhibition', enabling him to continue his studies part-time. This he did, gaining Ordinary and Higher National Certificates in electrical engineering with first-class passes once more.[50] He was also an avid reader of technical periodicals and purchased components to make his first crystal set and radiogram. George retired from Post Office Telecommunications in 1972, having attained the rank of Area Engineer.

George's formal schooling and subsequent part-time studies were instrumental in providing qualifications which underpinned his highly successful career in telecommunications. But his initial interest and confidence in practical matters stemmed from the influence of a substitute father figure, the porter in Peabody Buildings for whom George daily lit the lamps. It was he who taught George a range of useful household and potentially money-making skills, for example how to change a tap washer or repair a broken sash cord.

George's contributions to the family income, physical fitness and competence in practical matters were complemented by a confident manner and charitable approach. As he readily acknowledged, 'from an early age I became "bossy"'. Such bossiness, however, was frequently put to work in good causes. Thus George became senior sixer in the Wolf Cubs, troop leader in the Scouts and then a Rover 'Mate'. He was to the fore in organising Scout camps under the patronage of the local MP for North Southwark, Edward Strauss. He also became a server at Southwark Cathedral, where he had previously attended Sunday School and been confirmed.[51] His mother was a devout member of the Church of England and in return for various housekeeping duties secured a move to a Church property in Victoria Place in connection with an order of nuns. This modest terraced property, approached by a paved entrance under an arch from Union Street, Southwark, represented a distinct advance over Peabody Buildings. There was the principal use of a front sitting room, which also doubled as a 'quiet place' for clergymen and a transit lounge for girls passing through London from one main line station to another. The family also had sole use of a kitchen with inside tap and sink, two upstairs bedrooms and an outside lavatory. George's commitment to those whom he considered less fortunate than himself increased, and he became a helper with the Church Army. One of his major duties was to collect men sleeping rough on the Victoria Embankment and direct them to the hostel for homeless men in Waterloo Road where they could obtain free bed and breakfast for a limited period.[52]

Three points may be made in concluding this section. The first is that a small part of George Aldrich's life history, hitherto a matter of private concern, has by its inclusion in this book entered into a more public sphere.[53] The second is that George's account of his early years provides an important insight not only into his education, both familial and formal, but also into his understanding of what knowledge was of most worth. It confirms many of the points raised by Susan Williams in the previous chapter about the mother's role in education in respect of basic literacy, domestic economy and attitudes and values. Finally it is clear that the construction of George's life history, as represented in his autobiography, has been shaped by different conceptions of its historical significance. For George, the most memorable incidents in his life were the famous people whom he met, not least the fact that, 'During the war Mr Churchill spoke to me on a number of occasions, not always politely, about my work.' The final version of his autobiography, however, was modified by my comments about the importance and interest of more everyday matters – living conditions, money-making activities, the formal and informal acquisition of knowledge and of education.

CONCLUSION

Five brief conclusions may now be drawn. The first is that family history is of long standing and has principally been part of private knowledge. Second, during the latter half of the twentieth century in England, as in many other countries, there was a veritable explosion in family history. This explosion had both public and private dimensions. In the public sphere the history of the family became a matter for professional historians, both in higher education and in schools. The private dimensions of family history, however, soon came to predominate once more. The greater numbers of family historians of a private nature led both to the creation of specialist public facilities such as the Family Records Centre, and to a variety of private and public commercial provision, including search services and family history fairs.

There were some common features between private and public spheres. For example, both family historians and historians of the family were soon served by specialist journals, and both had strongly international frames of reference. Nevertheless, considerable differences also existed. Some professional historians and archivists looked askance at family historians and shuddered at the perceived naivety of their questions and working practices. In a preface to the 1977 paperback edition of *The Making of the Modern Family*, Edward Shorter recounted the criticisms of his book including the charge that 'I "pitch it low in the trough" in order to appeal to readers who aren't professional historians.'[54] Ten years later David Hey encouraged family historians to 'widen their interests', arguing that family history was 'in the same state of antiquarian development as local history was (with some outstanding exceptions) a generation or two ago'.[55]

In the twenty-first century, however, in family history, as in many other spheres of human activity, there is increasing evidence of a narrowing of the private and public divide. Archive projects such as AIM25 (Archives in London and the M25 Area) which offers networked access to the archives of some 50 institutions of higher education and other colleges and societies in the London area, provide the opportunity for a greater interaction between private and public approaches to knowledge and to education than ever before.[56] The CCED (Clergy of the Church of England Database 1540–1835), a project also based at King's College, London, will be available by internet to all researchers, including family historians. One of the most unusual features of this project is its use of amateur researchers.[57]

Finally, as the account of George Aldrich's life indicates, family and individual life histories of a private nature can complement traditional public histories of education which concentrate upon such issues as educational legislation, finance and the provision of formal schooling. For George, as for countless other boys whose fathers were killed in the First World War, from the age of 7 his education consisted primarily in the assumption and fulfilment of the role of 'man of the family'.

NOTES

1 D. Steel and L. Taylor, *Family History in Schools* (London: Phillimore, 1973), p. 5.
2 Quoted in J. Gillis, *A World of Their Own Making: Myth, Ritual, and the Quest for Family Values* (Cambridge, Mass: Harvard University Press, 1997), p. 238.
3 B. Laslett, 'The Family as a Public and Private Institution: An Historical Perspective', *Journal of Marriage and the Family*, 35, 3 (1973), p. 480.
4 D. Hey, *Family Names and Family History* (London: Hambledon and London), p. 13.
5 See the Introduction to *The History of the Family: An International Quarterly*, 5, 2 (2000), p. 154, a special issue edited by Guy Brunet and Alain Bideau entitled 'Surnames – History of the Family and History of Populations'.
6 D. Hey, *Family History and Local History in England* (London: Longman, 1987), p. 5.
7 D. Hey, *The Oxford Guide to Family History* (Oxford: Oxford University Press, 1998), p. 3.
8 P. Ariès, *L'Enfant et la vie familiale sous l'Ancien Régime* (Paris: Plon, 1960).
9 See the Introduction to the *Journal of Family History*, 12, 1–3 (1987), p. ix, a special tenth anniversary commemoration issue entitled 'Family History at the Crossroads: Linking Familial and Historical Change'.
10 M. Anderson, *Approaches to the History of the Western Family 1500–1914* (London: Macmillan, 1980), p. 13.
11 T. Hareven, 'The History of the Family as an Interdisciplinary Field', in T. Rabb and R. Rotberg (eds), *The Family In History: Interdisciplinary Essays* (New York: Harper & Row, 1973), p. 213.
12 Anderson, *History of the Western Family*, p. 15.
13 L. de Mause (ed.), *The History of Childhood* (New York: Psychohistory Press, 1974). See also the *History of Childhood Quarterly: The Journal of Psychohistory*, founded

in 1973, which in 1976 became *The Journal of Psychohistory*.

14   See, for example, P. Laslett (ed.), *Household and Family in Past Time* (Cambridge: Cambridge University Press, 1972) and E. Wrigley and R. Schofield, *The Population History of England 1541–1871* (London: Edward Arnold, 1981).

15   Anderson, *History of the Western Family*, p. 65.

16   Examples cited included his own, M. Anderson, *Family Structure in Nineteenth Century Lancashire* (London: Cambridge University Press, 1971), and J. Goody *et al.* (eds), *Family and Inheritance: Rural Society in Western Europe 1200–1800* (Cambridge: Cambridge University Press, 1976).

17   P. Ariès, *Centuries of Childhood: A Social History of Family Life* (Harmondsworth: Penguin, 1962), originally published as *L'Enfant et la vie familiale sous l'Ancien Régime* (Paris: Plon, 1960).

18   E. Shorter, *The Making of the Modern Family* (New York: Basic Books, 1975).

19   This is a gross over-simplification of what has become a very complex debate. See, for example, H. Cunningham, *The Children of the Poor: Representations of Childhood since the Seventeenth Century* (Oxford: Blackwell, 1991); H. Hendrick, *Children, Childhood and English Society 1880–1990* (Cambridge: Cambridge University Press, 1997); L. Pollock, *Forgotten Children: Parent–Child Relations from 1500 to 1900* (Cambridge: Cambridge University Press, 1983); S. Shahar, *Childhood in the Middle Ages* (London: Routledge, 1990).

20   Shorter, *Making of the Modern Family* (paperback edition, 1977), book cover.

21   Anderson, *History of the Western Family*, p. 85.

22   Ibid.

23   Shorter, *Making of the Modern Family* (1977 edn), p. xiii.

24   C. Dyhouse, *Feminism and the Family in England 1880–1939* (Oxford: Basil Blackwell, 1989), p. 6.

25   L. Tilly, 'Women's History and Family History: Fruitful Collaboration or Missed Connection?', *Journal of Family History*, 12, 1–3 (1987), p. 303.

26   Gillis, *A World of Their Own Making*, p. ix.

27   Ibid., p. x.

28   Ibid., p. xi.

29   R. Finnegan and M. Drake (eds), *From Family Tree to Family History* (Cambridge: Cambridge University Press in association with The Open University), p. x.

30   Ibid., p. 1.

31   Steel and Taylor, *Family History in Schools*, p. 1.

32   Ibid., pp. 5–6.

33   Ibid., p. 175.

34   Ibid., p. 8.

35   In the 1960s, the Conservative Party leader, Sir Alexander Douglas-Home, who in 1951 succeeded to the title of the fourteenth Earl of Home, responded to a gibe from the Labour Party leader, Harold Wilson, by referring to him as the fourteenth Mr Wilson.

36   Steel and Taylor, *Family History in Schools*, p. 20.

37   Hey, *Family History and Local History*, p. xii.

38   Ibid.

39   For a useful introduction to the last category see Hey, *Family Names and Family History*.

40   Finnegan and Drake, *From Family Tree to Family History*, p. ix.

41   Hey, *Oxford Guide to Family History*, p. 1.

42   R. Blatchford (ed.), *The Family and Local History Handbook* (York: The Genealogical Services Directory in collaboration with the British Association for Local History, 2002), pp. 260–72.

43 '1901 Census Online', *Ancestors*, 6 (2002), p. 4.
44 Quoted in M. Armstrong, '1901 Census Online Launch Sunk on First Day. Researchers Demand Availability in Other Formats', *Family Tree Magazine*, 18, 4 (2002), p. 4. See also articles and commentaries on the 1901 Census in *Ancestors*, *Practical Family History* and *Family History Monthly*.
45 *Family Tree Magazine*, 18, 4 (2002), pp. 4–5.
46 Much of the information in this section is derived from discussions with George during his compilation of an unpublished manuscript, 'My Life as a Telecommunications Engineer'.
47 His body now lies in the Oxford Road Cemetery in Weltje, within the city boundaries of Ypres.
48 George Peabody (1795–1869), an American philanthropist, established himself in London in 1837 and contributed more than £1.5 million to charitable works. The Peabody Trust was set up in 1862 to provide housing for the working classes of London.
49 George stated that his initial preference for the Borough Polytechnic was confirmed when at interview the headmaster of St Olave's made fun of his surname. For the background to the Borough Polytechnic, see E. Bayley, *The Borough Polytechnic Institute: Its Origin and Development* (London: Elliot Stock, 1910).
50 For several years after the Second World War at the invitation of Dr Rose, by then head of the mathematics department, George taught mathematics part-time for City and Guilds and National examinations at the Borough Polytechnic.
51 His father's name is included on the memorial to the fallen of the First World War at the East End of the Cathedral.
52 In the 1920s there were large numbers of unemployed men and women who travelled to London in search of work.
53 For a classic example of how the story of three generations of an 'ordinary' family became part of the public domain see M. Forster, *Hidden Lives. A Family Memoir* (London: Viking, 1995). For a recent discussion of many of the issues raised by autobiographical and biographical studies, life histories and oral history in the history of education, see *History of Education*, 32, 2 (2003), especially the contributions by Philip Gardner and Jane Martin.
54 Shorter, *Making of the Modern Family* (1977 edn), p. xiv.
55 Hey, *Family History and Local History*, p. 265.
56 For further information see the website, www.aim25.ac.uk
57 For further information see the website, www.kcl.ac.uk/humanities/cch/cce/

PART 3

8

CHANGING CONCEPTIONS OF PUBLIC AND PRIVATE IN AMERICAN EDUCATIONAL HISTORY

William J. Reese

INTRODUCTION

Something rather remarkable has occurred in the recent history of American education: a rediscovery of the public benefits of private education. The idea is an old one in the nation's history but has not been seriously entertained by mainstream political leaders or policymakers since the early nineteenth century. When dissenting Protestants, non-sectarian private school leaders, and Roman Catholics in particular protested against the monopolistic nature of public schooling by the mid-nineteenth century, they were loudly criticised and defeated in their efforts to divide the school fund for their competing systems of education. In effect, public schools became a virtual monopoly, and private networks of schooling existed without direct state aid. The public school, and not its private counterpart, became for most Americans the symbol of an indigenous democracy. And, until the final decades of the twentieth century, the majority of citizens and elected officials generally believed that the expansion and proliferation of tax-supported, compulsory public schools best served the common good.

During the past generation, a tidal wave of criticism has engulfed the public schools, leading to a reassessment of private schools and markets in the larger world of education. Concerns over low academic achievement, classroom violence, and the alleged weakening of moral and character education in the public schools, combined with an almost blind faith in the market place, have helped reorient popular perceptions of education in many sectors of society. In 2002, in a rancorous split decision, the US Supreme Court ruled in favour of a controversial voucher plan in Cleveland, Ohio, where public monies helped subsidise tuition at private religious schools. The long-range policy implications of this decision are unclear, but it breached the sometimes high wall separating public funds and private schools.

A diverse range of intellectuals, journalists, religious leaders, lobbying groups and politicians have increasingly publicised the benefits of private, not public, education. Whereas the famous nineteenth-century common school reformer, Horace Mann, believed that education should not be left to the whims of private enterprise or capriciousness of parents, today market-place solutions abound as a panacea for the ills of the schools. Competition in education, it is believed, will produce high academic achievement, strong moral character and overall excellence in schooling; at the same time, it will force the worst public schools (particularly in the cities) to improve or else disappear. Whether private schools and market-place competition will ensure scholastic excellence remains uncertain, but the idea has recently enjoyed considerable public appeal.

Exactly how did the public schools acquire their still dominant place in American education? Why have Americans revived an old notion, that private education and the market place should play an integral if not more central role in schools? An examination of changing popular conceptions of 'public' and 'private' in the American educational experience from the colonial period to the present can help to answer these questions.

EDUCATION IN COLONIAL AMERICA AND EARLY REPUBLIC

The creation of public school systems in the nineteenth century – state-controlled, compulsory, hierarchical and in theory standardised – stood in contrast to patterns of education that prevailed throughout the colonial and early national periods of American history. For no 'system' of education *per se* existed in America during these earlier eras. Moreover, 'the modern conception of public education, the very idea of a clear line of separation between "private" and "public", was unknown before the end of the eighteenth century', as Bernard Bailyn has written.[1] The newly ratified federal Constitution lacked specific provisions for state-controlled education or school systems, which helped contribute to decentralised and local control over formal education after political independence from Britain.[2]

While the idea that education and schooling are synonymous has considerable resonance in the modern Western world, the family served as the basic source of education and socialisation in America before the nineteenth century. The dominant nuclear family in the free colonies was both the centre of biological reproduction and material production, and it also served as an educational centre. If literate, parents normally taught their children to read; apprenticeship programmes, available for white youth in particular, were family based; and, together with the Church, neighbourhood and surrounding community, the family was central to life in colonial America. This was true of the Puritans of New England, of Quakers and other religious groups in the Middle Colonies, and even of the more geographically dispersed white settlers of the South. Child-rearing methods, shaped by diverse economic forces and religious sentiments, might differ widely, but the family remained ever dominant.[3]

Schools emerged as arms of local government, particularly in the seat of learning in the New World: New England. But the laws passed in seventeenth-century Massachusetts that mandated the creation of schools as population increased were widely ignored and often unenforceable. Whether in New England, the Middle Colonies, or the South – and regional differences would long prevail in schooling and social life generally – schools were an irregular and incidental part of a child's life. Schools were usually attended by children only for a few years, most often by boys during the regular term. The curriculum, heavily shaped by local religious norms, emphasised basic literacy skills, especially the ability to read Scripture and religious materials. As scholars repeatedly affirm, the American colonies had a diverse ethnic and racial character. The Puritans, however, were nevertheless pivotal in establishing community support for education and schooling, and the earliest and most extensive system of public education ultimately emerged among their descendants in New England states such as Massachusetts.[4]

Modern distinctions between 'public' and 'private' in the world of education were noticeably absent in the colonial or even early national era. Many town schools, for example, supplemented modest tax support with donations in kind and tuition from the parents of pupils. In addition, private venture schools emerged in the eighteenth century in many urban areas along the eastern seaboard. A private master in a growing metropolis such as New York City or Philadelphia might open a pay school that offered an array of subjects, such as accounting, cartography, or mathematics, to meet local demand. Citizens assumed that the teacher was performing a 'public' function and offering a 'public' education in the sense that anyone who could afford the tuition could presumably attend. Similarly, an enterprising woman who operated a dame 'school' in her home, a private teacher in charge of a writing 'school' in a rented room and other educational entrepreneurs all served the 'public' in a broad sense by contributing to the welfare of society even though they lacked any tax support. The lines separating public and private remained thin.[5]

SCHOOLING AND NINETEENTH-CENTURY AMERICA

After the 1790s, enormous social forces were unleashed that contributed to rising support for a public school monopoly during the next half century, especially in the free northern states. The informal, irregular, unsystematic character of educational arrangements in the colonial period soon disappeared. Schools became more influential in the lives of more children over the course of the nineteenth century, and every state in the Union built a single system of free schools. After the Civil War (1861–5), the South built separate school systems for whites and African-Americans, even though they were poorly funded and unequal. Across the nation, the family, the press, the Church and other agencies of education and socialisation retained their influence in everyday life, and the public school had yet to become a focal point in children's lives. But social change was endemic in the nineteenth century, ensuring momentous developments in the world of schooling.

Schools were not especially novel institutions by the 1830s, but the emergence of a school 'system' that monopolised tax dollars brought greater clarity to the meaning of 'public' and 'private'. State after state drafted constitutions that required the establishment of public schools; this was also a requirement for the readmission of the Confederate states into the Union in the 1870s. In the decades before the Civil War, especially in the North, locally controlled and financed systems of public education arose that increasingly eliminated the ability of assorted private schools (academies, female seminaries and colleges) to receive direct and indirect forms of public aid. Competition in education still existed, but institutions were not on an equal financial playing field. A public school system that attempted to advance the values of the dominant Anglo-Protestant culture increasingly gathered the majority of children into its embrace. As several historians have noted, critics by mid-century increasingly maligned private schools as un-American, culturally divisive and contrary to the common good.[6]

Only by the time of the Civil War did modern distinctions between 'public' and 'private' slowly emerge in important urban centres such as New York City and in other northern communities. In contrast, earlier in the century, the lines between public and private had been blurry throughout the nation. Colleges such as Harvard in the early 1800s were governed by private boards of control yet still received some public monies from the legislature. Even Dartmouth College enjoyed some public funding after the celebrated Dartmouth Case of 1819, which preserved its status as a 'private' school. In many cities, philanthropic, interdenominational Protestant voluntary associations operated charity schools for the unchurched poor and received varying levels of tax support. Before the 1820s, some northern districts continued to provide private sectarian schools, including Catholic elementary schools, with some tax support, a practice that soon became rare and then disappeared.[7]

Secondary education in the North also had a mixed public–private character before the Civil War. Academies (which often included lower grades, too) were ubiquitous and popular institutions, often established by evangelical Protestants, that frequently served as the predecessors of the modern high school; they numbered in the thousands in the northern states until after the Civil War, and they long retained a commanding presence south of the Mason–Dixon Line. Governed by private boards of trustees, academies survived thanks to a mix of tax support, public land grants, private bequests and tuition fees. 'States conceived of academies as public institutions', writes historian Michael B. Katz, and 'in the early national period, "public" implied a performance of broad social functions and the services of a large, hetero-geneous, nonexclusive clientele rather than control and ownership by the community or state'.[8] Only with the rise of actual state systems of education by the Civil War era would modern notions of 'public' and 'private' materialise.

Horace Mann, the most famous common school reformer of the nineteenth century, criticised non-public schools on many fronts, presenting arguments still heard today. Private schools, he warned, were hostile to the public interest, since they supposedly catered to the privileged few. He similarly condemned charity schooling for giving free education – which he wanted available for all (especially white) social classes – a pauper stigma. Everyone should be educated in a single public system. Education, Mann warned in 1848, should not be abandoned 'to the hazards of private enterprise, or to parental will, ability, or caprice'. Moreover, reflecting the heady nationalism of his times, he feared that 'the tendency of the private school system is to assimilate our modes of education to those of England, where churchmen and dissenters – each sect according to its own creed – maintain separate schools, in which children are taught, from their tenderest years to wield the sword of polemics with fatal dexterity'.[9]

Soon a free and 'public' education became equated with state-financed education, similar to the way the term is used today. One of Mann's contem-poraries, George Boutwell of Massachusetts, defined public schooling in an increasingly popular way: 'A *public school* I understand to be a school estab-lished by the public – supported chiefly or entirely by the public, controlled by the public, and accessible to the public under terms of equality, without special charge for tuition.'[10] A contributor to the *American Journal of Education* in 1873 provided a more elaborate definition. Public schools, he wrote, are state sponsored and reach all children in rural and urban areas, where they receive a common training in the same subjects and in good citizenship. Schooling was 'public' if 'it is established by the State through agencies of its providing, conducted according to the rules of its authorization, supported by funds protected or furnished by its legislation, accessible to the children of all citizens upon terms of equality, and subject to such inspection as the law may institute'.[11]

The public school establishment arose during a time of intense social and economic upheaval, when various political leaders feared for the very survival of the republic. Already in the 1780s and 1790s, national figures including Benjamin Rush and Thomas Jefferson called for finely articulated systems of education in the several states. Schools, they argued, would teach a diverse, newly independent people (especially the white citizenry) common moral principles and political values, a standardised language and basic citizenship skills. Despite the lofty rhetoric about national educational goals that infused the writings of the Founding Fathers, schooling remained a local affair: decentralised, ungraded and controlled by lay people who still often viewed the family and Church as the bedrock of society.[12]

While a national consciousness slowly developed, particularly in New England, the emerging state monopoly in education is best understood as a product of interlocking social changes transforming America. Of signal importance was the Second Great Awakening that began in the 1790s. The Awakening was a response by evangelical Protestants to the threat of political egalitarianism, rationalism and secularism spawned by the French Revolution, to the deism of the Founding Fathers, and to the then low levels of church membership. Since the Constitution did not provide for a national system of education, the task of constructing schools often fell upon Protestant evangelicals and their allies, who formed voluntary associations on the local level that greatly influenced the creation of public schools in the pre-Civil War era.[13]

Protestants from a variety of denominations dominated voluntary organisations, highlighting the intimate ties between 'private' organisations and the origins of 'public' education. Carl F. Kaestle's standard history of the rise of the common schools, *Pillars of the Republic*, demonstrates how in city after city, in response to ethnically and religiously diverse populations and growing fears of poverty and crime, Anglo-Protestant voluntary groups built charity schools for the children of the unchurched poor. Once these privately-controlled organisations successfully lobbied for more tax support, the basis for the modern public school system was fundamentally laid, however unintentionally. By mid-century, taxpayers in the North were increasingly expected to foot most of the bill for the common (public) schools.[14]

How this occurred was illuminated well in New York City. The Free School Society assembled there in 1805 and represented a range of elite philanthropic Protestants. In its attempt to inculcate morality and Protestant ethics in the children of the poor, the Society blended private resources and tax dollars to build what evolved into New York's public school system, open to everyone without charge. 'Free' education in the cities was long associated with the education of the poor, and it would take decades to weaken the stigmas attached to the concept of free schools. In addition, over time sectarian groups were denied access to public funds to run their own schools; state aid to Catholic schools, for example, ended in 1825. Local Baptists in the 1820s and Catholics in the 1840s battled for a division of the school fund for their own denominational schools – without success.[15]

Protestant charity school proponents such as the Free School Society (renamed the Public School Society in 1825) had therefore built a public system that gradually monopolised public taxes. The schools taught a non-denominational version of Protestant Christianity, often called 'non-sectarian' by friends but 'godless' by Catholics and a minority of Dissenting Protestants. These latter groups opposed the end of Church control over education and saw the public schools as essentially oriented around a bland Protestantism. Across the nation in the early 1800s, in both rural and urban areas, the majority of Protestants nevertheless successfully proselytised on behalf of a single system of free public education. In the public schools, children often began their day by reciting a non-denominational (Protestant) prayer, and teachers read to them from the King James version of the Bible and assigned textbooks filled with slurs on the Papacy and Catholic nations.[16]

Catholics frequently condemned these practices, but Protestant activists in state after state guaranteed that a single 'public' system of education enjoyed exclusive access to public taxes. They wrote provisions into many state con-stitutions that prohibited any spending of public monies on private schools, a policy aimed directly at the Catholics. (Such laws may continue to frustrate those who want to tap public funds, unless the US Supreme Court overturns these statutes.) After the Civil War, Republican leaders, including Ulysses S. Grant, criticised Catholics for demanding tax relief, adding to the bitter culture wars of the period. In a few short decades, then, the blurred lines once separating 'public' and 'private' education had disappeared. Catholics in particular and a minority of Dissenting Protestant denominations would estab-lish private schools as an alternative to the public system, but they would do it with their own funds.[17]

Catholic leaders continued to lobby unsuccessfully for public monies, provoking a nativist backlash. To the champions of public schools, private education was anathema. Catholics were singled out for building an expansive parochial school system, which grew impressively in many urban areas, especially in the northern states. One bigot in a leading educational journal in 1880 accused American Catholics of subservience to the Pope, who 'has ordered the destruction of our free non-sectarian system of popular education, and the substitution of his own system of church or parochial schools'.[18] Parochial schools in foreign countries, the writer added, were not only divisive but also spawned false doctrines, pauperism and criminality. In 1889, Republican activists in Illinois and Wisconsin passed legislation to regulate private schools, including prohibiting instruction in any language except English. Catholics and Lutherans joined forces to beat their opponents at the ballot box, but the place of private schools remained contested.[19]

By the late nineteenth century, competing systems of schooling had thus emerged – one labelled 'public', all others 'private' – and these finer distinctions long endured. Over the course of the century, the Protestant majority had scored impressive victories for the public system. By mid-century, in cities (as well as in the countryside) public schools were governed by elected or appointed school boards, not voluntary associations. By the 1880s, free public high schools replaced academies in the North as the main arena of secondary instruction; and the private sector became divided into self-funded religious schools and a small number of largely elite, often expensive independent schools.[20] Catholics built the largest segment of private schooling in the nation, but laws increasingly ensured that they would not receive public monies. It would take decades before they and other advocates of private schooling had the political leverage to reverse these developments.

SCHOOLING IN THE FIRST HALF OF THE TWENTIETH CENTURY

At the turn of the century, Theodore Roosevelt and other Republicans (unlike their party members in recent decades) applauded the free public schools and chastised those who wanted to share the public school fund. Immigration from central and southern Europe swelled between 1890 and the First World War, leading to a major increase in the Catholic population. Support for immigrant restriction intensified and finally led to legislation that shut off the spigot in the early 1920s. Catholic schools would nevertheless multiply, leading many native-born citizens to redouble their efforts to favour public over private schools.[21]

Nevertheless, in the early twentieth century changes in the public schools were under way that ultimately weakened their place in society. These changes form a broad backdrop to the rising criticisms of public schools in our own times. The basic changes – evident even today – included the growing centralisation of power in the hands of school superintendents, the centrality of vocational training (and not moral development *per se*) as a key aim of education and the overall secularisation of the schools, culminating in the banning of state-sponsored prayer by the US Supreme Court in the early 1960s. Even though many superintendents and teachers at mid-century were often Protestant or otherwise church members, the decline of religiously-based moral instruction in the schools also contributed to the rising chorus of criticism.

Schools, especially in urban areas, assumed a more corporate character in the first half of the twentieth century, as educators tried to adapt educational institutions to a more ethnically diverse as well as more urban and industrial society. Instead of only emphasising the values of the nineteenth-century school – basic Protestant morality and rudimentary literacy skills – the public system also prepared students for life in an expanding number of secondary schools; these high schools increasingly offered a more vocationally-oriented curriculum. After 1900, degree-holding school superintendents, not lay people on the school board, increasingly set policy. School boards themselves were centralised, reduced in size and elected at large, reducing the participation of local neighbourhoods in school governance. These trends spread to rural areas, where school districts were consolidated, superintendents grew more powerful and a more secular curriculum dominated.[22]

In the mid-nineteenth century, mainstream Protestants assumed that their descendants would continue to control the public schools, which would serve as a bulwark against Catholicism. Catholics themselves built a growing network of elementary and then secondary schools in the early twentieth century. Lutherans also sponsored an extensive parochial system in the Midwest, and a handful of smaller Protestant denominations also funded their own schools. But most Protestants remained within the fold of the public schools, unaware of how much their authority would slip over time.[23]

Some evangelical Protestants in the early twentieth century lamented the secularising trends already apparent in the public schools. Religious leaders such as Billy Sunday assailed the drift toward vocationalism in the schools, which they equated with a materialistic, Godless state. In reaction to these developments, they successfully lobbied state legislatures (largely controlled by rural Protestants) to pass laws that required (and thus re-affirmed) morning prayer and Bible reading in the public schools. In the 1920s, they also fought famous battles over the teaching of evolution and usually drove Darwin out of most high school biology classes. As a result, most evangelical and fundamentalist Protestants continued to support public over private education, even as they financed more Bible camps, Christian colleges and Sunday schools to ensure the survival of their religious beliefs.[24]

Hostility to private education remained potent in the 1920s, when the very survival of parochial schools became an issue in Oregon. Certainly the idea of providing public monies for private education during this period was virtually unthinkable among the Protestant majority. In an attempt to destroy the parochial school system, Protestant activists in Oregon successfully lobbied for legislation requiring all children to attend public schools. Backed by the Ku Klux Klan and other nativist groups, the legislation was ultimately ruled unconstitutional by the US Supreme Court in a landmark decision, *Pierce v. Society of School Sisters* (1925). The Court upheld compulsory school attendance but confirmed the right of parents to choose whether to send their children to public or private schools. While private (including Catholic and other religious) schools were protected by this ruling, the place of 'public' and 'private' schools in American society remained unsettled for the rest of the century.[25]

Debates over the relative merits of public and private schools continued in the coming decades. Contributors to a wide range of journals and in the popular press asked whether private schools produced higher academic achievement, whether private education was divisive and elitist and whether the public interest was best served by preserving a state monopoly or by expanding the private sector. Few prominent politicians suggested that private schools receive direct subsidies from the public coffers. The only Catholic ever elected President in American history, John F. Kennedy, had to assure voters during his political campaign in 1960 that he firmly endorsed the separation of Church and state and did not plan to provide tax support for Catholic schools.[26]

Certain trends had thus occurred in the first half of the twentieth century that opened the public schools to greater critical scrutiny. The rapid expansion of high schools, the greater secularisation of the curriculum, the centralisation of authority in the hands of educational experts and the rising importance of vocationalism often provoked debates about the role of school in society. Yet it was unclear where these criticisms would lead. Those who wrote popular jeremiads about the weak standards of the public schools in the early 1950s usually did not demand the dismantling of the system or the funnelling of tax monies to Catholic or other competing institutions. A handful of critics called for more market competition in education and tax reforms to aid families with children in private schools. But they were politically isolated and not part of the cultural and intellectual mainstream.

Indeed, the aura of public schooling in the 1960s was still strong enough that the sociologist, Christopher Jencks, who endorsed school vouchers, emphasised that opening the door to greater school choice would not be easy. 'Educators', Jencks warned in 1966, 'have taught us to use "public" as a synonym for "democratic" or just plain "good," and to associate "private" with "elitist" and "inequality"'. Decoupling these familiar associations, however, became increasingly common in the coming decades.[27]

PRIVATE AND PUBLIC SCHOOLS SINCE THE 1950s

What led more Americans to reappraise conceptions of 'public' and 'private' in the educational realm after the Second World War? As is usually true in history, the forces at work were multiple and mutually reinforcing: hostility among conservatives and then other Americans to rising federal authority in the public schools; the rejection of political liberalism at the ballot box by 1968; the popularity of market solutions to social ills within the revived Republican Party of the 1980s; the failure of inner-city schools to educate the poor well and the weakened wall separating Church and state that led to the recent voucher ruling by the US Supreme Court.

Without question, the growing influence of the federal government in the schools and domestic life in general after 1945 generated a conservative reaction that ultimately weakened political support for the public schools. The increased federal role in educational policy making became most dramatic in the 1950s and 1960s and fuelled a revival of interest in the private sector. Despite some precedents for federal activism in public education – stretching from the early national period, through Reconstruction, through the movement for federal aid for vocational education during the First World War – the USA has been unique among Western nations in its support for decentralised control over its schools. Nothing so stirs public controversy as federal intervention in social life, especially in school policy. After the Second World War, federal authority expanded so dramatically in particular areas (especially race, civil rights and religion) that more citizens found its rising power intrusive and subversive of local and states' rights.

Federal intervention in school affairs after 1945 was a response to two different developments: the Cold War and the emerging Civil Rights Movement. In response to the launching of the Soviet Sputniks, Congressional leaders with the support of President Dwight D. Eisenhower fashioned the National Defense Education Act (1958). This legislation provided financial support for curriculum development in the sciences, mathematics, foreign languages and to a lesser degree humanistic subjects deemed essential to the national interest. Some private foundations also joined multi-sided efforts to strengthen the academic character of the schools to undo the effects of 'progressive education' and other forces that had supposedly weakened the fibre of American youth.[28]

Federal involvement in education further accelerated in the 1960s, despite Republican opposition and the growing sense of many Americans that the individual states and not Washington should retain control over public education. Out of Lyndon B. Johnson's 'Great Society' reforms came not only an expansion of the power of various federal agencies (such as the Justice Department, to enforce desegregation), but also the Elementary and Secondary Education Act (1965), compensatory education programmes such as Head Start and other initiatives to enhance educational opportunity. By the 1970s, conservatives attacked this as federal meddling in school affairs while sometimes calling for constitutional amendments for school prayers (banned by the US Supreme Court in the early 1960s) and against mandatory court-ordered bussing. They were not pleased when Jimmy Carter, a moderate Democrat, successfully created the federal Department of Education, a new cabinet post, in 1979.[29]

Nothing so inflamed public opinion, first in the South and then in the North, as the federal government's role in the Civil Rights Movement. This, too, fuelled interest in private education in some quarters. Growing out of prominent efforts by African-Americans and white activists for racial justice, the movement was energised by the *Brown v. Board of Education* decision in 1954, which ruled segregated schools unconstitutional. Segregationist academies and private schools sprouted in many parts of the South. In addition, critics believed that the power of the US Office of Education and then Health, Education, and Welfare (precursors to the Department of Education) had increased too rapidly; public school districts that refused to comply with court-ordered desegregation in the 1960s were denied federal funds, which had been slowly growing as a percentage of local budgets since the Second World War. The effort to integrate public schools thus became yet another reason why some citizens looked more favourably on private school alternatives.[30]

If opposition to certain liberal policies of the federal government provoked more criticisms of the public schools, growing 'public' support for 'private' education also reflected something broader, a remarkable shift in popular attitudes. Since the Second World War, citizens have realised that success at school is more essential to success in the market place; employers increasingly used educational credentials to screen job applicants, and de-industrialisation eliminated many jobs once held by the less educated. The end of the Great Depression and renewed national prosperity in the 1950s also nurtured rising expectations among parents and society generally about the role of schools in society. The failure to raise academic standards or to increase test scores and graduation rates sufficiently became stock criticisms of city systems in the 1950s, at the very time when they increasingly served more poor and minority children. Public scrutiny of the schools thus intensified at every turn. It is not surprising that the most important voucher experiments later arose in Milwaukee and Cleveland, in the declining urban industrial heartland.[31]

In addition, older concerns about the importance of moral and religious instruction have not dissipated simply because the economic stakes of school success and failure have risen. As indicated earlier, nineteenth-century Americans expected schools to promote a range of social and political goals, especially the transmission of non-denominational Protestant values. Protestants once dominated the key educational and administrative posts in local schools, which gradually became more secular, expert controlled and centralised. In the cities, Catholic Democrats often ran the political machines that included schools as part of their bailiwick. The state system of education – so widely praised by the vast majority of nineteenth-century Protestants as supportive of a common faith – by the mid-twentieth century increasingly seemed hostile and alien to fundamentalist Christians.[32]

After the Second World War, more public monies indirectly reached more private schools through the creation of various student aid programmes, and some citizens soon realised that the concept of 'public' and 'private' needed revision. Like other writers, a contributor to the *Nation's Schools* in 1955 concluded that 'We do not have clear-cut conceptions of the respective roles of public and private education.'[33] The GI Bill allowed military veterans to use their grants to pay for higher education, including Church-based colleges and universities; school lunch, transportation and other new federal programmes also benefited both public and private school students, policies upheld when challenged in the courts. A writer in *School and Society* in 1957 sensed a more favourable atmosphere regarding public appreciation for private schools. 'Many recent discussions of private education', he noted, 'have stressed its public character. Indeed, some have recommended that the term "private" as applied to other than public schools should be abandoned because of historical and sociological connotations of the term.'[34] Such writers anticipated those who in the coming decades routinely applauded the public benefits of private schools in American society and often urged their expansion through various forms of government funding.

Before 1945, Roman Catholics primarily endorsed public aid for private education. But as a result of growing reactions against federal intervention in the black civil rights movement and the perception that public schools were overly secular and of declining quality, this lobbying base soon widened. Other factors nurturing greater respect for the private sector included the growing acceptance of Catholics in the American mainstream, the much-publicised failures of inner-city public schools, and the glorification of capitalism and the market place, particularly during the Reagan years but hardly dissipating during the Bush–Clinton–Bush era.

Again, these recent developments built upon important trends emerging by the 1950s. That aid to parochial education was a violation of the separation of Church and state was already contradicted by the 'child benefit' theory in the 1940s, which posited that indirect public aid to private schools benefited children, not Churches. After the Second World War, public monies were increasingly funnelled into private schools for school lunches, to help defray transportation costs, and for other services. What had long been mostly a 'Catholic' issue – public aid for private schools – now became a more mainstream national concern. Certainly Lyndon B. Johnson realised that the Education Bills at the heart of the 'Great Society' would fail to win Congressional approval if benefits were restricted to public school students. Each additional benefit to private school students, of course, only encouraged those who sought other forms of financial relief, from tuition tax credits to actual vouchers.[35]

The modern champions of public support for private schools were a mixed lot. Not all Catholics have supported public aid to their parochial schools, nor have all fundamentalist Protestants. Like many independent schools without sectarian affiliations, numerous Church-based schools oppose government aid, since it can lead to intrusive government regulations. An array of school choice and voucher activists had nevertheless arisen by the 1960s and 1970s, including voucher advocates on the left such as Christopher Jencks, free market economists such as Milton Friedman, traditional Catholic lobbies, new lobbies from the Protestant Christian right, and, by the 1980s, African-American activists disillusioned with inner-city public schools – all believing for slightly different reasons that the public schools had failed, that children needed an escape hatch, or that choice was simply desirable as a matter of principle. The Founding Fathers of public schools in the nineteenth century had turned their back on the market place, despite its potent influence in shaping the national economy. Now an assortment of people across an ideological spectrum, however, questioned the monopoly of public education.[36]

When Ronald Reagan was first elected president in 1980, the Republican Party increasingly positioned itself as the leading force for school choice and alternatives to the public schools. Reagan's endorsement of tuition tax credits, while tepid, helped solidify his appeal among many Catholics. The revival of the fortunes of the Republican Party following Watergate and the Ford–Carter interregnum drew sustenance from a wider disillusionment with the economy, military defeat in Vietnam, and the Welfare State. Criticisms of the federal government were commonplace, and they included numerous salvos against the public schools, including the famous Conservative manifesto, *A Nation at Risk* (1983), which blamed them for most social ills. The inability of the American economy to compete well with the Japanese and other friendly rivals was laid at the door of the public schools, not corporations, and private school alternatives and choice became increasingly fashionable and politically acceptable.[37]

The collapse of the Soviet Union by the late 1980s caused many Americans to believe that capitalism, choice and markets were the wave of the future, not only in newly liberated countries in Eastern Europe but also around the globe and with renewed vigour at home. In the 1970s and 1980s, the well-publicised successes of Catholic schools, with their bare-bones academic curriculum, firm discipline and attention to the needs of minorities in the inner cities, became the stuff of newspaper and magazine headlines and scholarly articles and books. Catholic school enrolments actually peaked in the mid-1960s, but the commitment of many parochial schools to the inner-city poor (including many non-Catholic African-Americans) understandably received attention and considerable praise.[38]

Good news about public schools became rarer, as complaints about low standards and test scores, undisciplined students and high drug use among many pupils remained very common. Christian fundamentalist schools and even home schooling grew more popular, and more citizens and elected officials came to doubt the wisdom of a monopolistic system of public schools.

CONCLUSION

Whether angry about rude students, desegregation, secular humanism, teacher unionism, or even with the concept of a state monopoly in an era that extolled markets, Americans by the early twenty-first century may have reached a crossroads in their thinking about the role of 'public' and 'private' education. The recent decision by the US Supreme Court that ruled the Cleveland voucher plan constitutional may prove to be a landmark, though its long-term influence remains unknown. Will private schools that receive public aid have to serve all children, including those with special educational needs? Do the public schools best promote the common good, or should the state fund a variety of alternatives to the traditional system?

To defenders of the public schools and those who want a high wall of separation between Church and state, the voucher decision was a major disappointment. Since the great majority of private schools are affiliated with Churches or have other religious attachments, liberals continue to argue that taxpayers are subsidising Churches, not children. How many citizens will press for more alternatives to public schools either through sectarian or non-sectarian choices remains unclear. Despite the continual complaint about the poor quality of America's public schools, public opinion polls frequently reveal that while citizens overall rate them as mediocre, parents rate their own children's public school higher. Grade inflation notwithstanding, this may mean that many citizens are fond of complaining about public services but not enough to end their traditional support for public education. In well-to-do suburbs, for example, the incentive to withdraw from the existing system may be negligible. And many religious denominations, as well as non-sectarian school administrators, remain wary of accepting tax monies for their private schools, fearful of government intrusiveness and regulations that may follow the public purse. Perhaps in the cities, where public school failure seems highest, school choice by means of vouchers and other familiar alternatives (such as magnet schools and charter schools) will become very appealing.

What is clear is that public and private schools are still a remarkably rich and diverse aspect of American culture. Criticisms of public schools are frequently directed against the worst achieving ones, usually in urban areas, where poverty, unemployment and other social ills compound the problems of the poor. In the suburbs, more frequent complaints are that students lack enough access to advanced college placement courses, to open the door wider to the most prestigious colleges and universities. There are tens of thousands of public schools in America, found in cities, suburbs, small towns and rural areas, all with some similarities but also many distinctive features and local traditions. Some public high schools, for example, have academic standards that exceed many non-selective colleges; others are chronically underfunded, serving the nation's neediest children, who may deserve the most but receive the least.

Similarly, private schools in America defy simple generalisations. A comprehensive survey of private schools for the 1999/2000 school year by the National Center for Educational Statistics, in the US Department of Education, vividly highlights the great diversity of non-public schools. In that year, as in many previous decades, about 10 per cent of all children who attended elementary and secondary schools were in private schools. More private schools existed in the South (30 per cent of the total) than in any other region, and the fewest were found in the West (20 per cent). The great majority of non-public schools have a religious affiliation, with Roman Catholics representing about 30 per cent of all private schools but 'almost half of all private school students'.[39] Another 36 per cent of all private school students are in other religious-based schools, mostly from a variety of Protestant denominations and sects. Adding further diversity to the mix are the remainder of non-sectarian and independent schools, ranging from progressive and child-centred to extremely competitive and traditional, among the various alternatives.[40]

The sheer variety of religious-based schools in America reveals considerable pluralism. In addition to the Catholic system, there are religiously-oriented schools that reflect the teachings of the Amish, Assembly of God, Baptists, Church of Christ, Church of God, Mennonites, Pentecostals, Jews and Black Muslims, to name just a few; Lutherans also support numerous schools. Within the category of 'Christian fundamentalist' and 'Christian day schools' one also finds much variety. Most private school pupils are non-Hispanic white. But about a quarter of all Catholic school students are members of a minority group, with Hispanics (11 per cent) slightly outnumbering African-Americans (8 per cent). The national study also found that nearly 22 per cent of students in conservative Christian (various Protestant evangelical or fundamentalist) schools were also from minority groups.[41]

What is apparent is that the new millennium has brought potentially dramatic changes to the world of public and private education. The popularity of school 'choice' and market solutions to education reflects the wider Western embrace of markets and globalisation. Entrepreneurs in the USA have even created for-profit companies that have been awarded contracts with several urban school districts, promising to raise test scores and make money for stock holders; neither goal has been reached, but it is a sign of the times. The US Supreme

Court ruling that allowed the use of public taxes to support attendance at private religious schools in Cleveland may have heralded a sea change in educational policy. President George W. Bush, thanks to a speech writer's flair for hyperbole, applauded the decision as equal in importance to the *Brown* decision of 1954. Historians can help explain the diverse, shifting views of 'public' and 'private' over the past few centuries, but where the current roads of educational reform lead is part of an unfolding contemporary drama.

NOTES

I would like to thank Story Matkin-Rawn, a graduate student in history at Wisconsin, for her invaluable research assistance.

1   B. Bailyn, *Education in the Forming of American Society* (New York: Basic Books, 1960), p. 11.
2   O.F. Kraushaar, *Private Schools: From the Puritans to the Present* (Bloomington, Indiana: Phi Delta Kappa Educational Foundation, 1976), p. 1, and C.F. Kaestle, *Pillars of the Republic: Common Schools and American Society, 1780–1860* (New York: Hill and Wang, 1983), ch. 1.
3   On the primacy of the family, see Bailyn, *Education*, and L.A. Cremin, *American Education: The Colonial Experience, 1607–1763* (New York: Harper and Row, 1970). On child-rearing, see J.W. Frost, 'As the Twig is Bent: Quaker Ideas of Childhood', *Quaker History*, 60 (1971), pp. 67–87, and especially P.W. Greven, *The Protestant Temperament: Patterns of Child-Rearing, Religious Experience, and the Self in Early American History* (Chicago: University of Chicago Press, 1977).
4   J. Axtell, *The School upon a Hill: Education and Society in Colonial New England* (New York: W.W. Norton, 1974), and A. Taylor, *American Colonies* (New York: Viking, 2001).
5   See especially, Axtell, *The School upon a Hill*; Kraushaar, *Private Schools*, pp. 11, 14; Cremin, *Colonial Experience*; C.F. Kaestle, *The Evolution of an Urban System: New York City, 1750–1850* (Cambridge: Harvard University Press, 1973).
6   M.B. Katz, *The Irony of Early School Reform: Educational Innovation in Mid-Nineteenth-Century Massachusetts* (Boston: Beacon Press, 1968), and Kaestle, *Pillars*, illuminate the breadth of social changes transforming American society.
7   On mass education, see Kraushaar, *Private Schools*, p. 30. On higher education, see J.S. Whitehead, *The Separation of College and State: Columbia, Dartmouth, Harvard, and Yale, 1776–1876* (New Haven: Yale University Press, 1973).
8   M.B. Katz, *Class, Bureaucracy, and the Schools: The Illusion of Educational Change in America* (New York: Praeger Publishers, 1975), p. 23, and T.R. Sizer (ed.), *The Age of the Academies* (New York: Teachers College Press, 1964).
9   Mann quoted in L.A. Cremin (ed.), *The Republic and the School: Horace Mann on the Education of Free Men* (New York: Teachers College Press, 1957), pp. 33, 107.
10   Boutwell quoted in Katz, *Class, Bureaucracy, and the Schools*, pp. 27–8.
11   'Common Schools and Public Instruction', *American Journal of Education*, 8 (1873), p. 225.
12   F. Rudolph, *Essays on Education in the Early Republic* (Cambridge: The Belknap Press of Harvard University Press, 1965), and Kaestle, *Pillars*.
13   D.G. Mathews, 'The Second Great Awakening as an Organizing Process', *American Quarterly*, 21 (1969), pp. 23–43.

14 Kaestle, *Pillars.*

15 On New York, see especially V.P. Lannie, *Public Money and Parochial Education: Bishop Hughes, Governor Seward, and the New York School Controversy* (Cleveland: Press of Case Western Reserve University, 1968); Kaestle, *The Evolution of an Urban System*; D. Ravitch, *The Great School Wars: New York City, 1805–1973* (New York: Basic Books, 1974).

16 On the role of Protestants in the creation of public schools, and religious compromises made among them in the process, see T.L. Smith, 'Protestant Schooling and American Nationality, 1800–1850', *Journal of American History*, 53 (1967), pp. 679–95; D.B. Tyack, 'The Kingdom of God and the Common School: Protestant Ministers and the Educational Awakening in the West', *Harvard Educational Review*, 33 (1966), pp. 447–69; D.B. Tyack, 'Onward Christian Soldiers: Religion in the Common School', in P. Nash (ed.), *History and Education: The Educational Uses of the Past* (New York: Random House, 1970), pp. 212–55; J.R. Bodo, *The Protestant Clergy and Public Issues* (Princeton: Princeton University Press, 1954); F.X. Curran, *The Churches and the Schools: American Protestantism and Popular Elementary Education* (Chicago: Loyola University Press, 1954).

17 W.M. McAffee, *Religion, Race, and Reconstruction: The Public School in the Politics of the 1870s* (Albany, New York: State University of New York, 1998), pp. 192–6, and T. Walch, *Parish School: American Catholic Parochial Education from Colonial Times to the Present* (New York: The Crossroad Publishing Company, 1996), pp. 62–3.

18 D.A. Hawkins, 'Compulsory School Attendance', *American Journal of Education*, 30 (1880), p. 825.

19 Walch, *Parish School*, pp. 63–5.

20 E.N. Saveth, 'Education of an Elite', *History of Education Quarterly*, 28 (1988), pp. 367–86.

21 On Roosevelt and public education, see W.H. Harbaugh, *The Life and Times of Theodore Roosevelt* (New York: Oxford University Press, 1975), pp. 28, 216.

22 J.H. Spring, *Education and the Rise of the Corporate State* (Boston: Beacon Press, 1972); D.B. Tyack, *The One Best System: A History of American Urban Education* (Cambridge: Harvard University Press, 1974); W.E. Fuller, *The Old Country School: The Story of Rural Education in the Middle West* (Chicago: University of Chicago Press, 1982); H.M. Kliebard, *Schooled to Work: Vocationalism and the American Curriculum, 1876–1946* (New York: Teachers College Press, 1999).

23 O.F. Kraushaar, *American Nonpublic Schools: Patterns of Diversity* (Baltimore: The Johns Hopkins University Press, 1972), chs 1–2.

24 Tyack, 'Onward', pp. 212–255; W.J. Reese, 'Public Schools and the Great Gates of Hell', *Educational Theory*, 32 (1982), pp. 9–18; J. Falwell, with E. Dobson and E. Hindson, *The Fundamentalist Phenomenon: The Resurgence of Conservative Christianity* (New York: Doubleday & Company, 1981); E.J. Larson, *Summer for the Gods: The Scopes Trial and America's Continuing Debate over Science and Religion* (New York: Basic Books, 1997).

25 D.B. Tyack, 'The Perils of Pluralism: The Background of the Pierce Case', *American Historical Review*, 74 (1968), pp. 74–98, and Kraushaar, *American Nonpublic Schools*, pp. 13–14.

26 P.F. Douglas, 'Keep the Public Schools Public', *Social Frontier*, 4 (1937), pp. 42–6; M.E. O'Connor, 'Are Private Schools So Superior?', *Journal of Education*, 120 (1937), pp. 321–2; 'Are Private Schools Better?', *Journal of Education*, 131 (1948), p. 47; J. L. Sherman, 'Is the Private Secondary School Undemocratic?', *School and Society*, 69 (1949), pp. 193–5; Revd P.C. Reinert, 'Does America Need Private Education?', *Vital Speeches*, 16 (1950), pp. 372–5; T.D. Martin, 'Are Private Schools

a Menace to our Democracy?', *Nation's Schools,* 46 (1950), p. 28; O.L. La Farge, 'We Need Private Schools', *The Atlantic Monthly,* 193 (1954), pp. 53–6. On Catholicism and the 1960 election, see Walch, *Parish School,* p. 209, and J.T. Patterson, *Grand Expectations: The United States, 1945–1974* (New York: Oxford University Press, 1996), p. 439.

27 C. Jencks, 'Is the Public School Obsolete?', in M.B. Katz (ed.), *School Reform: Past and Present* (Boston: Little Brown Company, 1971), p. 243.

28 J.H. Spring, *The Sorting Machine: National Education Policy Since 1945* (New York: Longman, 1976), and B. Clowse, *Brainpower for the Cold War: The Sputnik Crisis and National Defense Education Act of 1958* (Westport, Connecticut: Greenwood Press, 1981).

29 C.F. Kaestle and M.S. Smith, 'The Federal Role in Elementary and Secondary Education, 1940–1980', *Harvard Educational Review,* 52 (1982), pp. 384–409, and J.R. Jeffrey, *Education for the Children of the Poor: A Study of the Origins and Implementation of the Elementary and Secondary Education Act of 1965* (Columbus: Ohio State University Press, 1978).

30 While the literature on race and education after 1945 is vast, the starting place on the *Brown* decision is R. Kluger, *Simple Justice: The History of Brown v. Board of Education and Black America's Struggle for Equality* (New York: Alfred A. Knopf, 1976), and J.T. Patterson, *Brown v. Board of Education: A Civil Rights Milestone and Its Troubled Legacy* (New York: Oxford University Press, 2001). On segregationist academies, see D. Nevin and R.E. Bills, *The Schools That Fear Built: Segregationist Academies in the South* (Washington, D.C.: Acropolis Books, 1976); on the rise of Christian schools, see W.J. Reese, 'Soldiers for Christ in the Army of God: The Christian School Movement in America, *Educational Theory,* 35 (1985), pp. 174–94.

31 H. Kantor and B. Brenzel, 'Urban Education and the "Truly Disadvantaged": The Historical Roots of the Contemporary Crisis, 1945–1990', in M.B. Katz (ed.), *The 'Underclass' Debate: Views from History* (Princeton: Princeton University Press, 1993), pp. 366–402.

32 On concerns over morality, see B.E. McClellan, *Moral Education in America: Schools and the Shaping of Character from Colonial Times to the Present* (New York: Teachers College Press, 1999), ch. 5, and Reese, 'Public Schools', pp. 9–18.

33 H.M. Hamlin, 'Are We Returning to Private Education?', *Nation's Schools,* 55 (1955), p. 63.

34 B.J. Kohlbrenner, 'Some Practical Aspects of the Public Character of Private Education', *School and Society,* 86 (1958), p. 248; E.R. D'Allesio, 'Public Policy Implications of Public Assistance to Nonpublic Education', *Religious Education,* 70 (1975), pp. 174–84; E.G. Gaffney, Jr (ed.), *Private Schools and the Public Good: Policy Alternatives for the Eighties* (Notre Dame: University of Notre Dame Press, 1981).

35 On the 'child benefit theory', see D. Ravitch, *The Troubled Crusade: American Education, 1945–1980* (New York: Basic Books, 1983), pp. 30, 33, 41; on the support of private school groups for the Elementary and Secondary Education Act during the Johnson years, see Walch, *Parish School,* pp. 213–14.

36 See, for example, M. Friedman, *Free To Choose* (New York: Avon Books, c.1979), and J. Coons and S.D. Sugarman, *Education By Choice: The Case for Family Control* (Berkeley: University of California Press, 1978). Also see an early attempt to document the revival of conservatism in the 1970s, A. Crawford, *Thunder on the Right: The 'New Right' and the Politics of Resentment* (New York: Pantheon Books, 1980).

37 The rising power of the ideology of the market place is underscored in B.J. Schulman, *The Seventies: The Great Shift in American Culture, Society, and Politics* (New York: Da Capo Press, 2001). On Reagan and tax credits, see Walch, *Parish School,* pp. 221, 227.

38 The literature on Catholic education is vast; in addition to Walch, *Parish School*, see, for example, A.M. Greeley and P.H. Rossi, *The Education of Catholic Americans* (Chicago: Aldine, 1966); J. Coleman, T. Hoffer and S. Kilgore, *High School Achievement: Public, Catholic, and Private Schools Compared* (New York: Basic Books, 1982); A.S. Bryck, V.E. Lee and P.B. Holland, *Catholic Schools and the Common Good* (Cambridge: Harvard University Press, 1993).
39 National Center for Education Statistics, *Private School Universe Survey, 1999–2000* (Washington, D.C.: US Department of Education, Office of Educational Research and Improvement, 2001), p. 2.
40 *Private School Universe Survey*, pp.1–3. On the diversity of private schools in the past, see the overview in Kraushaar, *American Nonpublic Schools*, part 1; and the case studies in J.C. Carper and T. Hunt (eds), *Religious Schooling in America* (Birmingham, Alabama: Religious Education Press, 1984).
41 *Private School Universe Survey*, p. 20.

9

PUBLIC COMMITMENT AND PRIVATE CHOICE IN AUSTRALIAN SECONDARY EDUCATION

Geoffrey Sherington

INTRODUCTION

The history of education in Australia presents an apparent contradiction. During the nineteenth century, and for much of the twentieth century, the role of the state was crucial in creating a highly centralised 'public' education system, albeit one founded on clear social divisions of not only class and gender but also race and ethnicity.[1] Writing in the early 1980s, Bob Connell and his co-authors suggested that in Australia 'the ruling class and its schools are articulated mainly through a market, while the working class and its schools are articulated mainly through a bureaucracy (or to put it very strictly through the state via a bureaucracy)'.[2] In more recent decades, with the moves towards 'markets' and 'school choice' throughout much of the English-speaking world, it has been argued that Australia has developed one of the strongest commitments to 'private schools', while even the former public sector in Australia is seen as being increasingly privatised. The provision of education as a 'public good' for the foundation of a liberal-democratic society, it is suggested, has been replaced by education as 'a positional good' serving private advantage.[3]

The following discussion focuses not so much on the divide as the interaction between 'public' and 'private' in the history of secondary education in Australia. It concentrates on New South Wales, the largest of the Australian states and long reputed to have had the strongest public education sector.

Examining the structural and institutional provision of education, it pays particular attention to the colonial and constitutional contexts of Australian history. It emphasises the significance of curriculum and examination traditions in reinforcing the primacy of academic knowledge. Analysing some of the social class outcomes of secondary schooling, the discussion reveals the way public commitment has helped to sustain and even shape educational markets which have served private interests. Equally, it raises the question of how far the continuing existence of not only a public education system but also the persistence of private moral and religious values continue to influence, if not constrain, educational markets.

NINETEENTH-CENTURY ORIGINS

Created as a penal colony in the late eighteenth century, New South Wales inherited educational practices from Britain. While the early colonial adminis-tration provided some elementary schooling for children of convicts, the landed and commercial elite often employed family tutors as well as governesses to teach their children. There were also private venture schools to cater for the growing need for training in commercial practices, while the clergy and others established tuition in their own homes to provide elements of learning, includ-ing the study of classics. Governesses from Britain set up ladies academies to teach the polite accomplishments of music, art and an 'English education' in literature and the related humanities.[4] Australian colonial families thus purchased both knowledge and skills to ensure the future of their sons and daughters. As such, the needs of the emerging colonial elite helped to provide a basis of a market in education, although one that was essentially unregulated. Equally, however, these strategies were designed to form the character of the elite, albeit along gendered lines, and thereby to separate the education of the children of the privileged classes from that elementary schooling offered to the labouring class.

By the 1820s private interests had begun to merge with the corporate endeavours of Christian faiths. The Church of England attempted to form a Church and Schools Corporation which would be supported by land grants to help fund the establishment of schools. The venture failed due to the opposition of other Protestant denominations and the Roman Catholic Church. From out of this failure emerged attempts by the Anglican Church to found King's Schools modelled on the ancient establishment of similar name associated with Canterbury Cathedral. The King's School in the centre of Sydney opened in 1831 but soon collapsed. Its counterpart, at Parramatta, on the outskirts of Sydney, survived with a claim to be the first established boys' grammar school in Australia.[5]

The English grammar and public school tradition had a major influence on Australian male corporate schools. In some respects these were seen as Antipodean versions of the English public schools. The mid-nineteenth-century reforms in the male English public schools and even the later reform in the schooling of middle-class girls influenced the Australian colonies. Both the academic grammar school curriculum and the emphasis on character building and organised games would become important features of the late-nineteenth-century Australian versions of the English grammar and public schools. Much of this transplantation of ideals and forms was carried directly into the colonies with the appointment of school heads and staff. One example is seen in the non-denominational Sydney Grammar School, established in 1854 with state endowment as a feeder school to the recently founded University of Sydney. By the 1870s Sydney Grammar, which was primarily a town day boys' school, was exhibiting many of the features of the reformed English public school tradition with prefects, school colours and corporate spirit, and a specific emphasis on organised games which would constitute the creation of late-nineteenth-century middle-class masculinity.[6] Similar changes occurred in schools of all the major religious denominations, including the Catholic Church, despite other educational traditions imported from such areas as Scotland and even France.[7]

These foundations were not so much 'private' ventures but principally 'corporate' schools governed by religious or other organisations. Increasingly they supplanted the earlier establishments run principally for private profit. As in England, they assumed the form, if not the full substance, of the 'public school' by emphasising their role in the creation of future social leaders.[8] Amongst girls' schools the privately-run ladies academies lasted much longer, often well into the twentieth century, albeit now offering a curriculum founded on academic subjects as much as the female 'private accomplishments' in art and literature. Increasingly, all the major religious denominations followed the pattern of the Catholic convents in establishing girls' corporate schools.[9]

During the late nineteenth century similar schools began to emerge under state auspices. Despite the predominance in Australia of the English public school tradition with all the associations of that name, the concept of 'public education' became closely aligned with the establishment of state-provided schools, which first complemented and then competed with the schools of the religious denominations. In contrast to England and Canada, and much of Western Europe, the educational settlements reached in the Australian colonies in the late nineteenth century denied religious and social pluralism in the interests of establishing a common civic culture in schools founded and funded by the state. In New South Wales, as in the other Australian colonies, this cultural consensus was founded on agreement between the major Protestant Christian faiths but was equally vigorously resisted by the Catholic Church.

The situation was exacerbated even further by the composition of the Australian population, with many Australian Catholics owing allegiance to Ireland rather than the British Empire. At the same time, administrative arrangements of public education led to increasing control from state bureaucracies, with little allowance for local opinion. In part this related to matters of income for, rather than local rates and taxes financing public schools, funds came from the central state agencies. The 'compulsory, free and secular' systems of the Australian colonial state were highly centralised.[10] In these ways the apparent need for a common public education system prevailed over the private and local attachments to faith and community.

Initially, the state had only a limited role in founding schools beyond the stage of elementary education. In the wake of the New South Wales 1880 Public Instruction Act, which withdrew all state funds from Church schools, a number of state high schools were created in Sydney and major regional centres. In part, these new high schools introduced a form of meritocracy into secondary education in New South Wales with a process of selecting students by academic examination. It could be suggested that these meritocratic features, and even the concept of the 'high school', drew on the mythical egalitarian context of Scottish education rather than the aristocratic values of the English public and grammar schools, even though Scottish secondary education itself was becoming increasingly Anglicised during the nineteenth century.[11]

In the main the curriculum and values of the new public high schools were still modelled on the existing Australian corporate schools. All were single sex and the boys' schools in particular followed closely the traditional grammar school curriculum of the corporate sector, emphasising both academic subjects and character-building reinforced through organised sport and using such devices as the prefect system which was supposedly designed to produce future civic leaders. Significantly, Sydney Boys High School, founded in 1883, would be admitted into the elite Athletic Association of Great Public Schools. This was the organisation set up to regulate sporting competitions between the male corporate schools with a title which associated it with the English public school tradition while distinguishing its members from mere Australian public schools.[12] All the early public high schools also charged fees, but this proved an early disadvantage in local educational markets. In direct competition with the corporate sector only two high schools in Sydney, and two in the regional centre of Maitland, north of Sydney, where there was no local corporate school, survived into the twentieth century.[13]

At the same time, however, a system of non-fee-paying superior public schools emerged with a similar academic curriculum that even allowed pupils to matriculate to university. The most important of these was Fort Street School in the centre of Sydney, founded initially as a teacher training institution.[14] But even in regional rural centres a number of superior public schools offered academic studies leading to university.[15] Thus by the first two decades of the twentieth century the state had begun to establish a system of secondary education. Through a series of academic examinations, supplemented later by intelligence testing, students could climb an 'educational ladder', with scholarship support helping them to stay in school, and then proceed to university. New high schools were opened in Sydney and in the major country towns of New South Wales. Students not selected to attend these elite public institutions would have the opportunity to enrol in various forms of post-primary education with a vocational focus for boys and domestic science emphasis for girls. At the same time as these changes were instituted in public education, which now came under a Director-General, controls were tightened over schools outside the public sector which were required to meet certain standards of efficiency.[16]

The public high schools could promise essentially free education to those of academic talent. While both the corporate schools and public high schools were still closely associated with the tradition of 'character formation', with its accompanying gendered dimensions, the latter became more focused on a new secular and civic ethic which sought to supplant the corporate schools which were principally associated with specific Christian religious denominations. Some believed that the public high schools could help to produce a new aristocracy of talent and civic leadership.[17]

EARLY TO MID-TWENTIETH-CENTURY DEVELOPMENTS

From the early twentieth century public high schools were in direct competition with corporate schools in terms of both social values and academic performance. This competition was highly regulated through the examination system. From the mid-nineteenth century, centrally organised examinations had become one of the major features of New South Wales' secondary education. In 1867 the newly established University of Sydney had created a system of Junior and Senior Public Examinations. Similar to the examination system then being established in England, the Junior and Senior provided both a means of entry to the University and also helped maintain an academic emphasis in the secondary schools.[18]

By the early twentieth century, state-sponsored examinations, the Intermediate and the Leaving Certificate, based in part on Scottish models, had replaced the Junior and Senior Examinations, helping to enshrine a high school curriculum emphasising not only the classics and mathematics but also science, modern languages, the humanities and economics. Created to provide forms of certification for students graduating from the expanding public high schools, but also accepted by the corporate schools, these new examinations were also controlled by statutory boards which were generally dominated by university academics. With secondary education closely tied to the University, the curriculum in both the corporate and public high schools of New South Wales during the early to mid-twentieth century would remain closely focused on academic subjects.[19] As such, the examination system continued an academic tradition but also served private interests in creating pathways into the University as well as the expanding professions and white-collar occupations.

Increasingly, students from the public high schools not only constituted the majority of public examination candidates but were also achieving examination success beyond that of students from the corporate schools. In particular, the major boys' and girls' high schools in the city of Sydney began to dominate the examination results. By the 1920s, students from Sydney Boys High School and Fort Street High were outperforming those from the older established corporate schools such as Sydney Grammar School where many students did not even complete their studies but benefited from the social status attached to the school.[20] The state-provided public sector thus challenged the earlier domination of the corporate schools, particularly in Sydney, albeit with due regard for different interests of social class and region. The public high schools were more to be found in the inner city of Sydney or in selected areas of the expanding south-western suburbs, providing opportunities for sections of middle-class and bright working-class youth. In contrast, the corporate schools predominated in the established upper-middle-class suburbs of eastern and northern Sydney.[21]

Elsewhere in Sydney, different forms of public post-primary education emerged, including single-sex intermediate and junior high schools, commercial and junior technical schools for boys, and home science schools for girls, all of which had come to supplant the earlier superior public schools.[22] Many of these secondary schools were in the working-class areas of Sydney where the main competition to public education came from the Catholic schools which now formed the largest part of the non-public school sector. Denied funds from the state under the 1880 Public Instruction Act, the Catholic Church had set out to create its own system by relying on religious orders to provide teachers. By the 1950s, a series of separate Catholic secondary schools for boys and girls had been created throughout New South Wales. Based on local parish organisation, Catholic education attempted to create a system to rival that of the state public schools. These schools were single sex, generally offering a vocational curriculum for boys and domestic studies for girls. They were thus quite distinct from the more prestigious Catholic corporate boys' and girls' schools founded in the nineteenth century to create a Catholic elite.[23]

In rural regions a more complex pattern of interaction was occurring. Overall, more than three-quarters of the public high schools founded from 1910 to 1945 were in rural districts. The spread of the country high schools extended the educational ladder, often in response to rural community pressures on the political system. In particular, the leader of the Country Party in New South Wales, 1932–40, was also Minister for Education and especially committed to the extension of education in rural areas.[24] By the 1950s almost all major regional centres in New South Wales had a high school. In remote areas there were also 'Central' schools, combining both primary and junior secondary studies. As in working-class suburbs of Sydney the main competition to rural public schools came from Catholic secondary schools offering a more vocational curriculum than existed in the corporate schools. Yet there was also a form of tacit co-operation between the public and Catholic schools, with students often attending a rural Intermediate Catholic secondary school and then completing secondary school in a nearby country town high school.

As in Sydney, the spread of rural high schools had implications for the creation of an academic meritocracy drawn from the lower middle class or skilled working class. In the Illawarra region just south of Sydney, those entering the local Wollongong High School came increasingly from working-class backgrounds, particularly from the region's coal mining villages but also from families associated with industrial trades at the local iron and steel plant.[25] While the high schools in Sydney were single sex, however, country high schools were co-educational, although there were different patterns of discipline and control for males and females.[26]

Both rural and metropolitan high schools became a recruiting ground for future teachers in the public system, with bursaries and scholarships providing an opportunity to attend teachers' college and even the University. By the mid-1930s, almost 40 per cent of entrants to Sydney Teachers' College came from rural high schools and about 45 per cent from Sydney metropolitan high schools. The fathers of most of these students were in lower-middle-class white-collar occupations or skilled blue-collar work. The route from public high school to teaching provided new career opportunities, particularly for females who, by the late 1930s, constituted up to two-thirds of entrants to the teachers' colleges.[27]

Increasingly, and particularly in terms of academic status, the public high school system in New South Wales began to predominate over the older established corporate schools. Generally representing the social elite drawn from wealthy rural families or sections of the older professions, such as medicine, as well as parts of the emerging business class in the city of Sydney, a rather narrow process of social reproduction soon began to prevail within many of the corporate schools. For example, by the 1960s more than half the boys attending Sydney Church of England Grammar School, founded in the 1880s, were the sons of 'old boys'.[28] Recent research also suggests that in the immediate post-1945 period more than half the social elite of New South Wales had attended public high schools. Moreover, many of these successful public high school graduates were heavily concentrated in such areas as the universities and public service administration; a reflection, perhaps, in part of the creation of a new civic-minded elite who were employed within the public sector.[29] As elsewhere in Australia, public secondary education thus served to create and sustain a significant section of the Australian middle class.[30]

Within this context, and in the wake of the Second World War, there was a growing demand for public secondary schooling and the credentials it offered. Even in the 1920s students in schools offering a vocational curriculum had begun to sit for the Intermediate Certificate which had been designed for the selective academic high schools. With post-war economic growth and prosperity, enrolments in all forms of secondary education increased. Almost one-quarter of the public school population were now in some form of post-primary school, compared to only one-twentieth in 1910.[31] Since the mid-1930s there had been much discussion of both curriculum and examination reform in secondary education that might take account of these new circumstances. This came to fruition under a new Director of Education whose solution to the problem emanated from both internal and local experiences. Educated in New South Wales and California (Stanford University), Harold Wyndham, Director-General of Education, chaired a committee which recommended the creation of a comprehensive high school system. Drawing upon plans which had been developed first in the 1930s, the 'Wyndham scheme' was a response to growing demographic pressures on the existing public high schools, particularly in the era of post-1945 prosperity. It also reflected the commitment of Wyndham and others in the educational bureaucracy to expanding educational opportunities for all, and not merely to those who had managed to climb the educational ladder.[32]

Despite the example of the twentieth-century American comprehensive high school, and post-war British debates about comprehensive secondary education, many supporters of the comprehensive ideal in New South Wales simply looked to the local rural towns where co-educational high schools had long been seen to serve the interests of communities. The new system of comprehensive schools could thus be seen as bringing the rural ideal of a school set in its community to the city, albeit with due regard to the circumstances of a changing urban environment. In the inner city, older public schools and intermediate high schools were transformed into comprehensive high schools, some of which remained single sex. It was principally in the expanding middle-class suburbs or on the fringes of the city where working-class housing estates were being built that new co-educational comprehensive high schools were established.[33]

Highly assimilationist in aim, the 'Wyndham scheme' was designed to produce the modern citizen in ways that denied not only gender differences but also the cultural values of the new post-war migrants from Europe.[34] In

these ways it followed the path for public education laid down in the nineteenth century. The curriculum model was also not new. The comprehensive
school curriculum that now emerged both in the rural areas and in the suburbs
of Sydney still focused on academic subjects and was controlled by examinations administered by boards where university academics maintained an
important role. The organisation of schools also allowed for academic 'streams'
separating the academically-inclined students from the rest. The links between
the secondary schools and university education were thus maintained. It was
assumed that while all students should remain in school to complete a School
Certificate, after four years of secondary school only a minority would proceed to complete a Higher School Certificate and enter university. Moreover,
despite the opposition of Wyndham, a small number of older high schools and
one new agricultural high school in Sydney still used selective forms of entry
as a way of maintaining the elite but meritocratic academic tradition of the
public high school sector in New South Wales. Until the 1970s selective entry
in certain schools also continued in the regional centres of Newcastle and
Wollongong. Both the emphasis on formal external examinations and the
principle of academic selection of pupils would have major consequences for
the future of comprehensive public secondary education in New South Wales.

LATE TWENTIETH-CENTURY CHANGES

With the establishment of the comprehensive high school system, the 1950s
and 1960s may be seen as the apogee of centrally controlled and bureaucrati-
cally managed public education in New South Wales. The foundation of most
of the corporate schools had taken place in the period from the late nineteenth
century to the 1930s, with only a few new schools being established after the
Second World War. In New South Wales, 47 corporate schools, all single sex
and representing all major Christian religious denominations, were founded
and survived in the period from the 1830s to the 1930s; over the next four
decades only another 11 were established.[35] From 1880 to 1930, 38 public
high schools had opened in New South Wales and another 27 over the next
two decades. But from 1950 to 1970 more than 200 public comprehensive high
schools were established in New South Wales.[36] The public comprehensive
co-educational high school, recruiting from a local neighbourhood, seemed to
be the 'wave of the future'.

If the creation of the 'Wyndham scheme' was a culmination of more
than a century of public education in New South Wales, it also marked the
beginning of a process that would ultimately assert private interests over public
commitment. In part this emerged from changed political and constitutional
circumstances. When Australia had become a federation in 1901, education

remained the responsibility of the six individual federating Australian states. The Second World War helped to transform this situation. First, the crisis of the War led to new financial relations between the federal government and the individual states. The federal government assumed the prime powers of taxation with the states becoming increasingly dependent on federal grants to survive. Second, the federal government became directly involved in education by providing funds to Australian universities.[37] Finally, the post-war expansion of both primary and secondary education, stimulated by a rising birth-rate and a large-scale immigration programme, created a financial crisis for the resourcing of all schools. Facing the difficulties of building schools and finding teachers, Australian state governments urged the federal government to provide more finances to support public school systems and thereby establish further national investment in education.[38]

But the change in the balance of power between Australian federal and state governments was also associated with a challenge to the concept of public education itself. As Australia moved towards becoming a multi-cultural society with the impact of post-war immigration, issues were raised as to whose interests 'public' education was serving. The questions came first from the Catholic Church which had long maintained that public education systems created in the nineteenth century were essentially forms of 'common' Protestantism. Strained by increasing populations in its schools, and the possible impact of such changes as the 'Wyndham scheme', the Catholic Church and parent groups placed pressure on both state governments and federal authorities to provide financial aid to their schools. More generally, this campaign raised the issue of the rights of parents as individual taxpayers being able to benefit directly from the taxes they paid.[39]

By the early 1960s, federal aid was being extended to all Australian secondary schools, first for science laboratories and then for school libraries. Prompted initially by calls from industry and groups associated with the corporate schools, these programmes were aimed at modernising Australian education.[40] The federal government also introduced a series of scholarships to allow secondary school students to stay longer at school, so complementing a national scholarship system introduced in the 1940s and 1950s to provide support for university students. In part this policy continued the ideology of meritocracy which had prevailed in the initial creation of public high schools. Following the election of the new Labor Government with Gough Whitlam as Prime Minister in 1972, these tentative steps of federal support for schools were soon consolidated into a new national policy framework. It was now determined that federal aid would be distributed to schools on the basis of need. All Australian schools received some form of federal aid, even though the policy was designed to distribute more to schools of social and economic disadvantage and less to schools of wealth and social privilege.[41]

Federal aid to all schools was planned initially as a national public commitment to education which even involved the establishment of national institutions in the area of educational policy. A federal Schools Commission was established in 1973 to develop policies in support of principles of social and gender equity and the recognition of cultural and ethnic differences. Within a decade-and-a-half economic rationalism in the context of changed economic circumstances led to a new emphasis on policies which tended to favour school choice rather than those which sought to create social justice and equity. Despite certain efforts to restrict state aid to the wealthy corporate schools, and to contain the growth of new non-government schools, in the mid-1980s fiscal restraints led even the Australian Labor governments towards policies which benefited schools outside the public sector. By the mid-1990s, a newly elected national conservative coalition had introduced policies which not only supported private choice but also withdrew resources from schools in the public sector.[42]

Public funds now virtually subsidised school fees, not only allowing schools outside the public system to survive but ultimately encouraging their growth. The costs of sending a child to a Catholic or corporate secondary school had actually increased in the immediate post-war years; by the late 1970s, with the introduction of state aid, they had declined dramatically.[43] Over the last three decades of the twentieth century there was a major shift in the balance between public and non-government schools. In 1970, more than three-quarters of secondary school enrolments in New South Wales were in public schools; by 2000 this had fallen to less than two-thirds. While Catholic schools remained the most significant part of the non-government sector, contributing over half the growth in secondary school enrolments, much of the expansion in the number of non-government secondary school pupils came from the establishment of new religious schools. Most of these new schools were in areas of population growth in the outer suburbs of Sydney, but some were in rural areas and along the New South Wales coastline. Many of these new foundations were 'combined' primary–secondary schools, often small in size at first but growing as the schools expanded their enrolments to include all primary and secondary grades. Through processes of demographic change and rationalisation the number of public secondary and even Catholic schools declined, although there was an overall increase of 55 schools in New South Wales in the period 1991–2000. About one-third of these were schools under the newly created Anglican Board of Education. The rest were primarily schools associated with fundamentalist Christian sects or the Islamic faith.[44]

The growth of schools outside the public sector was assisted not only by a new federal and political context but also by fundamental economic change. By the mid-1980s, with the collapse of the full-time youth labour market, more than 70 per cent of pupils were remaining to the end of high school, twice the proportion of the 1960s when public comprehensive high schooling was introduced.[45] With the subsequent expansion in the Australian higher education system there was an increasing move towards academic selection in tertiary entry. Rather than leading to a major revision of the curriculum, this growth in numbers of school pupils led to an increasing quest for credentials, strengthening the role of the Higher School Certificate. Nevertheless, in the 1980s, despite the growth in retention rates, the share of students in higher education coming from the public sector declined from 60 to 50 per cent.[46]

Parents who had themselves attended public high schools often now chose to send their own children elsewhere. Indeed, there is clear evidence of a drift away from public secondary schools as early as the introduction of the 'Wyndham scheme' of comprehensive education in the 1960s.[47] Recent research suggests that this trend was itself associated with apparent changes amongst the middle class that had previously benefited from the growth of the public high schools in New South Wales. For much of the twentieth century the Australian middle class had been composed principally of a strong segment of professionals tied to state funding, particularly in the social services area, with a weaker managerial sector located in the private business sector. By the 1980s the private sector amongst the Australian middle class became much stronger while even in the declining public sector those associated with entrepreneurial management expanded.[48] As in Britain, there were signs that the composition of the Australian middle class was being re-constituted with a shift towards those associated with a more entrepreneurial outlook who coincidentally shared greater anxiety about the future of their own children.[49] The increasing ethnic and cultural diversity of Australian cities in the 1970s and 1980s probably reinforced these trends, with many recent middle-class immigrants looking to education as a way for social advancement for their children.

By the late 1980s schools outside the traditional public system had an increasing appeal while public education seemed in decline. The corporate schools began to assume the space previously held by the selective high schools. By the late 1970s Sydney Grammar School, having shaken off its poor academic performances of the early to mid-twentieth century, and having introduced partial selective academic entry tests, was being recognised as the top performing school in the Higher School Certificate.[50] In response to this challenge, during the last decade of the twentieth century, under governments drawn from both non-Labor and Labor backgrounds, public secondary education in New South Wales was restructured. Ministerial authority was increased and the former educational bureaucracy was in part supplanted by a new form of managerial expertise. To oversee the curriculum and public examinations, new legislation created a statutory Board of Studies which was independent of the state Department of Education. In place of the ideal of comprehensive neighbourhood high schools, there was now the policy of selectivity and choice within public education with parents being able to enrol their children in schools outside their local area.[51] In particular, amongst other changes, it was decided to create a number of former comprehensive high schools as academically selective public high schools to complement the few that had survived the 'Wyndham scheme'. The intention was to allow public schooling to compete directly with the private sector, even though the drift to schools outside the public sector continued unabated.[52]

By the end of the 1990s public education was again being restructured, with further school closures and creation of senior colleges for the last two years of schooling. The new policies of selectivity and differentiation only served to encourage further private quests for the 'positional goods' public education now apparently offered. A market emerged for privately-paid tutors to coach students for the selective schools entry tests. In 2002, over 15,000 applicants were sitting for 2,500 places available in the 28 selective high schools in New South Wales. Of those who failed to receive a place, three-quarters would abandon the public high schools and enrol in a fee-paying school.[53]

The impact of these changes on local comprehensive high schools was profound. Signs of residualisation of the comprehensive schools in terms of regions if not social class began to appear. In remote rural areas, where the comprehensive ideal had been first formed, and where there was little competition from either the Catholic sector or other low-fee religious schools, the local public high school often survived to fulfil its long-term mission in educating the children of the local community. In the far outer west of New South Wales, where there were many Aboriginal communities and pockets of rural poverty, almost 90 per cent of the school populations were in public schools. In urban areas and in the coastal regions, where the population was growing, there was often intense competition not only between public high schools and a variety of religious and non government schools but within the public sector itself. In Sydney, where enrolments in public schools had declined to about 60 per cent of the total school population, the impact of migration and other patterns of settlement meant that many local schools had become associated with certain ethnic groups, often to their disadvantage in terms of how they were perceived by the media and parents. Changing perceptions of gender relations in education led to single-sex girls' schools being favoured while public single-sex boys' schools often suffered in enrolments. Public schools in middle-class areas promoted their success in examinations and other performances. With the virtual end to school zones students could now cross the city, enrolling not only in selective and other specialist high schools but also in those comprehensive high schools regarded as having a good reputation. The rising property market in Sydney in the late 1990s only served to give a new meaning to 'positional goods', with recent immigrants attracted to suburbs with a reputation for 'good' schools.[54]

In an area such as the expanding outer western suburbs of Sydney, where new comprehensive schools had been founded in the 1960s and 1970s, there was a marked shift in the distribution of enrolments between the public and non-government schools and an intense competition between all schools. Of the 21 schools founded in outer western Sydney in the quarter century from 1950 to 1975, 18 had been public secondary schools and all but two of these were new comprehensive co-educational schools. Over the ensuing quarter of a century from 1975 to 2000, 24 new schools were established of which only one-third were public comprehensive high schools; of the rest, one was a senior college in the public sector, six were Catholic schools and nine were 'Christian community' schools.[55]

At the end of the twentieth century, the concept of a universal commitment to public education seemed in continuing decline. Even the older selective principle in public education had, in effect, not been revived but transformed. The early twentieth-century civic ideal of the ladder of educational oppor-tunities, supported by scholarships and other forms of assistance, had been replaced by a league table of schools judged by academic and examination performance. In the early twenty-first century the top performing school in New South Wales was James Ruse Agricultural High, a co-educational but selective public high school established in the then semi-rural outer suburbs of Sydney at the time of the 'Wyndham scheme'. Originally designed to pro-duce students to go into rural careers, James Ruse High, surrounded now by expanding suburbia, had become prominent as a public selective school where most of the successful entrants were children of recent immigrants and particularly those from East Asia. In 2002, James Ruse led the list of the 'top' ten at the Higher School Certificate exam, having now supplanted the male single-sex Sydney Grammar School. Of the next eight schools on the unofficial 'league table', two were Jewish co-educational schools, three were selective public high schools, two of which were single-sex girls and one co-educational, and three were long-established girls' corporate schools.[56] In this sense market competition had changed the pattern of secondary schooling in a way unimag-ined only a generation previously.

CONCLUSION

The above discussion suggests a complex interaction between public commit-ment and private choice in Australian secondary education. Founded principally on religion and with associations based on relationships of social class and gender, the Australian corporate schools certainly played a major part in the early history and formation of Australian secondary education. Tied closely to entry to higher education, they offered formal qualifications and a curriculum that would help shape the coming generation of the social elite. In this way, private choice became institutionalised, as the corporate schools increasingly replaced the early colonial informal markets of tutors, governesses and private schoolmasters and schoolmistresses.

By adopting for public secondary education the academic and other aspects of the corporate model, the state obviously had its own interests in creating a school system that would help sustain the civic culture of which the educational bureaucracy was itself an important part. It is not insignificant that many of the early twentieth-century state high schools in New South Wales were the recruiting grounds for the teachers who would staff the expanding public school system. But the bureaucratic state also regulated and shaped the educational market, in the process helping to produce a new social elite. Through the principle of merit selection the early public high schools in New South Wales met the aspirations of not only bright working-class children but also a significant section of the Australian middle class. Eventually the graduates of the early high schools of New South Wales would come to play a major role in the civic and social life of the nation.

Introduced in ways which retained an essentially academic curriculum, the establishment of public comprehensive secondary schools marked the culmination of the state's role in secondary education which had first begun in the early twentieth century.[57] Public comprehensive education was also a way to control, if not dominate, the market in secondary schooling, offering not so much school choice as universal provision of a common form of secondary schooling. This was a challenge not only to the older corporate schools and much of the Catholic sector with its limited resources, but also to the principle of academic selection on which the urban, if not the rural, public high schools had been built. While the public comprehensive high school model in New South Wales drew upon the experience of the country high schools based on rural communities, the public system itself lacked the local administrative and financial context to sustain the universal ideal of comprehensive school linked closely to its geographic neighbourhood in an urban environment. Public secondary education could only succeed with a federal funding commitment that went beyond state boundaries.

For a brief time it did seem that the public comprehensive secondary education would receive the support of a national public commitment of resources. That moment soon passed as national policies in education acted increasingly to subsidise private choice rather than maintain a public system of schools. In this way changing political commitments now responded to, but also shaped, the nature of the changing middle class in Australia. By the end of the twentieth century, even public education in individual states was being stripped of both its former educational bureaucratic expertise and the institutional forms which had sustained a civic culture of schooling. Increasingly public education had become more a limited service of state governments still principally centrally resourced but managed more at the local level in an effort to respond to different educational markets. While most students still attended public comprehensive high schools there was now a range of choice and differentiation and competition within public education which seemed to indicate the triumph of the ideology of the market place.

What has remained constant in Australian secondary education is the primacy of academic knowledge. In contrast to North America, which invented its own forms of the secondary school curriculum, Australia has remained tied to its colonial past and traditions which originated in England. Even the promise of the Australian public high school was principally for the few not the many.[58] The creation of the Australian model of the comprehensive secondary school, with its continuing commitment to academic examinations, may have actually strengthened the race for credentials as much as in North America. The search for credentials may have become more pronounced as Australia moved more towards a society of recent immigrants seeking social advancement through schooling.[59] Academic studies now served to provide increasing private benefit rather than the liberal civic culture intended when the 'Wyndham scheme' of comprehensive education was introduced in the 1960s. The academic credential has become the principal confirmation of private aspirations, replacing even the informal credentials of the 'old school tie' associated with the corporate schools that had survived even beyond the Second World War.[60] In Australia generally, academic success tested by examination and thereby leading into the expanded higher education system provided the main way to preserve or attain social power and position.[61] What has marked out New South Wales is the strong tradition of selective public high schools and their success in academic examinations, a tradition which has been revived in recent years with other forms of school differentiation deemed necessary within the contexts of new educational markets.

Despite these fundamental changes, there remained a number of constraints on educational markets. First, there was the continuing bureaucratic legacy in the public education system which educates more than two-thirds of the secondary school population in New South Wales. In 2002, with more than 2,200 primary and secondary schools and 60,000 teachers, the formal public education system in New South Wales remained the largest and most highly centralised system in Australia. In resources alone, it more than matches some of the larger provincial and local systems in North America and Europe. Even the supporters of traditional public education still see not only the lack of public resources but also continuing bureaucratic forms as restraining educational innovation and the ability to respond to change.[62]

There was also the constraint of past traditions. Even with the decline of the cachet of the 'old school tie', many of the corporate schools continued to draw status from sporting achievements, even though amateur sport in schools was itself becoming more professionalised and subject to the market. Within the transformed public sector there was similar continuing attachment to some of the values of the past. In early 2002, concerned at the sporting performance of the oldest boys' selective high school which remained a member of the Association of Great Public Schools, a group of old boys from Sydney Boys High School were considering ways to re-assert the values of 'Renaissance Man', even proposing to revive a policy discriminating in favour of the enrolment of the sons of former students at the school. Behind this campaign lay concerns that the large numbers of boys from Asia now enrolling in the school had little interest in or talent for 'manly' sports such as rugby.[63] Responding in part to this campaign, in May 2002 the New South Wales Government announced a review of the entry tests to selective schools that would reinforce examination in the English language.[64] The incident seemed to reveal some continuing problems of public education coming to terms with cultural diversity. It also showed that male elites, influenced by even older ideals drawn from the colonial past, could feel threatened by the 'pure operation' of the market favouring the emergence of new elites whose original homeland and values owed little to Australia's colonial origins.

This particular incident seems to suggest that private choices were influenced not only simply by the 'positional goods' of academic credentials. It is significant, therefore, to consider finally the prevalence and continuing strength of schools founded on religious faith. While much attention has focused recently on the new fundamental Christian and Islamic schools, the best example of religious schools surviving over time remains the Catholic system. Denied the resources of the state, a few elite Catholic schools sought identity with the corporate schools, but the majority of the early twentieth-century Catholic secondary schools in New South Wales emulated and competed with state secondary schooling. Depending upon local parish support and the non-paid labour of the teaching orders, Catholic schools could claim certain success in academic attainments. By the 1960s the representation of Catholics amongst the social elite of New South Wales had more than doubled since the early twentieth century, by then constituting the respective proportion of Catholics in the overall population.[65] With the introduction of state aid, Catholic education, with its heavily subsidised fees, now appealed to many parents not so much on grounds of promised academic success, or even for specific denominational faith, but often because of the order, discipline and values that Catholic schools apparently represented. By 2002 one-fifth of the parents of pupils in Catholic secondary schools were not Catholic.[66]

Provided with access to national funds, the Catholic system has developed its own educational bureaucracy to supplement and largely replace its earlier reliance on local parish endeavours. While it thus seems to have emulated parts of the older bureaucratic form of the public system, even some supporters of the public ideal of education suggest that the Catholic system now represents not only a community of faith but some of the best features of the former civic culture of public education. Certainly, in New South Wales at least, Catholic education has held to the comprehensive secondary school as being able to embrace all, retaining a 'non-market system based on systemic notions of equity and co-operation, rather than competition between institutions in the system'.[67]

Such a view could lead to a re-definition of public education embracing multiple religious faiths and cultural diversities within separate institutions. It would thereby help to meet such views as that of the executive officer of the New South Wales Parents Council, who has suggested that the drift to schools of religious faiths was not so much dissatisfaction with the public schools or a search for social privilege but rather that such schools offered a definite 'religious and philosophical environment'.[68] It could also form a basis to replace the settlement about public education that was created in the nineteenth-century colonial context, long before Australia became a society of many different religions and cultures. For if democracy is now not so much about state institutions but rather process and rights, including school choice, then those who still hold to the civic values they see in public education will need to find ways to recognise individual and social diversities that avoid the old assimilationist models of the past.

NOTES

The author acknowledges support from the Australian Research Council. He is also indebted to his research colleague Dr Craig Campbell for comments and to Ms Dorothy Straesser for research assistance.

1   As one example see P. Miller, *Long Division: State Schooling in South Australian Society* (Adelaide: Wakefield Press, 1986). For a recent review of the state and secondary schooling in Australia, see C. Campbell, C. Hooper and M. Fearnley-Sander, *Toward the State High School in Australia: Social Histories of State Secondary Schooling in Victoria, Tasmania and South Australia 1850–1925* (Australia and New Zealand History of Education Society, 1999).
2   R.W. Connell, D.J. Ashenden, S. Kessler and G.W. Dowsett, *Making the Difference: Schools, Families and School Division* (Sydney: George Allen and Unwin, 1982), p. 133. See also R.W. Connell, *Ruling Class, Ruling Culture* (Melbourne: Cambridge University Press, 1977).
3   S. Marginson, *Markets in Education* (Sydney: Allen and Unwin, 1997), and A. Reid and E. Cox (eds), *Going Public: Education Policy and Public Education in Australia*

(Canberra: Australian Curriculum Studies Association, 1998). See also D. Anderson, 'The Interaction of Public and Private School Systems', *Australian Journal of Education*, 36, 3 (1992), pp. 213–36.

4   C. Mooney, 'Securing a Private Classical Education in and around Sydney: 1830–1850', *History of Education Review*, 25, 1 (1996), pp. 38–53, and E. Windschuttle, 'Educating the Daughters of the Ruling Class Colonial in Colonial New South Wales, 1788–1850', *Melbourne Studies in Education 1980* (Melbourne: Melbourne University Press, 1980), pp. 105–33.

5   S.M. Johnstone, *The History of The King's School* (Sydney: Angus and Robertson, 1931).

6   C. Turney, *Grammar: A History of Sydney Grammar School 1819–1988* (Sydney: Allen and Unwin, 1989). See also C. Turney, 'The Advent and Adaptation of the Arnold Public School Tradition in New South Wales', *Australian Journal of Education*, 10, 2 (1966), pp. 133–44 and 11, 1 (1967), pp. 29–43.

7   For the transformation of Scottish and French traditions under the influence of the reformed English public school, see G. Sherington and M. Prentis, *Scots to the Fore: A History of The Scots College, Sydney, 1893–1993* (Sydney: Hale and Iremonger, 1993), and G. Sherington and M. Connellan, 'Socialisation, Imperialism and War: Ideology and Ethnicity in Australian Corporate Schools 1880–1918', in J.A. Mangan (ed.), *'Benefits Bestowed'? Education and British Imperialism* (Manchester: Manchester University Press, 1988), pp. 132–49. See also M. Crotty, *Making the Australian Male: Middle-Class Masculinity 1870–1920* (Melbourne: Melbourne University Press, 2001).

8   G. Sherington, R.C. Petersen and I. Brice, *Learning to Lead: A History of Girls' and Boys' Corporate Schools in Australia* (Sydney: Allen and Unwin, 1987). See also C.E.W. Bean, *Here My Son: An Account of the Independent and Other Corporate Boys' Schools of Australia* (Sydney: Angus and Robertson, 1950).

9   M. Theobald, *Knowing Women: Origins of Women's Education in Nineteenth-Century Australia* (Melbourne: Cambridge University Press, 1996), and N. Kyle, *Her Natural Destiny: The Education of Women in New South Wales* (Sydney: University of New South Wales Press, 1986).

10 The literature on this topic is vast, but for New South Wales see A.G. Austin and R.J.W. Selleck, *The Australian Government School 1830–1914. Select Documents with Commentary* (Melbourne: Pitman, 1975), and A. Barcan, *Two Centuries of Education in New South Wales* (Sydney: New South Wales University Press, 1988), pp. 106–50.

11 R. Anderson, *Education and Opportunity in Victorian Scotland* (Oxford: Clarendon, 1983).

12 G. Sherington, 'Athleticism in the Antipodes: The AAGPS of New South Wales', *History of Education Review*, 12, 2 (1983), pp. 16–28. By the early twentieth century there were similar elite sporting organisations for girls, but these did not admit Sydney Girls High School, also founded in 1883. Nor did elite Catholic girls' schools join these organisations.

13 E.W. Dunlop, 'The Early High Schools of New South Wales 1883–1912', *Journal of Royal Australian Historical Society*, 51, 1 (1965), pp. 155–80.

14 R.S. Horan, *Fort Street, The School* (Sydney: Honeyset Publications, 1989), and C. Morris, *'The School on the Hill': A Saga of Australian Life* (Sydney: The Wentworth Press, 1984). Founded in 1849 and originally co-educational, the school split into a boys' and girls' school in 1911.

15 For the example of Kiama, just south of Sydney, see W. Mitchell and G. Sherington, 'Families and Children in Nineteenth-Century Illawarra', in P. Grimshaw, C. McConville and E. McEwen (eds), *Families in Colonial Australia* (Sydney: George Allen and

Unwin, 1985), pp. 105–11, and G. Sherington, 'Families and State Schooling in the Illawarra 1840–1940', in M. Theobald and R.J.W. Selleck (eds), *Family, School and State in Australian History* (Sydney: Allen and Unwin, 1990), pp. 114–33.

16 For the architect of many of the early twentieth-century reforms see A.R. Crane and W. Walker, *Peter Board* (Melbourne: Australian Council for Educational Research, 1957).

17 D.L. Webster, 'Kilgour of Fort Street: The English Headmaster Ideal in Australian State Secondary Education', in *Melbourne Studies in Education 1981* (Melbourne: Melbourne University Press, 1981), pp. 184–206.

18 Barcan, *Two Centuries of Education in New South Wales*, p. 131. See also P.W. Musgrave, *From Humanity to Utility: Melbourne University and Public Examinations 1856–1964* (Melbourne: ACER, 1992).

19 Barcan, *Two Centuries of Education in New South Wales*, pp.189–90.

20 Horan, *Fort Street*, pp. 164–74, and Turney, *Grammar*, pp. 176–86.

21 P. Spearritt, *Sydney Since the Twenties* (Sydney: Hale and Iremonger, 1978), pp. 203–8.

22 *Government Schools of New South Wales 1848 to 1993* (New South Wales Department of School Education, 1993).

23 R. Fogarty, *Catholic Education in Australia 1806–1950* (Melbourne: Melbourne University Press, 1950), vol. II, pp. 311–51.

24 Barcan, *Two Centuries of Education in New South Wales*, pp. 214–15.

25 Sherington, 'Families and State Schooling in the Illawarra', pp. 124–31. In contrast, the proportion of those from farming backgrounds going to the public high school in the Illawarra declined throughout the twentieth century.

26 H. Proctor, 'Gender Grievance and Bad Behaviour at a NSW State High School, 1913–22', *Change: Monograph 2000*, pp. 53–65. Parramatta is to the west of Sydney. North of Sydney was the coal and iron city of Newcastle where until 1930 there was a co-educational high school founded in 1906. In 1930 two single-sex high schools replaced this original school so leading to different patterns of gender formation within the two schools on separate sites: J. May, 'Gender, Memory and the Experience of Selective Secondary Schooling in New South Wales from the 1930s to the 1950s', University of Newcastle, PhD thesis, 2000.

27 G. Sherington, 'Student Life, 1918–1945', in G. Boardman *et al.*, *Sydney Teachers' College, A History 1906–1981* (Sydney: Hale and Iremonger, 1995), pp. 96–100. See also G.W. Bassett, 'The Occupational Background of Teachers', *Australian Journal of Education*, 2, 2 (1958), pp. 79–90. For the general importance of teaching as a secure career to the middle class even after 1945, see C. Campbell, 'Family Strategy, Secondary Schooling and Making Adolescents: The Indian Summer of the Old Middle Class, 1945–1960', *History of Education Review*, 22, 2 (1993), pp. 18–44.

28 G. Sherington, *Shore: A History of Sydney Church of England Grammar School* (Sydney: George Allen and Unwin, 1983), p. 289.

29 M. Peel and J. McCalman, *Who Went Where: The Schooling of the Australian Elite* (Melbourne: Melbourne University History Research Series, no. 1, 1992), pp. 12–23.

30 C. Campbell, 'Secondary Schooling, Modern Adolescence and the Reconstitution of the Middle Class', *History of Education Review*, 24, 1 (1995), pp. 12–27.

31 *Government Schools of New South Wales*, p. 221. See also Barcan, *Two Centuries of Education in New South Wales*, pp. 238–40.

32 J. Hughes, 'Harold Wyndham: A Study in Education and Administration', University of Sydney, PhD thesis, 1999. See also J. Duffield, 'The Making of the Wyndham Scheme in New South Wales', *History of Education Review*, 19, 1 (1990), pp. 29–42.

33 Preliminary findings from Craig Campbell and Geoffrey Sherington, 'Residualisation, Regionalism and the Recent History of the State Comprehensive High School', Australian Research Council funded project.

34 L. Johnson, *Modern Girl: Childhood and Growing Up* (London: Open University Press, 1993), and T. Irving, D. Maunders and G. Sherington, *Youth in Australia, Policy, Administration and Politics: A History Since World War II* (Melbourne: Macmillan, 1995), Part I.
35 See Sherington, *Learning to Lead*, Appendix II, pp. 184–5.
36 A. Nation, 'Selective Growth: An Examination of the Expansion of Academically-Selective Schooling during the Metherell Era of Education in New South Wales 1988–1990', University of Sydney, M.Teach (Hons) Special Study, 2001, Appendices A and B.
37 A. Spaull, *Australian Education in the Second World War* (St Lucia: University of Queensland Press, 1982).
38 D. Smart, *Federal Aid for Australian Education* (St Lucia: University of Queensland Press, 1978), and A. Spaull, *The Australian Education Council 1936–1986* (Sydney: Allen and Unwin, 1986).
39 M. Hogan, *The Catholic Campaign for State Aid* (Sydney: Catholic Theological Faculty, 1978), pp. 187–98. It has been suggested that in contrast to the state planning of the War, the 1950s in Australia saw an emphasis on the rights of individual consumers and taxpayers: N. Brown, *Governing Prosperity. Social Change and Social Analysis in Australia in the 1950s* (Melbourne: Cambridge University Press, 1995).
40 D. Smart, 'The Industrial Fund: A Highly Successful Model of Big Business Collaboration with the Headmasters' Conference in the Interests of School Science', *Melbourne Studies in Education 1984* (Melbourne: Melbourne University Press, 1984), pp. 81–105.
41 For a recent analysis of the growth in federal funding from 1960 and the Karmel Committee which laid the foundation for this national policy after 1973, see S. Marginson, *Educating Australia, Government, Economy and Citizen since 1960* (Melbourne: Cambridge University Press, 1998), Part I.
42 J. Dudley and L. Vidovich, *The Politics of Education: Commonwealth Schools Policy, 1973–1995* (Melbourne: ACER, 1995), and A. Morrow, J. Blackburn and J. Gill, 'Public Education: From Public Domain to Private Enterprise?', in Reid and Cox (eds), *Going Public*, pp. 9–17.
43 See R.A. Williams, *The Economic Determinants of Private Schooling in Australia* (Canberra: The Australian National University Centre for Economic Policy Research, Paper 94, 1984), and *Interaction between Government and Private Outlays: Education in Australia 1949–50 to 1981–82* (Canberra: The Australian National University Centre for Economic Policy Research, Paper 79, 1982).
44 *Review of Non-Government Schools in NSW: Report 1* (Sydney: New South Wales Department of Education, 2002), pp. 19–36.
45 Irving, *et al. Youth in Australia*, Part III.
46 Marginson, *Markets in Education*, p. 169.
47 Ibid., p. 19.
48 B. Martin, 'The Australian Middle Class, 1986–1995: Stable, Declining or Restructuring', *Journal of Sociology*, 34, 2 (1998), pp.136–51.
49 S. Ball and C. Vincent, 'New Class Relations in Education: The Strategies of the "Fearful" Middle Classes', and S. Power, 'Missing: A Sociology of Educating the Middle Class', in J. Demaine (ed.), *Sociology of Education Today* (London: Palgrave, 2001), pp. 180–95 and 196–205.
50 Turney, *Grammar*, pp. 297–370.
51 For a study of the beginnings of this change in emphasis see G. Sherington, 'Education Policy', in M. Laffin and M. Painter (eds), *Reform and Reversal: Lessons from the Coalition Government in New South Wales 1988–1995* (Melbourne: Macmillan, 1995), pp. 171–87.

52   Nation, 'Selective Growth', pp. 70–7.
53   Report in *Sydney Morning Herald*, 6–7 April 2002, p. 31.
54   Findings from Campbell and Sherington, 'Residualisation, Regionalism and the Recent History of the State Comprehensive High School'.
55   Ibid.
56   Analysis in *Sydney Morning Herald*, 4 February 2002. The success of girls was now marked, although recent research suggests that proportionately females have consistently outperformed males in the centrally controlled exams: G. Kamperos, 'Gender Equity: Academic Performance of Girls and Boys in Public Matriculation Examinations in New South Wales 1884–1995', University of Sydney, PhD thesis, 2002.
57   B. Bessant and A. Spaull, *The Politics of Schooling* (Melbourne: Pitman, 1976), pp. 45–96.
58   W.J. Reese, *The Origins of the American High School* (New Haven: Yale University Press, 1995), and R.D. Gidney, *Inventing Secondary Education: The Rise of the High School in Nineteenth-Century Ontario* (London: McGill-Queen's University Press, 1990). See also D.L. Angus and J.E. Mirel, *The Failed Promise of the American High School 1890–1995* (New York: Teachers College Press, 1999), and J. Herbst, *The Once and Future School* (New York: Routledge, 1996).
59   D. Labaree, *How to Succeed in School Without Really Trying: The Credentials Race in American Education* (New Haven: Yale University Press, 1997).
60   G. Maslen, *School Ties: Private Schools in Australia* (Melbourne: Methuen, 1982).
61   R. Teese, *Academic Success and Social Power: Examinations and Inequality* (Melbourne: Melbourne University Press, 2000).
62   *Inquiry into the Public Provision of Public Education in NSW* (Vinson Enquiry) First Report May 2002, Sponsored by NSW Teachers Federation and Federation of P & C Association of NSW.
63   This item attracted much attention in the *Sydney Morning Herald* during April 2002.
64   New South Wales Department of Education and Training, 'Student Assessment and School Accountability Unit, Year 7 Placement Process, A Discussion Paper', May 2002.
65   Peel and McCalman, *Who Went Where,* p. 15.
66   *Sydney Morning Herald*, 9 May 2002 and 25–26 May 2002.
67   S. Marginson, 'Putting Public Back into Public Education', in Reid and Cox (eds), *Going Public*, p. 76.
68   *Sydney Morning Herald*, 25–26 May 2002.

descriptor stretches between utopian-idealist and functional-realist poles. International education reflects these competing currents and has long ceased to be understood as an idealist enterprise dedicated to increasing international understanding, fed by tributaries from peace and conflict studies and development studies.[4] Realist, descriptive perspectives would best characterise the major expansion in international education over the last 25 years of the twentieth century.

International education is understood to occur whenever a cross-border or transnational dimension is incorporated into facets of educational activity. Such activities can have cognitive, physical mobility and organisational-institutional dimensions; the outcomes of such activities may have curricular, research, fiscal, student, faculty or administrative manifestations. This definition also allows for subjective perceptions from all involved in the field.

To provide greater precision as we consider the public–private dimensions of international education, it is useful to approach the phenomenon from three interrelated perspectives – orientation, function and form. The *orientation* perspective allows us to distinguish the various purposes that international education advocacy and delivery address. For example, international education discourse frequently legitimates itself in relation to nationalist criteria such as the bolstering of national prosperity, power and competencies as in the case of the US NDEA (National Defense Education Act) of 1958 and the more recent NSEP (National Security Education Program) of 1991.[5] It can also reflect regional and integrationist agendas, as in the case of the European Union's Erasmus and Socrates programmes, and it may also reflect polycentric (cross-cultural, environmental) objectives. Orientation also provides a perspective from which we can analyse and categorise the content of international education.

The *functions* perspective highlights the knowledge, skills and values inputs and outcomes of international education. These are closely related to orientation characteristics as well as to perceptions of market value and the hierarchies of education and training. The functions perspective also informs our view of content.

Finally, the *forms* of international education relate to the particular way in which the product or service is delivered. The range of forms is enormous – student or faculty exchange, study abroad, franchised degree or sub-degree programmes, open and distance learning, branch campuses, dual-validated courses and qualifications, joint research across national boundaries, curricular innovations, to name a few.

Using an orientation/functions/forms approach enhances our ability to assess developments in this sector. For instance, the impact of globalisation and the increased activity of private actors in the sector have led to the inclusion of international education in the WTO domain. This has manifested itself initially in the forms (modes of delivery/education as a tradeable commodity) but also has rapid and inevitable consequences in terms of the functions and orientations of what is supplied and consumed.

It is worth noting that these perspectives are by no means static. The orientations and functions of international education have, for example, shifted dramatically in the UK. Up to 1987 it may be argued that a primary objective was cultural diplomacy in that the education of potential overseas elites within the UK was conceived of as a mechanism that would ensure positive perceptions of the UK in a post-colonial reality. The introduction of differential (higher) fees for overseas students created a shift from diplomacy towards commerce in that it created the necessary precondition (potential for profit) that would allow governments to reduce the basic level of support for higher education, while empowering universities to earn income to supplement state funding.[6]

In contrast, it may be argued that Japan's post-war strategy in this area was driven by the desire to create some positive perceptions of that nation following the Second World War. The emphasis on fully funded scholarship schemes and, particularly, the JET (Japan Exchange and Teaching Programme) had, implicitly or explicitly, the intention of countering anti-Japanese feelings relating to Japan's aggressive activities in the region during the war. In short, the orientations, functions and forms – the patterns and purposes – of international education shift in relation to perceived imperatives drawn from political and economic realities.

PUBLIC AND PRIVATE IN INTERNATIONAL EDUCATION

The starting point of this discussion is the assertion that in the context of international higher education the distinction between the public and the private is fast becoming irrelevant. This, of course, paints the picture with too broad a brush but it establishes the position from which the authors will examine the issues arising in greater detail.

In Europe we retain, at least the residue of, a sense that the public sector in higher education is somehow the guardian of 'values'. In this perception, the gatekeepers of 'quality' reside in the public sector where they are untroubled by the demands of the market: there exists a perceived gulf between education and commerce. Although five minutes spent in an international office at a British university would convince most onlookers of the redundancy of this perception, there still remains a suspicion of the private sector (especially of the for-profit private institutions) which is sustained at some level by the kinds of prejudice implied in the sense that education has nothing to do with commerce.

The persistence of this myth is, of course, uneven. It tends to be most prevalent in the, as yet, unreformed systems of some parts of continental Europe where even tuition fees are seen as some kind of compromise with Mammon. That this will undoubtedly change over the next few years is inevitable due to the demands of commerce and the international educational markets, and because of the reforms generated within Europe over the last few years. The creation of a European Higher Education 'space' by 2010 (envisioned in the Bologna Declaration of 1999 and examined later in this chapter) will challenge these ancient prejudices, as universities will have to learn to become more transparent and competitive. In short, what we take to be the traditional association of quality and value with the public sector has become irrelevant in that educational quality has necessarily become a key part of the agenda of all institutions, be they public or private, non-profit or for-profit.[7] The public–private dichotomies cease to be meaningful because the key factor is the capacity to compete effectively in the international education market. In most cases, this is not a future projection but a current reality.

At the root of this reality are a number of processes and dynamics that are irresistible. In the first case, the demand for education throughout the world has grown beyond the capacity of most national resources that can be funded through public expenditure. It is simply not possible to raise the taxes necessary to meet the increasing demand for higher education anywhere in the world. This fact has meant that education has become a commodity where demand outstrips supply. The inevitable consequence (albeit an unpalatable one) is that those who can afford it buy quality education. Those who cannot afford it either go without or make do with an inferior product. This is equally true for individuals as it is for nations. The gap between educational opportunity in Western Europe and, for example, East Africa, is a chasm.

This would be less of an issue if education were less important but, generally, individual fates are closely tied to skills acquired. If that is true for individuals, it is also relevant to nations where development is recognised to be dependent on human as well as natural resources. If a national labour force is under-educated in the new global market place, that nation has no chance of moving towards prosperity and equity with the more developed nations. Furthermore, that nation has no chance of satisfying the demands of its (under-educated) citizens for the commodities and services that, through technology, are almost universally known but are not universally available. In these circumstances the potential for social and political unrest is entirely apparent.

Universities throughout the world have either realised the reality of the international educational market, or they have not. Those that have (pre-eminently in Australia, UK and USA), have learnt to market themselves inter-nationally and to sell their commodity to those who want to have it and can afford to buy it, either because it is not available at home, or because its value is perceived as better, or more desirable.

In a domestic UK context, the same broad reality can be quite simply demonstrated by a review of the personnel needs of any international office in a market-driven university. A cursory review of advertisements for staff indicates that the qualities required are usually: an international outlook; a grasp of various educational systems and their requirements around the world; a nose for lucrative markets where local demand is not satisfied by local supply; a willingness to identify and work with local partners once common status and prestige criteria are satisfied; above all, the capacity to communicate effectively and to represent (sell) the university's courses (products) abroad. This combination of entrepreneurial ability, technical knowledge and communicative ability is comparable to that required in any situation (public or private) where a commodity or service is being promoted across national boundaries. Such qualities would, we believe, be just as essential to the successful corporate international marketing director as they would be for the Director of International Education at the University of X.

International education is ultimately, therefore, not significantly different from other international commercial activity. Products perceived as having 'quality', 'style', 'substance', 'image' will sell better, be in greater demand and can probably command a higher price. The difference between education and commerce in this context is that, usually, the commercial business will understand this better and be better at it, or it will have ceased to exist. Roger L. Geiger suggests that private sectors are more responsive to a range of diverse factors because they are more finely attuned to the exigencies of the market place, whereas public sectors are mainly sensitive to demands mediated through formal political processes.[8] Interestingly, some of the earliest 'modern' attempts to create international universities were private initiatives.[9]

The market-driven university will, at least in intent if not in achievement, be competitive and ambitious to establish its 'brand'. In short, that university will try to employ the techniques and strategies that are characteristic of effective private commerce. Its status as a public or private sector institution has become, in this context, largely a technical irrelevance. What matters is how well it operates.

It should, of course, be recognised that most universities throughout the world operate in a regulated environment. They exist to serve, firstly, the national interest and are subject usually to government regulation and funding for some of their needs. It is also inevitable that this source of funding will never meet the demands made upon the institution, and consequently its role in the competitive international market will be crucial for the gathering of necessary supplemental resources. The plethora of subsidiary companies founded by public universities signifies this reality. This can be illustrated by reference, for example, to the University of Westminster in London. The international activity of the University is, for the most part, centralised under the control of a private company wholly owned by the University. This company recruits students from abroad and buys courses, classes and services from the University departments. In this sense, it employs the commercial techniques of a private company to streamline its operation, cut through university bureaucracy, increase efficiency, and, thus, better serve its clients (students and sending universities). The intention is to gain a greater share of the market with consequent commercial benefits. Murdoch International at Murdoch University in Western Australia operates precisely with the same structure and has the same objectives and intended outcomes. There are numerous other institutions that could be cited in this context.

The proliferation of these arrangements in many parts of the world signifies the perceived need to learn from, and apply, commercial techniques (usually associated with the private sector) in a public sector activity that is, increasingly, highly competitive. This privatisation within the public sector signals a major shift in practice and perception: the ivory tower crumbles while financial imperatives force institutions into, what two decades ago, would have been seen as the grubby alleyways of commerce. The widespread use of commercial agents overseas to represent public sector higher education institutions (particularly those in Australia, UK and USA) reflects precisely the same journey from indifferent isolation to committed engagement in the realities of commercial competition. Market-driven institutions will compete for research grants, students, the best teachers, private funding and so on using at least some of the techniques and mechanisms associated with private commerce.

PUBLIC, PRIVATE AND 'PERFORMATIVITY'

This section takes us into contentious terrain where the deeper resonances of public and private domains are explored. At its simplest, the advocates of the private sector contend that the choices consumers make in the market place are a more valid reflection of their true interests and priorities than are the political mechanisms regulated through and by the state. However, defenders of the 'public sphere' suggest that the market economy distorts and erodes traditional public sphere goals of creating a space in which public opinion (rather than the interests of powerful, wealthy elites and private interests) may be articulated. Jürgen Habermas has argued that the corruption of the public sphere – and this would include the universities – occurs because the market can only present citizens/consumers with technical choices, related to efficiency.[10] This is what Jean-François Lyotard has termed 'performativity – operational efficiency, determined by cost/benefit or input/output analyses – [the] fundamental principle of capitalism'.[11] For Habermas, the universities have to remain within the public domain, since only their public status can guarantee their residual relative autonomy that resists 'threats to the growth of knowledge from the "terroristic" demands of performativity ... which recognises no other goals than instrumental effectiveness and efficiency'.[12] In this way, universities can continue to work on their revised role as the arena within which little narratives can be generated to contest the totalising power of the market.

In Europe, the distinction between public and private remains more salient than in the USA precisely because the USA already has a well-developed and well-respected private higher education sector. Distinctions between private and public are, in that sector, well established. They are not, however, distinctions drawn on the assumed and illusory qualitative differences between commercial and non-commercial. In Europe there is still the tendency to associate private with commercial (with connotations of shabbiness) and public with non-commercial (and therefore good). In the USA, the whole of the higher education sector is thoroughly commercial in the sense that it is market-driven with a basic grasp of education as a commodity. Distinctions between the private and public sectors are usually matters of function, location, philosophy, size and so on. The sources of funding (state, fees or whatever) are obviously highly significant to the specific institution, but they are not perceived signifiers of quality or, as in parts of Europe, of moral purpose.

The 'accreditation' systems applied in the USA constitute mechanisms that exist to establish standards and ensure quality. These operate across both private and public sectors. The legal status of the institution is not an issue in relation to quality assurance. Indeed it can be argued that, in any system, the private sector, where it operates, is more likely to be responsive to questions of quality simply because it knows that it is dependent on student enrolment rather than government funding.

Geoffrey Alderman goes a step further when he implies that the existence of a 'for-profit', private sector in the UK would bring greater diversity and, by implication, wider representation into higher education:

> A lot of nonsense is talked about 'for-profit' higher education providers. All universities in Britain have shareholders. In most cases, there is only one shareholder, the government, which enjoys absolute control over all taxpayer funded higher education institutions. In the for-profit sector, universities have many shareholders to whom institutions answer. This structure widens opportunities for funding and also acts as a safeguard for the institution against dominance by just one political stakeholder.[13]

In England, the example of the EFL (English as a Foreign Language) industry is instructive. From the 1960s onwards, there was a huge growth in private language schools (profit and not-for-profit) offering courses for foreign students. In a highly competitive market, most of the shabby operators have gone under while better institutions innovated teaching methods and offered small classes, personalised services and depended for their existence on a high level of customer satisfaction. As the public universities entered the field, they had to adopt the techniques of the private sector (rather than those of the traditional academic departments) so as to offer the kind of quality that students had come to expect from their experiences in the private sector. The competition between private and public sectors has driven up standards and driven out the incompetent operators, whether private or public.

Traditionally, public demands are politically expressed through nationally and sub-nationally organised political institutions, and we are all aware of the laments about loss of sovereignty and efficacy that have been directed at these institutions over the past two decades. The public sector has serious difficulties keeping up fiscally with the demand for adequate quantity and quality of provision in such areas as health and education, pensions and similar areas of 'public good'. In the USA, the state's acceptance of responsibility in many of these areas has long been minimal and even grudging. In Europe all manner of formulae are being applied, but more and more there is a trend towards blurring the public–private line, with private funding and supply initiatives even being promoted by centre-left governments.

The new public arena for the expression of values and choice is the market place where through consumption aggregations of individual choice make themselves felt. Some of the political and ethical consequences of this will be explored in the last section. At some risk of aggregating all European states, it could be suggested that the historical relative weakness of the private sector in Europe is significant because it has led to a stronger identification with the politically-defined needs of the state. Those issues are by no means solely of concern in Australia, Europe or the USA. Indeed, as the picture elsewhere indicates, the private sector has an increasing role to play in those countries (often in the developing world) where demand dramatically exceeds the capacity of the state to supply it.

If, as we have argued, higher education is an expensive commodity where demand exceeds supply, it stands to reason that, simply, a market will emerge that may behave much like other markets. This market, will like others, be driven and shaped by the forces that apply to all markets. This is broadly the case with the important proviso that higher education is necessarily still a sector more regulated than most; the educational system as a whole is a mechanism that serves national interest and is, therefore, directly within the parameters of the political process. It will inevitably be subject to some level of centralised concern.

That said, Bangladesh offers an interesting case study where some 22 private universities have been developed. As in many developing environments, the private university is a means of supplementing the inadequate provision that the state itself can offer. Similarly in Pakistan, the nationalisation of the university system in 1973 proved to be an unsustainable burden on a government already overburdened by problems of poverty, international debt and so forth. By the late 1980s, the implication of nationalisation in Pakistan was clear. Educational quality had fallen and the system allowed of minimal diversity. The brightest and best students who had some funds available went abroad. Centralised public control of higher education created the necessary precondition for the loss of a potential leadership group to the universities of the developed world. In response to this reality, the government chartered The Aga Khan University in Karachi. Within 20 years, the number of private universities in Pakistan has grown to around 40. Neither the governments of Pakistan or Bangladesh have allowed complete deregulation but they have, in a number of ways, liberalised the system to allow diversity through private provision.

What these developments exemplify is that national bureaucracies cannot possibly meet the demands for higher education in the developing world. The choice is broadly to allow the growth of private provision (often originating from, and funded by, institutions from Australia, UK or USA) to meet the needs of a potential leadership group, or to see the best of that group go abroad to study. In the latter scenario, the result is likely to be an increasing brain drain from the developing world to the developed. National interest is demonstrably better served by having a diverse system in which the public and private co-exist and mutually enhance available provision.

In the newly independent states of the old Soviet Empire, the growth of private institutions (over 120 in the Ukraine alone) has had an impact that goes beyond the economic. As Eastern Europe moves out of an ideologically driven model that serves to support a 'grand narrative' of history, economics and culture, a proliferation of diverse institutions supports the notion of pluralism wherein culture can be contested and debate encouraged. If the ideological defeat of Communism is a reality, the educational systems necessarily have to express ethnic, cultural, political and economic pluralism. National governments are, in the nature of things, committed to a national narrative and to the proliferation of national myths that minimise issues such as ethnic diversity and regional aspirations: the whole range of conflicting notions of culture that are characteristic of a pluralist society. In this context, the private universities are potentially agencies for intellectual liberalisation: gateways to free thought.

In societies as diverse as Armenia, Egypt, Estonia, Malaysia, Nigeria and Syria the private sector complements public provision, creates choice through diversity, and, incidentally, serves to drive standards up as the public sector tries to compete with the private. In Taiwan, where a mature private sector exists, expansion has been almost solely through the growth of private institutions. In Japan the private sector has been widely recognised as the leading force in driving change and, above all, in pioneering approaches in student-centred learning.

Without labouring the point, it is apparent that the private sector has been a significant force in shifting attitudes in higher education throughout the world. The impact has been intellectual, pedagogical, economic and political. Above all, it is clear that private sector institutions are better suited to the enhanced pace of change that is apparent in the new international environment. Unburdened by undue state intervention they are more likely to serve the real needs of the climate in which they operate otherwise, quite simply, they will disappear. Unprotected by government subsidy (for the most part), private institutions will need to serve their 'clients' (the students) because they understand that otherwise those clients will move to a competitor.

Clearly, the growth of the private sector in higher education is an established international trend. In those areas where the process has been resisted, in Ontario, Canada for example, the protests seem at some profound level to be anachronistic, in that they try to resist the inevitable. Technological advances, the reality of borderless education, demands from students, international competition: these forces cohere to make objection to a private sector futile.

As demonstrated above, the opportunities to supply private HE (higher education) services locally have proliferated over the past few years; these opportunities are paralleled on a global terrain. US companies (see below) have identified global markets in private HE as a profitable sector, growing in response to increased demand for skills and knowledge across the global economy. Again, the ability of private enterprises to regard global rather than national space as a legitimate arena for the marketing and supply of educational services reinforces the homology between public/national and private/global. The closer relationship of performativity to the private sector also reinforces the ability of the latter to innovate, to identify and respond to shifts in demand across the globe for skills and knowledge.

Brenda Gourley, Vice Chancellor of Britain's Open University, recently noted that 'higher education has embraced the concept of global delivery in less than a decade', before going on to flag 'public–private partnerships and opening up education to world trade – possibly through recognition by the WTO and bridging the educational divide', as a major contemporary topic in HE.[14]

A good example of this would be Sylvan Learning Systems, a US Nasdaq-listed corporation which, like smaller predecessors Edutrack and Career Education Corporation, sees itself as an international provider of US educational services rather than a provider of international education services. On its website, Sylvan describes itself as a venture expecting to benefit from the 'significant supply–demand imbalance in most post-secondary education markets ... and worldwide trends in educational deregulation and the needs for career-oriented education in an ever-growing knowledge-based economy'.[15] Two of Sylvan's five business divisions are involved in international education. SIU (Sylvan International Universities) owns and operates universities in Chile, India, Mexico, Spain and Switzerland, and Sylvan Ventures invests in and fosters links with existing universities and new communication technologies. SIU typifies the private approach to the international sector, deliberately aimed at securing, in the words of Doug Becker, Chairman and Chief Executive Officer, Sylvan Learning Systems, 'a distinct competitive advantage in the global high growth sector of private education'.[16]

Sylvan pitches its programmes towards practical, career-oriented curricula and also utilises two other features of the global economy – English as one of the major global vernacular languages, and the expansion of ICT (information and communications technologies). Another characteristic of such institutions is the contractual relationship to faculty (as just another human resource). Such flexible ownership of faculty, unthinkable in more traditional universities, is a hallmark of the new private learning corporations such as the University of Phoenix that are increasingly active in the domestic US sector.

The main significance of the private in international education, we suggest, is that the private sector has a greater ability to exploit globalised supply and demand trends, whereas expressions of the public good (outside of aggregations of consumer choice) are experiencing greater and greater difficulties in being articulated through older, nationally organised political channels and institutions. Hence, the greater the extent of globalisation, the more the private sector is empowered.

REGIONAL AND GLOBAL DIMENSIONS OF INTERNATIONAL EDUCATION

While international education is both a reflection of, and an agent in, the growing interdependence of economies, nations, polities and cultures, it continues to reflect regional and national histories, strategic interests and capabilities, social institutions and political projects.

International education activities expanded in the last four decades of the twentieth century primarily because they meshed with national or regional perceptions of interest. International education initiatives and activities are often based on such macro-level rhetorical underpinnings as, in the US case, competitiveness and market-orientation coupled with the American ability to exploit globalised markets or, in the European case, regional integration and the growing acceptability of private initiatives. Lower down the socio-economic system, the agents of international education (universities, corporations) operate and advocate with reference to these larger rhetorical devices, but may primarily be pursuing self-interest.

European international education still largely emanates from public sector (state or sub-state) dominated HE systems. Market linkage, while growing in Europe, has never been as strongly developed as in the USA. The regiocentric and integrationist orientation of European Union international education is explained as part of a tertiary sector adaptation to the European educational market or space envisaged by 2010 in the Bologna Declaration of 1999.[17] US international education is better adapted to seeking global markets partly because American business and university cultures traditionally have more of an overlap, thus creating greater US educational entrepreneurialism, decentralisation and partnership with private organisations. This results in the virtual dominance of US 'global players' in HE, with European institutions, no matter how entrepreneurial they may have become, playing more to regional than global markets. Moreover, US entities orientate themselves more consciously to missions that evoke ideals of internationalisation, mutual understanding and global competence.

However, within Europe, significant developments signal a future in which the private sector will become increasingly important while the public sector will inexorably operate in ways that approximate to those of the private. As the public sector necessarily learns the need to compete, it will increasingly adopt the techniques of the private: developing a marketing strategy, and creating a 'client-driven' mode of operation. At the heart of the process of change in European higher education is a trend identified by Stephen Adam: 'The structures of many European domestic education systems are rapidly changing under the impact of globalisation and market forces. The Bologna declaration is, in part, a response to these pressures.'[18]

The Bologna declaration and subsequent conferences brought into focus the fact that European higher education is at a point of significant development. It recognised the impact of international education and, above all, signalled the need for a new competitive spirit throughout the continent. As a first step, European higher education was encouraged to develop systems that would enhance convergence and transparency within the diverse systems of conti nental Europe. The underlying objectives are apparent:

> The combined impact of the suggested action lines would also make European higher education more understandable and attractive to students, scholars and employers from other continents; they would enhance European competitiveness and thus help to consolidate (or in the eyes of many, to re-establish) its role and influence in the world.[19]

Guy Haug contended that the Bologna declaration was not simply a European statement of intent but a necessary response to changes within the global environment. Key factors are, first, that the demographics of most of Europe are changing and that universities will need to develop strategies for recruiting students both at home and overseas. Second, the growing challenge from non-traditional providers will inevitably challenge the traditional practices of higher education in Europe:

> Many universities will have to do something which they were not at all accustomed to do i.e. compete for students, especially since public funding in most countries is in one way or another dependent on student enrolment. This is something really new in many higher education communities; it can be expected that students' choice will increase and that institutions will have to pay more attention to their needs and satisfaction than in the past.[20]

The implications are apparent: if the European universities are to prosper, or even survive, in the emerging international educational market, they will need to learn techniques that recognise that the environment is competitive and that students are, in some senses, clients. In short, they will need to adopt the kinds of marketing strategies that are commonplace in the private sector, and that have been assimilated in much of the USA, UK and Australia but remain an anathema in some parts of continental Europe. Perhaps the greatest challenge will be that of perception. The university can no longer be the guardian of the Holy Grail of knowledge, protected by arcane regulations and complex, obscure practices. That role will need to give way to a mode of operation characterised by transparency, accessibility, student service and competitiveness in the international market.

Moreover, when it comes to mechanisms of mobility, the long-established US credit system facilitates a high degree of transferability, compared with the fledgling ECTS (European Credit Transfer System) scheme which, moreover, is institutionally- rather than student-owned. ECTS is predominantly a 'transfer' system that permits movement between institutions that have established mutual levels of understanding about curriculum, standards and so on. It is, therefore, a system operated and owned by institutions. In contrast, the US credit system is an accumulation and transfer mechanism owned by both institutions and, significantly, by students. Unlike their European counterparts, US students are empowered to choose mobility (with some reservations) within the USA and internationally.

GLOBALISED INTERNATIONAL EDUCATION

Although international education has been imbued with varied meanings and practices over the past centuries, the single greatest influence in the field over the past two decades has been globalisation. We use globalisation in this context to refer to the process of ever-closer integration and interdependence of economic, social and cultural systems and the shrinkage of spatial and temporal dimensions. In a world where globalisation has accelerated and increased the volume of transglobal interactions, one of the many domains reflecting these changes is education, and *ipso facto*, international education too.

The linkage between education and the nation-state has been so close for so long that one of the earlier pleasures of the narrative of international education was that it opened up the possibilities of thinking about educational activities outside and beyond national boundaries. Now, as we contemplate an emerging global order that is increasingly all-encompassing and undermines our sense of nationally-bounded space and systems, some of the fundamental entanglements between education and globalisation become traceable.

In the global order we grew accustomed to until the late twentieth century, the nation was the reality and the category that enabled and legitimised the socialisation of subjects and the structuralisation of cultures. However, in the context of strong contemporary currents of transnationality, the nation has lost some of its capabilities and is starting to become an absent structure. Although still an apparatus of enormous power, many nation-states no longer possess the ability or even the desire to monopolise the forms and content of tertiary education. In terms of their primary orientation to international education, nations are shifting their focus from the state to the region and from the region to the global.

As it is proving increasingly difficult for traditional, state-organised manifestations of power to articulate their interests in a global arena characterised by fast capital and investment flows and surging cultural and consumer trends, it seems reasonable to conclude that globalisation processes favour the private domain. If globalisation is both a cause and a consequence of increasingly borderless transactions, this suggests that education will become increasingly market-sensitive. The knowledge sector of the globalised system concerned with the creation and dissemination of cognitive insights, information and related skills is clearly impacted by both the technologies of communication and the growth of the international market place for products and services, ideas and finance.[21]

The content, delivery and ethos of international education have themselves become globalised over the last few years in many ways, yet it is in the *forms* of international education that globalisation has had the greatest impact. We believe that, thus far, globalisation has most effected the delivery and distribution modalities through which international education products or services are delivered – study abroad, ODL (open and distance learning), student or faculty exchange, changes to curriculum, shifts in institutional mission and activities, policy shifts within parts of or entire educational systems. Examples of such impacts can be seen in the following ways:

- Technological and commercial developments since the 1980s have led to more overseas delivery of entire courses or course elements through franchising, the establishment of branch campuses, dual accreditation and cross-national consortia.
- Communications technology has fuelled a huge increase in open and distance learning and web-based educational activities. It has also inevitably undermined notions of national, centralised control of subject matter. Students in country A are, in many circumstances, able to access educational material produced anywhere in the world. This challenges both the idea of a national educational policy and the kinds of knowledge control aspirations associated with totalitarian objectives.
- The arrival of commercial players, not themselves universities, as agents of and purveyors of international education.

Some national idioms in tertiary level education lend themselves more effectively to globalisation as do certain aspects of business culture. The readily exported, recognisable and desirable aspects of US HE, combined with a particularly effective entrepreneurial approach, has created optimum growth conditions for privatised US HE. Expanded opportunities for British and primarily Australasian systems also exist.

It is also necessary to consider the ways in which international higher education has not been 'globalised', despite the rhetorical flourishes that colour this area of debate. There are, in practice, very few institutions that are 'international' in structure. Most universities operate within a national set of guidelines (be they public or private). Accreditation is, for the most part, nationally based. Degrees are still largely defined by country or region. Quality control mechanisms almost invariably derive from within a single national context. Thus, New York University, for example, describes itself as 'The Global University' but it is, in practice, a private US university with many international activities. The reality is that there are a multitude of universities with widespread interests in international education. That does not make them international or global universities in so far as they are still governed by systems and practices deriving from their particular national context.

That said, the non-territoriality of capitalism was clear from the earliest epoch. As Thomas Jefferson remarked, 'Merchants have no country. The mere spot they stand upon does not constitute so strong an attachment as that from which they draw their gain.'[22] Unlike the state-based educational systems that were funded within state boundaries and catered to populations that for the most part resided within national boundaries, capitalism 'was from the beginning an affair of the world economy and not of nation states'.[23] It is as though the Comtean vision of John Eaton, the second US Commissioner of Education speaking before the Centennial Exposition in Philadelphia in 1876, 'gentlemen, before the time of universal peace can come, the schoolmaster must be abroad over the whole world',[24] has somehow, in the last 120 years, been squeezed through a new prism to become that of the entrepreneurs marketing their educational wares across the globe.

An ascendant USA with a set of cultural, economic and educational orientations congruent with a more globalised educational market place is best placed to be successful in the next phase of globalised international education. This will be characterised by more ODL and more private US-local partnerships and branch campuses. More localised European regional activity will continue to both harmonise and privatise the European educational space and will continue to fill niche markets in other parts of the world, based on linguistic affinities or post-colonial affiliations, through franchising, accreditation and similar partnerships.

Ernest Gellner (1983) argued that through such agencies as educational systems, nations were able to define what is meant by nation and nationalism.[25] Perhaps this can now be extended to suggest that certain nations and some forms of commerce, when allied to the idioms of international education, play a formative role in the shared rhetoric of globalisation.

CONCLUSION

It is clear that the developments we have discussed above will have an uneven social and educational impact around the world. Perspectives that critique global inequalities and re-focus attention on inequality of provision and inequality of access issues return us to fundamental aspects of the public/private arena.

Gourley seems to agree with Manuel Castells' contention that the consequences of globalised digital networks will be greater inequality and greater social exclusion which, in the long run, will be socially and politically unsustainable. In the same article, as part of an extended discussion of the de-nationalisation of polities and economies, she utilises Thomas Friedman's notion of skilled elites disconnecting from their less fortunate fellow countrymen and women and plugging into the global 'electronic herd' – 'the equivalent of taking your country public, only the shareholders are no longer just your own citizens'.[26] She does, however, offer a more optimistic view, suggesting that the moral and practical imperatives might blend since the expansion of the global market place for education will suck in enterprises that 'have stuff to sell' and they in turn will assist in [social and economic] development if:

> they believe that in the process they are creating markets. All who specify, buy or produce the materials, systems and ideas that are traded in the world education market must recognise that we are part of this process

and that we have responsibilities. Those of us who deal in the internationalisation of higher education must share a vision that derives from
the idea that the world will be better off, healed by educational intervention
that engages rich and poor, capitalists and subalterns, metropolis and
hamlets. ... It is a massive task and a noble one if it does not lapse into
the acquisitiveness that characterises so many initiatives that ride the
spirit of globalisation.[27]

This tension between the idealist and realist/instrumentalist concepts of
international is not new, but it is given a new twist in the era of globalisation.
Peter Berger and Thomas Luckmann (1967) suggest that 'real factors'
determine or regulate the conditions under which 'ideal factors' can operate
in history, but they cannot affect the *content* of ideal factors.[28] Society deter-
mines the presence but not the nature of ideal factors. Thus we have a new
generation of international educators envisioning the globalised version of
their project through somewhat differently tinted spectacles than their
entrepreneurial cousins in the private sector. Different actors and agents in
international education invent their own 'international' discourse, inserting it
where necessary to justify or enhance what they are already doing. In increasingly competitive higher education markets, both within national and regional
borders and in the global space beyond them, free-floating international
idealism or disregard for the profitability of institutions and ventures would
lead to the early demise of international education. Instead, international
education has become coupled with technology, communications, supply
deficiencies and bottlenecks in the delivery of education, and thus is itself
becoming globalised and privatised.

Given this, and given that the culture of corporate capitalism takes it as
read that the maximisation of profit is the sole purpose of the corporation, the
issue of how the public good or the development of human capital is placed
on the agenda is problematic. Sylvan Learning System's primary concern
cannot be the needs of developing nation-states, since the dominant needs of
the American investment community and corporate America point to their
providing services only to the sub-sector in developing countries that has the
ability to pay. We could, however, take the view that the impact of globalisation
on domestic, national tertiary systems is to galvanise them into greater market
sensitivity and responsiveness to 'society's' needs as opposed to those of the
politically entrenched elites and bureaucrats.

Access and equality of provision issues are always problematic in the context
of a perceived public good like education, and are even more contentious
when played out in terms of the inequalities between the global north and the
global south. Developing countries are hard put to develop their human capital
at a basic level, let alone educate and train their populations at the tertiary

level. The elites of these countries, therefore, come to the rich north at high cost to receive education and then often stay detached from the productive sectors of their home countries. International education is not an evenly distributed good: those who already have are getting more; those who have little are getting less, leading to Saskia Sassen's apt description of the view from the south as being a 'landscape of despair'.

However, a further impact of these processes might be to redefine traditional global dichotomies. Friedman asserted that the real divisions among nations and regions may emerge along revised lines, that is between the fast and the slow world. If that is true the new divisions will be between those nations developing technological capacities that will empower them to participate in, and benefit from, the new dynamics, and those who, for reasons of politics, economics, or whatever, are unable to exploit the inherent potential. The case of India indicates that a traditionally 'poor' nation may move into the 'fast' world, with resulting economic benefit, in the not-too-distant future.

Education is a public as well as a private good, but neither the definition nor the guardianship of the public good is as straightforward as it appeared to be in past eras. Who are the guardians now? If the grand narrative is dead, what role can universities play? Since universities, like all social institutions, require legitimacy, what small narratives will globalised universities of the twenty-first century deploy to legitimate themselves? Lyotard and Habermas both speculate on the consequences of the erosion of the autonomy of higher education as it becomes subordinated to the irresistible logic of performativity. The winners in this current phase of globalised international education are private educational entrepreneurs in the USA, UK and Australasia plus the relatively affluent student populations of the global north. We have also suggested that greater pluralism and diversity in the educational sectors of transitional societies are both likely and desirable outcomes. Probable losers include monolithic state-dominated systems and culturally static entities, as well as the majority of students in the global south.

Nevertheless, we have entered a period of development so rapid that all that can be confidently predicted is that current predictions are, at best, attempts to peer into a future that will not look like the present. In this context we can only suggest that the boundaries between public and private educational provision will diminish and that the borders between nations and regions will become increasingly fluid. This emerging world is likely to be one in which what we now know to be true may no longer be so. As was noted about another, more distant revolution, 'all that is solid melts into air'.[29]

NOTES

1 T. Friedman, *The Lexus and the Olive Tree* (New York: Anchor Books, 2000), p. 336.
2 M. Mann, 'Nationalism and Internationalism: A Critique of Economic and Defence Policies', in J. Griffith and T. Atkinson (eds), *Socialism in a Cold Climate* (London: Unwin, 1983), p. 196.
3 For a discussion of the controversy surrounding the proposal see 'Colleges, Fighting US Trade Proposal, Say It Favours For-Profit Distance Education', *The Chronicle of Higher Education*, 18 January, 2002, pp. A33–5. The proposal can be viewed at: www.ustr.gov/sectors/services/educ.pdf
4 Useful earlier discussions of the various categories of international education can be found in S. Arum, *International Education: What is it?* (New York: Council on International Educational Exchange, Occasional Paper 23, 1987); E.L. Backman, *Approaches to International Education* (New York: Macmillan/ACE, 1984); D. Heater, *World Studies: Education for International Understanding in Britain* (London: Harrap, 1980); D. Hicks and C. Townley, *Teaching World Studies: An Introduction to Global Perspectives in the Curriculum* (London: Longman, 1982); D.P. Huden, *Some Factors in International Irrelevance: The Failures of International Educational Organisations* (New Haven: Yale, 1977); M. Zweig, *The Idea of a World University* (London: Feffere and Simon, 1967).
5 For the NDEA see http://ishi.lib.berkeley.edu/cshe/ndea and for the NSEP see http://extranet.ndu/nsep/index.html
6 All of the European colonial powers practiced some form of cultural diplomacy through public domain higher education. In addition to the education of colonial elites through the metropolitan universities, many colonies also saw the establishment of 'extension colleges' such as the University of London's external degree courses in Lagos, Nigeria, Legon, Ghana, and Salisbury, Rhodesia.
7 We note that, in the case of such English universities as Bristol, Leeds, Liverpool and Manchester, the sources of their growth and consolidation in the nineteenth century were 'public' only in terms of municipal pride leading to local government-launched public subscription campaigns. The sources of financial support were private and the largest donors were industrialists and merchants. The oldest English universities predated the state and though subsequent state authority gave legal status to Oxford and Cambridge, the state was not responsible for financial support.
8 R.L. Geiger, 'Public and Private Sectors in Higher Education: A Comparison of International Patterns', *Higher Education*, 17, 6 (1988), pp. 699–711.
9 Zweig, *World University*.
10 J. Bernstein, *Recovering Ethical Life: Jurgen Habermas and the Future of Critical Theory* (London: Routledge, 1995).
11 J. Fritzman, 'Overcoming Capitalism: Lyotard's Pessimism and Rorty's Prophecy', in P. Dhillon and P. Standish (eds), *Lyotard: Just Education* (London: Routledge, 2000).
12 N. Blake, 'Parology, Validity Claims and the Politics of Knowledge: Habermas, Lyotard and Higher Education', in Dhillon and Standish, *Lyotard: Just Education*, pp. 55–8.
13 Geoffrey Alderman, 'Lots To Gain From For-Profits', *Times Higher Education Supplement*, 22 March 2002.
14 B. Gourley, 'Digital Deprivation', *Times Higher Education Supplement*, 17 May 2002.
15 www.sylvanu.com/company/company_article_011801.asp Career Education Corporation, a smaller US corporation that has recently ventured into international education with universities in Dubai and London, can be viewed at www.collegeview.com
16 www.sylvanu.com/company/company_article_011801.asp
17 http://europa.eu.int/comm/education/socrates/erasmus/bologna.pdf

18   S. Adam, *Transnational Education Project Report and Recommendations*, (Confederation of European Union Rectors' Conference, March 2001), p. 5.

19   G. Haug, *Trends and Issues in Learning Structures in Higher Education in Europe*, Beitrage von Hochschulpolitik, (Bonn, February 2002), p. 11.

20   G. Haug, 'Visions of a European Future: Bologna and Beyond', an address to the 11th Annual European Association of International Education Conference, 1999.

21   S. Strange, *States and Markets* (London: Pinter, 1988). Strange's analysis of the power structures in the international political and economic order suggests a model with four different structural dimensions of power – security, production, finance and knowledge. We suggest that recent developments in international education are usefully seen in the context of convergence between the finance and knowledge sectors.

22   W. Mueller, 'Corporate Secrecy v. Corporate Disclosure', in R. Nader and M.J. Green (eds), *Corporate Power in America* (New York: Grossman, 1973), p. 118.

23   I. Wallerstein, *The Capitalist World Economy* (Cambridge: Cambridge University Press, 1979), p. 19.

24   Huden, *Some Factors*, p. 4.

25   E. Gellner, *Nations and Nationalism* (Oxford: Blackwell, 1983).

26   Gourley, 'Digital Deprivation'.

27   Ibid.

28   P.L. Berger and T. Luckmann, *The Social Construction of Reality* (London: Penguin Books, 1971).

29   K. Marx and F. Engels, *The Communist Manifesto* [1848] (Oxford: Oxford University Press, 1992), p. 6

INDEX